NATURE GUIDES
ROCKS
AND MINERALS

NATURE GUIDES
ROCKS
AND MINERALS

MONICA PRICE
KEVIN WALSH

DK

LONDON, NEW YORK, MUNICH, MELBOURNE, AND DELHI

DK LONDON
Senior Art Editor Ina Stradins
Senior Editor Ros Walford
Editors Georgina Garner, Bella Pringle
DTP Designer John Goldsmid
Production Editor Kavita Varma
Production Controller Lucy Sims
Managing Art Editor Phil Ormerod
Publishing Manager Liz Wheeler
Art Director Bryn Walls
Publishing Director Jonathan Metcalf

DK DELHI
Designers Romi Chakraborty,
Malavika Talukdar
DTP Designers Balwant Singh,
Sunil Sharma, Pankaj Sharma
Editors Glenda Fernandes, Rohan Sinha
Managing Art Editor Aparna Sharma

This edition published in 2011
First published in Great Britain in 2005 by
Dorling Kindersley Limited
80 Strand, London WC2R 0RL
A Penguin Company (UK)

001-PD051-Jul/11

Copyright © 2005
Dorling Kindersley Limited

A CIP catalogue record for this book
is available from the British Library

ISBN 978-1-4053-9084-2

Reproduced by Colourscan, Singapore
Printed and bound by Hung Hing, China

Discover more at
www.dk.com

CONTENTS

How this book works

This guide covers over 320 of the most important rocks and minerals found all over the world. The book begins with a short introduction, which focuses on the process of identifying different rocks and minerals. The following pages divide rocks into three groups: sedimentary, igneous, and metamorphic; and minerals into two groups: ore minerals and rock-forming minerals. Introductions to each of these sections define the groups and explain how entries are organized within them.

CHAPTER HEADING

ROCK OR MINERAL NAME

CHEMICAL FORMULA OF THE MINERAL

LOCALITIES AND ASSOCIATIONS
Shows important rock or mineral localities, or shows the rock or mineral in a typical association.

▽ **GROUP INTRODUCTIONS**
Each chapter opens with an introductory page describing the parameters of the group, as well as any further sub-groups.

CAPTION
Describes the featured area or association in which the rock or mineral may be found.

PHOTOGRAPHS
The main images illustrate typical examples of the rock or mineral. Secondary pictures show named varieties.

STAUROLITE is often associated with kyanite, as in this muscovite schist from St Gotthard, Switzerland.

pseudo-orthorhombic crystals

Rock-forming Minerals

The bulk of minerals that constitute rocks are not ores, although some have important uses in industry. This chapter features minerals that are found in a wide range of rock types (pp.143–67), and those found mainly or exclusively in sedimentary rocks (pp.168–75), igneous rocks (pp.176–96), and metamorphic rocks (pp.197–216). Talc, for example, is found exclusively in metamorphic rocks, such as the cliffs of Kynance Cove, England (below). Hydrothermal minerals that are neither ores nor their secondary minerals are also included in this chapter.

PICTURES
Photographs of representative specimens show the diversity within the group.

ROCK-FORMING MINERALS 215

Lazurite
(Na,Ca)$_8$Al$_6$Si$_6$O$_{24}$[(SO$_4$),S,Cl,(OH)]$_2$

Since ancient times, lazurite has been highly prized for its exquisite blue coloration as the principal mineral in the rock known as lapis lazuli. Lazurite is a member of the feldspathoid group. It is always deep or vibrant blue, and it was once the source of the artist's pigment ultramarine. Most lazurite is massive or in disseminated grains, and distinct crystals – which are usually dodecahedral – are much sought after. Lapis lazuli forms by contact metamorphism of limestones. At its finest, this rock consists of lazurite speckled with golden pyrite, but white calcite and other feldspathoids are normally present too.

THE RICH mountains of Badakhshan in Afghanistan have been a rich source of lapis lazuli for thousands of years.

ULTRAMARINE

LAPIS LAZULI CABOCHONS

polished surface

dodecahedral crystals with dull lustre

white calcite

SECTION SHOWN

rich blue colour

golden pyrite grains

POLISHED LAPIS LAZULI

ROUGH LAPIS LAZULI

NOTES
The sard lapis for a crystals came from Badakhshan Province in Afghanistan, which is also the source of the many lapis lazuli specimens in old collections said to be from Persia (now Iran). The stone was traded, but not mined, in Persia. Other deposits of lapis lazuli...

COMPOSITION Silicate.
CRYSTAL SYSTEM Cubic.
CLEAVAGE/FRACTURE Imperfect/Uneven.
LUSTRE/STREAK Vitreous to dull/Bright blue.
HARDNESS/DENSITY 5-5.5 / 2.38–2.45.
KEY PROPERTIES Bright blue streak; does not fizz in dilute HCl like azurite (p.123). Should not be confused with lazulite (p.148).

NOTES
Describe unique features, or provide interesting historical or contextual background.

K
Al$_2$-

Blue and crys har its l of i mic vein

THE FIRST descriptions of kyanite were of crystals from the schists of Zillertal in the Austrian Alps.

triclin prism cryst

shades of blue

bladed crystals

▷ **FULL-PAGE ENTRIES**
Rocks or minerals that exhibit a more varied or complex range, are of special interest, or are particularly important, are all given full-page entries.

▽ ▷ ROCK AND MINERAL ENTRIES

The typical page features two entries. Each has a main image, which is supported by one or more secondary pictures. Annotations, scale artworks, and a data box add key information for each entry.

OTHER KEY INFORMATION – ROCKS

These panels provide consistent information on the following points:
GRAIN SIZE: *the typical size or size range of the rock grains.*
ESSENTIAL COMPONENTS: *lists the essential mineral constituents.*
ADDITIONAL COMPONENTS: *lists minerals that may appear in the rock, but that are not essential.*
ORIGIN: *describes the process by which the rock type is formed.*
SIMILAR ROCKS: *lists rocks that look similar to the one featured, and often provides distinguishing features to help tell them apart.*

MICROGRAPHS

Shows a section through the rock, seen through a microscope, to show the constituent minerals.

G MINERALS

$(Si,Al)_8O_{48}H_{2-4}$

wn, yellowish brown, or nearly s as prismatic crystals, which are haped in section, often with rough enetration twins are common. It ns by regional metamorphism of argillaceous (or clay) rocks, and is found in medium-grade schists and gneisses.

muscovite schist

cross-shaped twin

COMPOSITION *Silicate.*
YSTAL SYSTEM *Monoclinic, pseudo-horhombic.*
EAVAGE/FRACTURE *Distinct/Nearly nchoidal.*
STRE/STREAK *Vitreous to dull/Pale grey.*
RDNESS/DENSITY *7–7.5 / 3.74–3.83.*
Y PROPERTIES *Brown; cr*

1s.

DESCRIPTION

Conveys the main features and the distinguishing characteristics of the rock or mineral.

DETAIL PICTURES

These tinted boxes show different aspects of the rock or mineral, including gem cuts, different habits, and colour variations.

ANNOTATION

Characteristic features of the rock or mineral are picked out in the annotation.

COLOUR BANDS

Bands are colour-coded, with a different colour for each of the five chapters.

e the usual colours of kyanite, ixed or zoned within a single , bladed crystals are often bent; ater across a crystal than along at temperatures between those site and sillimanite. It occurs in d associated hydrothermal quartz

vitreous lustre

MPOSITION *Silicate*
STAL SYSTEM *Triclinic.*
AVAGE/FRACTURE *Perfect and distinct vages at 90°/Splintery.*
TRE/STREAK *Vitreous to pearly/Colourless.*
RDNESS/ DENSITY *5.5 along crystal, 7 ss crystal / 3.53–3.65.*
PROPERTIES *Bladed, blue crystals.*

SCALE MEASUREMENTS

Two small scale drawings are placed next to each other in every entry, as a rough indication of the size of the featured specimen. The hand represents an average adult hand of 18cm height.

OTHER KEY INFORMATION – MINERALS

These panels provide consistent information on the following points:
COMPOSITION: *the mineral class to which the entry belongs. Some silicate minerals also inlude an additional group classification.*
CRYSTAL SYSTEM: *the crystal system to which it belongs.*
CLEAVAGE: *the grading, from poor to perfect, of the way in which the mineral splits along flat planes.*
FRACTURE: *the description of the typical appearance of a surface where a specimen has broken.*
LUSTRE: *the different ways the mineral typically reflects light, from dull to adamantine or metallic.*
STREAK: *the colour of the mineral when it is in fine powdered form.*
HARDNESS: *the hardness of the mineral when compared to the standard minerals on Mohs' scale.*
DENSITY: *the typical weight of the mineral, measured in grams per cubic centimetre.*
KEY PROPERTIES: *the key identifying characters of the mineral, sometimes suggesting similar-looking minerals and distinguishing features to help tell them apart.*

What are Minerals?

Minerals are natural, inorganic substances, composed of the atoms of either one single chemical element or a number of different elements. There are over 4,000 different minerals, and each one is distinguished by its chemical composition (the particular ratio of its chemical elements) and its crystal structure. Nearly all minerals are crystalline: the atoms are arranged in a regular pattern; when allowed to grow freely, they form symmetric crystals with flat faces.

tabular crystals with triclinic symmetry

COMPOSITION
Microcline is composed of potassium, aluminium, silicon, and oxygen atoms in the ratio 1:1:3:8, giving it the chemical formula $KAlSi_3O_8$. It is a silicate mineral, and a member of the feldspar group.

flat-faced crystal

solid (like virtually all minerals)

MICROCLINE

Rock-forming and Ore Minerals

Minerals are in all the rocks of the Earth. They can be found wherever rocks have been exposed, either naturally or by man. Some minerals are rich in those metals we use in our everyday lives, and we exploit these as ores.

ROCK-FORMING MINERALS
Most minerals that make up the bulk of rocks and veins are neither metallic nor noticeably heavy, and many are not particularly colourful. There are important exceptions, however, and some of the most richly coloured are gem minerals that are beautiful, durable, and rare.

ORE MINERALS
Ores and their secondary minerals frequently occur in mineral veins, which are sheet-like structures that result when minerals fill fractures within existing rocks. Many ore minerals look metallic, and some are noticeably heavy. Secondary minerals may be formed when primary ore minerals are altered by rain and groundwater. They are often brightly coloured, and some may themselves be of economic value.

ROCK FORMATIONS

Calcite

ROCKS AND CAVES
Calcite makes up the bulk of rocks such as limestone and marble, as well as forming stalagmites and stalactites in limestone caves.

MINERAL VEINS

Galena

LEAD ORE
Galena, the principal ore of lead, can be seen as a metallic grey band in this mineral vein.

What are Rocks?

Rocks are naturally-occurring consolidated substances, which may be made up of minerals, other rock pieces, and fossil materials, such as shells or plants. Rocks are the result of various geological processes that occur both at and beneath the Earth's surface or, in the case of meteorites, in other parts of the Universe. Rocks can be studied and differentiated between by grouping together those types that share a similar appearance, similar composition, and the same process of formation.

COMPOSITION
Granite is always made up of three different kinds of minerals: white or beige-coloured feldspar, clear or grey quartz, and black mica (biotite).

quartz

biotite   feldspar   GRANITE

thin sheets and dark colour

transparent and glassy

light colour and square corners

BIOTITE   FELDSPAR   QUARTZ

The Rock Cycle

Dynamic processes acting on the Earth's crust allows rock material to be recycled. At the Earth's surface, weathering and erosion break down pre-existing rocks into sediments, which form new rocks such as sandstone. These rocks may be buried beneath the Earth's surface; heat and pressure of large-scale movements in turn cause fracture, deformation (alteration caused by stress), and eventually, melting. For example, sandstone is transformed into gneiss, and melted gneiss solidifies into granite. Uplift of deeper parts of the Earth's crust bring these new rocks to the surface.

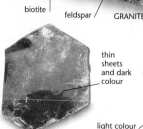

sandstone

EROSION

SEDIMENTARY

BURIAL

granite

gneiss

MELTING

IGNEOUS   METAMORPHIC

Rock Identification

There are many features of rocks that can be used in identification; the size and shape of the grains, the colour, and determination of the constituent minerals are all important. The processes that produce rocks also give rise to characteristic textures and structures, for example, lava can produce glassy rocks with flow structures.

Types of Rock

Examples of the three main types of rock – sedimentary, igneous, and metamorphic – are shown below, but some other types of rock also feature in this book: deformation rocks, which result from Earth movements; meteorites; and surface impact rocks, which are produced when meteorites strike the Earth.

SEDIMENTARY ROCKS

Sedimentary rocks result from the consolidation of sediments. One type of sediment is deposited as grains by water or wind, in layers known as bedding; another is formed from biological material, producing rocks such as limestone.

| CHALK | TRAVERTINE | SANDSTONE | FLAGSTONE | CROSS-BEDDED SANDSTONE | TURBIDITE |

IGNEOUS ROCKS

Intrusive igneous rocks form when magma (molten rock beneath the Earth's surface) solidifies, and are made up of crystals, which can be aligned or layered. Volcanic rocks are extrusive and form when lava solidifies; they may contain glass, gas bubbles, or show flow structure.

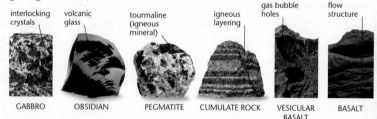

| GABBRO | OBSIDIAN | PEGMATITE | CUMULATE ROCK | VESICULAR BASALT | BASALT |

METAMORPHIC ROCKS

These rocks are produced by alteration due to increased heat and pressure. They often show features of deformation, such as flattening, streaking, or folding. Distinctive minerals, such as garnet, are good indicators of this type of rock.

| TECTONITE | GARNET SCHIST | MIGMATITE | SCHIST | METATUFF | MYLONITE |

Mineral Content

Some minerals are restricted to particular types of rock, and determining mineral content can help identification. Obvious mineral grains can give a clue to a rock's identity, for example, garnet only appears in metamorphic rocks.

TRAVERTINE (SED.) PEGMATITE (IG.) ECLOGITE (META.)

Grain Size

In sedimentary rocks, grain size depends on how far the grains have travelled; for igneous rocks it is determined by how long the rock took to crystallise; metamorphic grain size depends on the pre-existing rock. Size limits for coarse, medium, and fine grains vary according to the group of rocks.

	COARSE	MEDIUM	FINE
SEDIMENTARY ROCKS	CONGLOMERATE	IRONSTONE	CLAY
IGNEOUS ROCKS	GRANITE	MICROGRANITE	RHYOLITE
METAMORPHIC ROCKS	PARAGNEISS	QUARTZITE	SLATE

Grain Shape

The shape of individual grains are more easily observed using a hand lens. Some features to consider include the degree of roundness, whether all the grains are similar in shape, and how well developed any crystals are. Well-developed crystals have their flat faces intact and straight edges.

CONGLOMERATE BRECCIA GRANITE AUGEN GNEISS TEKTITE

Texture

Texture refers to the rock's surface appearance or the relationship between the individual grains in a rock. If the rock has no visible grains and is a single mass of mineral or glass, it is known as massive. Many igneous rocks are made up of interlocking grains – a texture known as granular.

massive

ROCK GYPSUM

porphyritic (crystals in fine matrix)

PORPHYRY

oolitic (small, rounded grains)

PISOLITE

glassy

FLINT

crystalline

GRANODIORITE

Structure

Structure refers to those features produced by geological processes. Some structures, such as bedding, igneous layering, and gneissic banding, are formed at the same time as the rock itself, but others, such as folding and shearing (stretching of mineral grains), occur later. Many structures exist over a vast range of scale, for example, folding can be seen in microscopic crystal grains as well as across entire cliff faces. Geologists use structural information to construct geological histories and produce geological maps.

folding

shearing

TECTONITE

banding

bedding

FOLDED MYLONITE

GNEISS

layering

CUMULATE ROCK

SANDSTONE

Colour

Colour is an obvious but useful property in rock identification. It can be used to tell apart different varieties of a rock, and it can also provide information on the composition of the rock. In many cases, the colour of a rock will be affected by weathering, so a fresh surface should always be exposed.

red sandstone

green sandstone

pink sandstone

grey sandstone

DESERT SANDSTONE

GREENSAND

ORTHOQUARTZITE

GREYWACKE

VARIETIES
Each sandstone colour is determined by its constituent minerals; these depend on the original sediment and the geological history.

light

intermediate

mainly dark

dark

GRANITE

DIORITE

GABBRO

PYROXENITE

IGNEOUS ROCKS
In general, the higher the silica content of an igneous rock, the lighter its colour should be.

Geological Environments

Rock types rarely occur in isolation. Normally, several different but related types of rock form together in one geological environment. For example, basalt, scoria, spilite, and volcanic bombs are found together in the volcanoes of Hawaii. Knowing these associations can help to identify rocks that occur together and, also, to recognise their ancient environment – greensand and chalk of the Cretaceous Period are evidence of warm, calm seas of 100 million years ago.

VOLCANOES
scoria

RIVERS
conglomerate

LAKES
siltstone

CAVES
travertine

DESERT
loess

OCEANS AND SEAS
greensand

Where to find Rocks

Rocks are found everywhere, but the best examples are found where the effects of weathering are least, often in settings created by human activity, such as road-cuts, mine dumps, and quarries. Good examples are also found where nature has recently exposed fresh rock, such as on sea cliffs, beaches, mountains, and volcanic terrains. Many of the harder, more resistant, and more attractive rocks are used for building; these can be seen as support structures, as well as interior and exterior decoration. Geological maps show the distribution of rocks in particular areas, and can be important and useful tools for finding and recognising rocks.

BUILDINGS
oolitic limestone

MOUNTAINS
dolomite

VOLCANIC REGIONS
tuff

BEACHES
amber

ROAD CUTS
volcanic bomb

MINES
kimberlite

QUARRIES
slate

Mineral Identification

The fact that a single mineral can occur in a variety of crystal shapes and in a range of colours can be confusing. However, every mineral can be identified by investigating a combination of properties. Some properties, such as colour, are visible to the eye; others, such as hardness, need to be measured using simple pieces of equipment.

Mineral Composition

Minerals are divided into the following classes according to their negatively charged component, for example, carbonates (CO_3^{2-}). Many properties of a mineral result from its chemical make-up, for example, colour, streak, and magnetism. Chemical elements and their symbols appear on p.19.

silver
cobaltite
chalcocopyrite

ELEMENTS
Native elements occur uncombined with any other chemical elements.

SULPHIDES AND SULPHOSALTS
Many sulphides (-S) and sulphosalts (-AsS or -SbS) are ores.

halite
manganite
calcite
borax

OXIDES AND HYDROXIDES
Oxides (-O) and hydroxides (-OH) vary widely in appearance, and may be metallic.

HALIDES
These include fluorides (-F) and chlorides (-Cl); they often have cubic symmetry.

CARBONATES
The carbonates (-CO_3) include rock-forming minerals such as calcite and dolomite.

BORATES
Borates are mainly white or grey; their complex structures link -BO_3 units together.

crocoite
pyromorphite
kyanite
baryte

SULPHATES
Most sulphates (-SO_4) are secondary minerals, but some, like gypsum and baryte, make up rocks and veins.

CHROMATES, MOLYBDATES, AND TUNGSTATES
These minerals (-CrO_4, -MoO_4, and -WO_4) include important ores.

PHOSPHATES, ARSENATES, AND VANADATES
-PO_4, -AsO_4, and -VO_4 minerals are often brightly coloured.

SILICATES
SiO_4 units connect to form a range of structures. Most rock-forming minerals are from this huge class.

Mineral Groups

Some minerals are grouped together because they have closely related chemical compositions and crystal structures. As a result of this, they share certain key properties and may be difficult to tell apart. Many silicate minerals belong to groups, which include the feldspars, garnets, micas, amphiboles, and pyroxenes.

THE GARNET GROUP
Grossular, almandine, and spessartine all belong to this group. The group name is useful to use when unsure what member mineral you have.

GROSSULAR

ALMANDINE

SPESSARTINE

Crystal Forms

A crystal's form is its geometric shape. Some crystals are single forms, such as octahedrons; others are more complex and combine two or more forms, for example, the quartz crystal (below right) combines a prism with two pyramids.

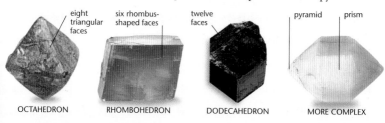

eight triangular faces

six rhombus-shaped faces

twelve faces

pyramid | prism

OCTAHEDRON | RHOMBOHEDRON | DODECAHEDRON | MORE COMPLEX

Twinned Crystals

Twinned crystals form when different parts of one crystal grow as mirror images of each other. These may join at a crystal face, edge, or internal plane. Simple twins have two parts; multiple twins have three or more. Twinning gives a mineral different crystal forms, for example, this aragonite appears hexagonal.

interpenetrant twin

simple contact twin

multiple twin

CALCITE | STAUROLITE | ARAGONITE

Crystal Systems

The crystal forms of a mineral indicate which crystal system the mineral belongs to. For example, elongate crystals with a square cross-section, such as that of the vesuvianite below, are found in minerals that belong to the tetragonal system. There are seven crystal systems, and each has certain elements of symmetry. Each of a mineral's forms will always have the elements of symmetry of the system to which it belongs.

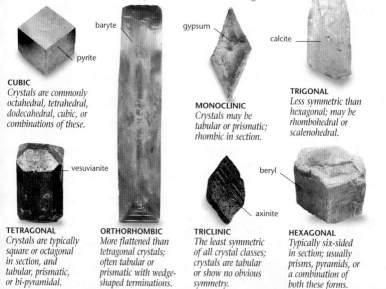

baryte

gypsum

calcite

pyrite

CUBIC
Crystals are commonly octahedral, tetrahedral, dodecahedral, cubic, or combinations of these.

MONOCLINIC
Crystals may be tabular or prismatic; rhombic in section.

TRIGONAL
Less symmetric than hexagonal; may be rhombohedral or scalenohedral.

vesuvianite

beryl

axinite

TETRAGONAL
Crystals are typically square or octagonal in section, and tabular, prismatic, or bi-pyramidal.

ORTHORHOMBIC
More flattened than tetragonal crystals; often tabular or prismatic with wedge-shaped terminations.

TRICLINIC
The least symmetric of all crystal classes; crystals are tabular or show no obvious symmetry.

HEXAGONAL
Typically six-sided in section; usually prisms, pyramids, or a combination of both these forms.

Mineral Habits

The habit of a mineral describes the general appearance of its crystals or clusters of crystals. A mineral can have more than one habit. For example, actinolite can be bladed, acicular, fibrous, or massive, depending on the conditions in which it forms. A massive habit indicates not the size but the absence of any visible crystal shape. Consequently, a tiny sample of a mineral can be massive.

splaying out from a central point

hair-like

FIBROUS AND RADIATING

very thin and tabular

PLATY

flattened, but not very elongated

TABULAR

flattened and elongated

BLADED

same size in all directions

EQUANT

thin flat sheets

LAMELLAR

bent masses of lamellar crystals

FOLIATED

parallel prismatic crystals

COLUMNAR

needle-like

ACICULAR

irregular grains

GRANULAR

sphere-shaped

SPHERULAR

rounded, kidney-like

RENIFORM

like a bunch of grapes

BOTRYOIDAL

elongate parallel faces

PRISMATIC

tree-like

DENDRITIC

powdery mass

EARTHY

no visible crystals

MASSIVE

Cleavage and Fracture

These terms describe the way a mineral breaks. Cleavage refers to the flat planes along which a crystal tends to split; it is graded from poor to perfect depending on how clean and easy the break is. Fracture describes the surface where a mineral has broken, but where it has not cleaved. A parting looks like a cleavage, but has other causes.

perfect cubic cleavage

GALENA

perfect micaceous cleavage

MUSCOVITE

uneven fracture

EPIDOTE

hackly fracture

GOLD

conchoidal (shell-like) fracture

CITRINE

parting (looks like a cleavage)

SAPPHIRE

Transparency

All minerals featured in this book are transparent or translucent unless stated otherwise. Sometimes transparency may only be seen when looking through thin slivers of the mineral.

transparent

translucent

CARNELIAN

opaque

ROSE QUARTZ

CHALCOCITE

Colour

green

purple

yellow

FLUORITE

Some minerals are always of the same colour, as a consequence of their chemical composition and structure. Their colour is a useful aid to identification. Other minerals, such as fluorite, can be different colours due to tiny amounts of chemical impurities, structural flaws, or to their different habits. Certain minerals are fluorescent – they glow different colours under ultraviolet (UV) light.

Lustre

Lustre describes the way a mineral reflects light. Adamantine is the most brilliant lustre shown by transparent or translucent minerals. The glass-like vitreous lustre is less brilliant. Slightly inferior lustres are prefixed 'sub', for example, a subadamantine lustre is slightly less bright than adamantine. A mineral's lustre may be different on certain faces or cleavages, and it should always be examined on a clean, unweathered part of the mineral.

adamantine

vitreous

metallic

DIAMOND

TOPAZ

GALENA

pearly

waxy

resinous

HEULANDITE

OPAL

OLIVINE PERIDOT

greasy

dull

silky

NEPHELINE

MICROCLINE

HAWK'S EYE

Streak

The colour of the finely powdered mineral is called the streak. Even if a mineral's colour varies, the streak will always the same for a mineral. For example, no matter the variety, hematite has a reddish brown streak. Streak is tested by drawing the mineral across a streak plate, which is the white unglazed back of a ceramic tile.

crystal

kidney ore

HEMATITE

USEFUL KIT
Some properties are easier to see with a hand lens or magnifying glass. hand lens
Other useful tools include a streak plate, a compass for detecting magnetism, a soft brush for cleaning minerals, and coins and a knife for testing hardness. Schools, clubs, and societies may be able to provide chemicals for acidity testing and Geiger counters.

coins

streak plate

soft brush

Hardness

How hard a mineral is depends on the way its atoms are arranged. Hardness is measured by reference to the ten standard minerals on Mohs' scale, the softest mineral being talc, and the hardest, diamond. On Mohs' scale, a crystal that scratches calcite but is scratched by fluorite would be 3.5 on the scale. It may be possible to distinguish similar looking minerals by measuring their hardness.

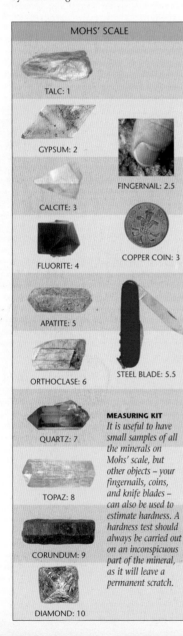

MOHS' SCALE

TALC: 1

GYPSUM: 2

FINGERNAIL: 2.5

CALCITE: 3

COPPER COIN: 3

FLUORITE: 4

APATITE: 5

ORTHOCLASE: 6

STEEL BLADE: 5.5

QUARTZ: 7

TOPAZ: 8

CORUNDUM: 9

DIAMOND: 10

MEASURING KIT
It is useful to have small samples of all the minerals on Mohs' scale, but other objects – your fingernails, coins, and knife blades – can also be used to estimate hardness. A hardness test should always be carried out on an inconspicuous part of the mineral, as it will leave a permanent scratch.

Density

Most minerals have a density of between 2 and 4, but some are conspicuously lighter or heavier. For example, the crystal of baryte, below, would feel distinctly heavy compared to gypsum. Density is measured in number of grams per cubic centimetre.

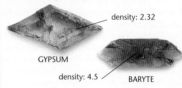

density: 2.32

GYPSUM

density: 4.5

BARYTE

Magnetism

A few iron-bearing minerals are magnetic; when placed beside a compass, they deflect the needle from the north. Magnetite, a particularly strong natural magnet, attracts iron or steel objects.

iron filings

MAGNETITE

attracts the paperclip

Acid Tests

If a tiny drop of dilute hydrochloric acid (dil. HCl) is placed on certain carbonate minerals, it fizzes and gives off bubbles of carbon dioxide gas. Certain other minerals react to spot acid tests in other distinctive ways, by

HCl fizzes on calcite

changing colour or dissolving. Please note, all acids can be dangerous: they must always be handled with great care.

Radioactivity

Minerals that contain uranium or thorium are radioactive. Radioactivity is detected using a Geiger counter. All radioactive minerals require special handling and storage.

Geological Association

Some of the most important clues to
the identity of a mineral come from
the rock matrix in which it occurs and
the other minerals that occur with it.
Some minerals only occur in particular
types of rocks; others are
typically associated with
certain other minerals. For
example, apophyllite often
occurs with stilbite.

apophyllite

basalt

BASALT ASSOCIATION

elbaite
tourmaline

quartz

rhodochrosite

kyanite

muscovite
mica

albite
feldspar

staurolite

sphalerite

pyrite

PEGMATITE ASSOCIATION

MICA SCHIST ASSOCIATION

**HYDROTHERMAL VEIN
ASSOCIATION**

TABLE OF ELEMENTS

Ac	Actinium	Ge	Germanium	Po	Polonium
Ag	Silver	H	Hydrogen	Pr	Praseodymium
Al	Aluminium	He	Helium	Pt	Platinum
Am	Americium	Hf	Hafnium	Pu	Plutonium
Ar	Argon	Hg	Mercury	Ra	Radium
As	Arsenic	Ho	Holmium	Rb	Rubidium
At	Astatine	I	Iodine	Re	Rhenium
Au	Gold	In	Indium	Rh	Rhodium
B	Boron	Ir	Iridium	Rn	Radon
Ba	Barium	K	Potassium	S	Sulphur
Be	Beryllium	Kr	Krypton	Sb	Antimony
Bi	Bismuth	La	Lanthanum	Sc	Scandium
Bk	Berkelium	Li	Lithium	Se	Selenium
Br	Bromine	Lu	Lutetium	Si	Silicon
C	Carbon	Lw	Lawrencium	Sm	Samarium
Ca	Calcium	Md	Mendelevium	Sn	Tin
Cd	Cadmium	Mg	Magnesium	Sr	Strontium
Ce	Cerium	Mn	Manganese	Ta	Tantalum
Cf	Californium	Mo	Molybdenum	Tb	Terbium
Cl	Chlorine	N	Nitrogen	Tc	Technetium
Cm	Curium	Na	Sodium	Te	Tellurium
Co	Cobalt	Nb	Niobium	Th	Thorium
Cr	Chromium	Nd	Neodymium	Ti	Titanium
Cs	Cesium	Ne	Neon	Tl	Thallium
Cu	Copper	Ni	Nickel	Tm	Thulium
Dy	Dysprosium	No	Nobelium	U	Uranium
Er	Erbium	Np	Neptunium	V	Vanadium
Es	Einsteinium	O	Oxygen	W	Tungsten
F	Fluorine	Os	Osmium	Xe	Xenon
Fe	Iron	P	Phosphorous	Y	Yttrium
Fm	Fermium	Pa	Protactinium	Yb	Ytterbium
Fr	Francium	Pb	Lead	Zn	Zinc
Ga	Gallium	Pd	Palladium	Zr	Zirconium
Gd	Gadolinium	Pm	Promethium		

Sedimentary Rocks

Sedimentary rocks are produced by the movement of water or wind. There are two groups: detrital, which result from the settling of rock grains, and chemical/organic, such as the chalk that forms the cliffs of England's south coast (below), which are produced by water-deposited chemicals or from organic remains. Here, the detrital sedimentary rocks are arranged in order of decreasing grain size. This may depend on how far the grains have travelled before deposition, or on the energy levels of their environment. For example, only large grains can settle in fast-moving water. The chemical/organic rocks are grouped by composition.

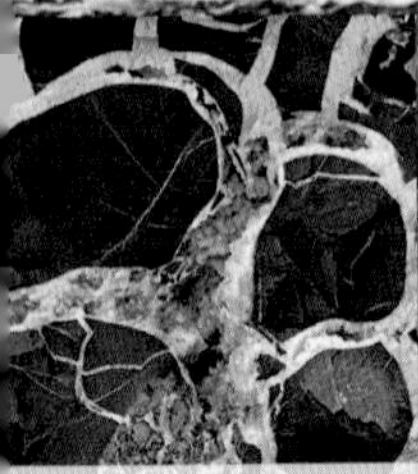

SEPTARIAN NODULE

TUFA

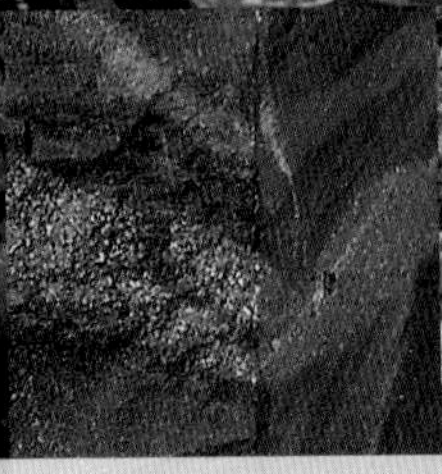

BANDED IRONSTONE

LIMESTON

Conglomerate

This common rock type is easily recognized by its large rounded clasts. The clasts, which were pebbles, may be of one type, such as all quartz or limestone, or more. These clasts are in a finer matrix made up of smaller grains (typically sand-sized) and cement. Conglomerates are found with sandstone in rock formed in large river systems.

CONGLOMERATE, *inter-bedded with sandstones, was formed in a river channel and flood plain.*

rounded clast

different clast types

POLYGENETIC CONGLOMERATE

sandy matrix

GRAIN SIZE *2mm to several cm, in finer matrix.*
ESSENTIAL COMPONENTS *Commonly quartz, chalcedony, and rock fragments.*
ADDITIONAL COMPONENTS *Sometimes gold, uranium minerals.*
ORIGIN *Detrital, from pebbles.*
SIMILAR ROCKS *Breccia (below).*

Breccia

Unlike the clasts in conglomerate, those in breccia are angular, which indicates that they have not travelled far from their source. Breccias may form in volcanic systems and in faults. Sedimentary breccias, however, are formed from screes in mountains and along coasts, or in deserts due to flash floods.

WELL-DEVELOPED *screes on cliffs in southern Morocco; such deposits may be the source of the clasts in breccia.*

fine matrix

different clast types

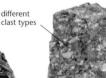

POLYGENETIC BRECCIA

angular clast

GRAIN SIZE *2mm to several cm, in finer matrix.*
ESSENTIAL COMPONENTS *Commonly rock fragments.*
ADDITIONAL COMPONENTS *None.*
ORIGIN *Detrital, from coarse sediment.*
SIMILAR ROCKS *Fault breccia (matrix is a mineral), volcanic breccia (occurs next to lava).*

Tillite

MELTING *glaciers and the deposition of their ice-carried sediment produce tillite rock.*

A large variation in grain size – from powder to clasts of several metres – is typical in this rock and gives rise to tillite's other name: boulder clay. In the past, material was ground up and transported as a result of a glacier moving down a valley; when the glacier melted, it deposited its entire load of materials or till. The resultant rock, tillite, is common in geologically recent deposits of ice ages in northern Europe and North America, but also found in older rocks.

large clast

grey clay matrix

SECTION SHOWN

GRAIN SIZE *Less than 0.005mm to many metres.*
ESSENTIAL COMPONENTS *Commonly rock fragments.*
ADDITIONAL COMPONENTS *None.*
ORIGIN *Detrital, from coarse angular sediment.*
SIMILAR ROCKS *Breccia (p.21).*

Gritstone

COARSE *bedding and blocky jointing is typical in gritstone outcrops.*

Gritstone is made up of the cemented deposits of rounded grains. These are the size of coarse sand to gravel. In some gritstones the grains can be easily rubbed out, while in others a strong cement makes the rock suitable for use as a grinding stone, such as Millstone Grit. Quartz is always the greatest component, but it often contains iron oxides giving it a yellow, brown, or red colour.

reddish colour from iron oxides

coarse quartz grains

FELDSPATHIC GRITSTONE

GRAIN SIZE *1–4mm.*
ESSENTIAL COMPONENTS *Quartz, feldspar.*
ADDITIONAL COMPONENTS *Mica and many heavy and resistant minerals, such as garnet, rutile, and titanite.*
ORIGIN *Detrital, from grit.*
SIMILAR ROCKS *Sandstone (p.23) is finer; feldspathic gritstone contains more feldspar.*

Sandstone

One of the most common sedimentary rocks, sandstone is usually quartz-dominated with visible sandy grains. These grains may be of various shapes when viewed with a hand lens. Well-rounded grains are typical of desert sandstone, while river sands are usually angular, and beach sands somewhere in between. The colour is also an indication of how the sandstone formed and can be shades of white, red, grey, or green. Bedding is often seen in sandstones as a series of layers representing successive deposits of grains. Bedding surfaces may show other depositional features, such as ripples.

RED *sandstones with well-developed bedding are found in the desert of Arizona, USA.*

fine sandstone

rounded quartz grains

IRON-RICH SANDSTONE

coarse upper layer

folded bedding planes

SLUMP-BEDDED SANDSTONE

MICACEOUS SANDSTONE

GRAIN SIZE *0.1–2mm.*
ESSENTIAL COMPONENTS *Quartz, feldspar.*
ADDITIONAL COMPONENTS *Mica and many others.*
ORIGIN *Detrital, from sand.*
SIMILAR ROCKS *Orthoquartzite (p.25), arkose (p.25), greensand (p.26), flagstone (p.28).*

NOTE

Sandstone is an attractive building stone and, since ancient times, it has been carved into monuments, such as the Great Sphinx at Al-Jizah in Egypt. Its resistance to weathering depends on the nature and strength of the mineral cement that holds together the grains of sand.

Cross-bedded Sandstone

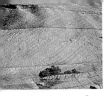

CROSS-BEDDED *units in a series of yellow sandstone are parallel at the base of each unit and truncated at the top.*

When one set of beds is inclined to another it is known as cross-bedding. It forms in deserts where wind deposition creates beds at different angles along dune surfaces, and it forms in water-lain sediments as competing currents drop sediments at different angles. Desert sandstone is usually red due to the deposition of a thin hematite layer over the quartz grains.

truncated bedding

mud-rich layer

CROSS-BEDDED MUDDY SANDSTONE

GRAIN SIZE *0.1–2mm.*
ESSENTIAL COMPONENTS *Quartz, feldspar.*
ADDITIONAL COMPONENTS *Hematite, mica.*
ORIGIN *Detrital, from desert wind or water.*
SIMILAR ROCKS *In other sandstones (p.23), the layers are parallel and not truncated. Cross bedding can occur in quartzites (p.76) and gritstones (p.22).*

Loess

LOESS *is formed from the lightest fragments of sediment carried by desert winds.*

This is a yellow or brown, soft and crumbly, low-density rock. It comprises very fine rock and mineral material. It contains few clay minerals, so feels smooth but not sticky when wet. It is another rock formed by the deposition of material carried by the wind. The largest deposits are found next to the Gobi desert in China. European examples are often accumulations of wind-blown debris from glacial deposits.

yellow colour

spongy texture

SECTION SHOWN

GRAIN SIZE *Less than 0.005mm.*
ESSENTIAL COMPONENTS *Quartz, feldspar.*
ADDITIONAL COMPONENTS *None.*
ORIGIN *Detrital, from wind-blown sediment in a desert.*
SIMILAR ROCKS *Clay (p.29), which is sticky when wet, has also a far greater density.*

Orthoquartzite

White or pinkish sandstones composed of more than 95 per cent quartz are known as orthoquartzites to differentiate them from similar metamorphic rocks. They are hard rocks and often form ridges. The quartz grains have been naturally sorted and have travelled far.

ORTHOQUARTZITE *forms prominent white ridges in this landscape.*

darker weathered surface

GREY ORTHOQUARTZITE

quartz grains

GRAIN SIZE *0.1–2mm.*
ESSENTIAL COMPONENTS *Quartz.*
ADDITIONAL COMPONENTS *Heavy minerals, such as zircon, rutile and titanite.*
ORIGIN *Detrital, from a quartz-rich sand.*
SIMILAR ROCKS *Other sandstones (pp.23–27) have a lower proportion of quartz (p.143), and are darker coloured.*

Arkose

A pink sandstone, the colour of which is due to an abundance of feldspar, especially pink alkali feldspars. The flat cleavage faces and angular grain shape of the feldspars reflect light under a hand lens. Arkose forms by the fast deposition of sand weathered from granites and gneisses.

TORRIDONIAN *arkose from northwest Scotland covers large areas of flat-topped mountainland.*

pink colour of feldspar

small resistant veinlet

GRAIN SIZE *0.1–2mm.*
ESSENTIAL COMPONENTS *Feldspar, quartz.*
ADDITIONAL COMPONENTS *None.*
ORIGIN *Detrital, from a feldspar-rich sand.*
SIMILAR ROCKS *Other sandstones (pp.23-27) have more quartz (p.143) and less feldspar. Unlike other sandstones, most arkoses occur in ancient rock sequences.*

grey colour of many ancient arkoses

GREY ARKOSE

Greensand

GREENSAND *forms in quiet, shallow marine conditions. The green colour is due to ferrous iron.*

Green-coloured sandstones are usually the result of the presence of sand-sized and smaller grains of the iron mineral glauconite. They typically weather to a brown colour on surface exposures. They are formed in shallow marine conditions and may contain shell fragments and larger fossils. Cretaceous and younger rocks of southern England and North America have many greensand beds.

glauconite

green colour from glauconite

quartz

MICROGRAPH

paler grains mainly quartz

GRAIN SIZE *0.1–2mm.*
ESSENTIAL COMPONENTS *Quartz, feldspar, glauconite.*
ADDITIONAL COMPONENTS *None.*
ORIGIN *Detrital, from glauconite-rich marine sand.*
SIMILAR ROCKS *Rounded green grains of glauconite (p.170) are unique to greensand.*

Phosphorite

GUANO *deposits on Navassa Island, in the Caribbean, have produced a brown phosphorite.*

Sedimentary rocks rich in phosphate minerals are known as phosphorites. Several of these consist of phosphates derived from animals, such as bone beds and guano, where the phosphorites are dark brown. Others are made of black phosphates: deep sea nodules, pebble beds, and sandstones. Another common type is pale-coloured and rich in apatite.

phosphatic grain (fish bone)

brown calcareous mudstone

SECTION SHOWN

NODULAR PHOSPHORITE

GRAIN SIZE *Some are not granular; others have grains up to and greater than 1cm.*
ESSENTIAL COMPONENTS *Phosphate minerals (apatite, variscite, vivianite, etc.).*
ADDITIONAL COMPONENTS *Bones, guano.*
ORIGIN *Organic or chemical precipitate.*
SIMILAR ROCKS *Dark phosphorites may resemble ironstone (p.35).*

Greywacke

Greywacke has formed from a mixture of sand and, proportionately less, mud. It is a dark-coloured rock: grey, dark green, or black. Sand-sized grains of rock fragments and minerals are visible, and may be randomly distributed or in graded layers with coarser fragments at the base, fining upwards. It is especially abundant in Lower Palaeozoic rocks worldwide.

GREYWACKE *appears as a dirty-grey coloured series of beds in a coastal outcrop.*

grains of many different sizes and types

dirty grey colour

MICROGRAPH

mixed angular fragments

GRAIN SIZE *0.005–2mm.*
ESSENTIAL COMPONENTS *Rock and mineral fragments.*
ADDITIONAL COMPONENTS *None.*
ORIGIN *Detrital, from muddy sand.*
SIMILAR ROCKS *Other sandstones (pp.23-27) have less angular grains; turbidites (below) contain both greywackes and finer rocks.*

Turbidite

A turbidite is a unit of rock formed from a turbidity current: a fast-moving turbulent mass of water and sediment that travels over the continental shelf into deeper ocean. Turbidites have a repeated series of different types of bed in a particular order. It starts with a thick greywacke, followed by thin graded greywackes, then siltstone, then mudstone. The last two rocks may show ripples on bedding surfaces.

TURBIDITE *units, each tens of centimetres thick, represent successive influxes of sediment.*

dark, coarse grains

fine grains

graded bedding

SECTION SHOWN

GRAIN SIZE *0.005–2mm.*
ESSENTIAL COMPONENTS *Rock and mineral fragments.*
ADDITIONAL COMPONENTS *None.*
ORIGIN *Detrital, from a turbidity current.*
SIMILAR ROCKS *Turbidites are a mixture of greywacke (above), siltstone (p.28), and mudstone (p.29) present in repeating layers.*

Flagstone

This is a type of sandstone that easily splits into flat sheets along certain bedding planes. These surfaces are rich in small, flat-lying grains of mica, chiefly muscovite, which may sparkle as they reflect light. Mica grains are concentrated because they settle through water more slowly than quartz and other minerals. Flagstones are often used as paving stones and for building walls.

flat surface

bed a few centimetres thick

> **GRAIN SIZE** *0.1–2mm.*
> **ESSENTIAL COMPONENTS** *Quartz, feldspar, mica.*
> **ADDITIONAL COMPONENTS** *None.*
> **ORIGIN** *Detrital, from a mica-rich sand.*
> **SIMILAR ROCKS** *Flagstones are differentiated from other sandstones (pp.23-27) by a higher content of mica, and the ability to be split.*

Siltstone

POLYGONAL *dessication cracks, seen here in silt, are often preserved in siltstones.*

Siltstone is another detrital sedimentary rock, lying in grain size between sandstone and mudstone. Like sandstone, it can form in different environments and have different colours and textures, but reds and greys, and planar bedding are typical. Plant fossils and other carbonaceous matter are common in darker-coloured siltstones.

The presence of mica may produce a flaggy siltstone.

silt-sized grains

dark colour from carbon

SECTION SHOWN

> **GRAIN SIZE** *0.005–0.1mm.*
> **ESSENTIAL COMPONENTS** *Quartz, feldspar.*
> **ADDITIONAL COMPONENTS** *Plant fossils, coal, mica.*
> **ORIGIN** *Detrital, from silt.*
> **SIMILAR ROCKS** *Sandstone (p.23) is coarser, mudstone (p.29) is finer, but siltstone can grade into either.*

Mudstone

A grey or black rock formed from mud, mudstones contain both detrital minerals, such as quartz and feldspar, and clay minerals and carbonaceous matter. Individual grains, however, are too small to be seen without a hand lens. Some mudstones are fossiliferous, others are calcareous and react with acid.

A PILLAR *of more-resistant sandstone is perched on grey mudstones, in Namibia.*

paler colour

mud-sized grains

curved fracture

CALCAREOUS MUDSTONE

GRAIN SIZE *Less than 0.1mm.*
ESSENTIAL COMPONENTS *Quartz, feldspar.*
ADDITIONAL COMPONENTS *Fossils are commonly well-preserved.*
ORIGIN *Detrital, from mud.*
SIMILAR ROCKS *Greywacke (p.27), which has a greater range of grain size.*

Clay

Clay is a rock made of minerals such as kaolinite, illite, and montmorillonite. When damp, clay has a sticky feel. Adding water allows it to be moulded by hand, but more water will cause it to disintegrate. Clay is typically dark to light grey but a pure white variety called china clay can occur. Individual grains may be seen only under powerful microscopes.

SHRINKAGE *cracks can be seen in this quarry face of grey clay.*

limonite gives yellowish colour

KAOLINITE

extremely fine grains

GRAIN SIZE *Less than 0.005mm.*
ESSENTIAL COMPONENTS *Clay minerals, such as kaolinite, illite, and montmorillonite.*
ADDITIONAL COMPONENTS *None.*
ORIGIN *Detrital, from products of chemical weathering.*
SIMILAR ROCKS *Loess (p.24).*

Septarian Nodule

SECTION *through a septarian nodule in brown clay on a beach cliff.*

Septarian nodules are structures that form within calcareous mudstones and marls. They are boulder-shaped areas within the rock, typically 20–50cm in diameter, and comprise of harder rock than the surrounding matrix. The nodule is often a dark brown colour due to the presence of iron oxides. Within each nodule, concentric and radial shrinkage cracks are lined with light-coloured minerals, such as white or yellow calcite.

calcite infill of shrinkage crack

brown calcareous mudstone

GRAIN SIZE *Nodules 10cm–1m.*
ESSENTIAL COMPONENTS *Calcite, celestine.*
ADDITIONAL COMPONENTS *None.*
ORIGIN *Dehydration effects during rock formation.*
SIMILAR ROCKS *Nodules are common in many rocks; "septaria" are the infilled cracks.*

Iron Sulphide Nodule

IRON *sulphide nodules can form around or replace a fossil, as seen in this ammonite.*

Both pyrite and marcasite form similar nodules in clays, mudstones, shales, and chalk. These are often spherical and usually about 5cm in diameter. The sulphide mineral forms a radiating structure and, on first exposure to air, has an attractive yellow colour and metallic lustre. This lustre is soon lost as both minerals are unstable.

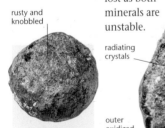

rusty and knobbled

radiating crystals

EXTERNAL SURFACE

outer oxidized edge

metalic lustre of pyrite

GRAIN SIZE *Nodules 1–10cm.*
ESSENTIAL COMPONENTS *Pyrite or marcasite.*
ADDITIONAL COMPONENTS *Fossils, such as ammonites.*
ORIGIN *Chemical reactions in host rock.*
SIMILAR ROCKS *Meteorites (p.84) but these have a furrowed surface.*

Shale

Shale is a highly fissile rock, meaning that it breaks up readily into thin sheets. Otherwise it resembles mudstone in grain size and colour. Shales are frequently fossiliferous and may contain bivalves, other molluscs, and plant fossils. Oil shales are rich in hydrocarbons and are of economic importance. Black shales, also rich in carbon and its compounds, form in muddy water. They often have concretions of pyrite or gypsum that have formed after sedimentation. Alum shales, common in northern Europe, contain aluminium salts. These salts were once used in the tanning and dyeing industries.

SHALE *forms irregular, crumbling cliffs of loose weathered fragments, due to its fissile nature.*

fine, grey rock

hydrocarbon drops

OIL SHALE

aluminium-rich mineral

ALUM SHALE

brachiopod

fissile sheets

FOSSILIFEROUS SHALE

GRAIN SIZE *Less than 0.1mm.*
ESSENTIAL COMPONENTS *Quartz, clays, mica.*
ADDITIONAL COMPONENTS *Carbon (graphite), alum, fossils common.*
ORIGIN *Detrital, from mud, clay, and organic material.*
SIMILAR ROCKS *Mudstone (p.29).*

NOTE

The Burgess Shales of British Columbia, Canada, are 505 million years old and contain finely-preserved fossils. These are among the earliest examples of complex life recorded on Earth and include a large range of organisms, some related to modern species and other strange animals long since extinct.

Limestone

KARST *topography is typical of limestone outcrops, here the light grey stone is Carboniferous Limestone.*

Limestones are yellow, white, or grey rocks composed primarily of the mineral calcite. They can easily be identified by their reaction with dilute hydrochloric acid, which results in a rapid release of carbon dioxide gas and a fizzing sound. Calcite may be in the form of lime mud (micrite), detrital grains (calcarenite), tiny spheres (oolites), calcite crystals (sparite), and/or fossils. The combination of these, leads to a large number of textures, which give important clues to the environment in which the limestone was formed.

brachiopod
fossil

gastropod
(snail)

crinoid
stem

SHELLY LIMESTONE

FRESHWATER LIMESTONE

CRINOIDAL LIMESTONE

very fine
grains

grey
colour

SECTION SHOWN

shell fragment

GRAIN SIZE *0.005–2mm.*
ESSENTIAL COMPONENTS *Calcite.*
ADDITIONAL COMPONENTS *Dolomite, aragonite, quartz, and fossils common.*
ORIGIN *Chemical and organic precipitation.*
SIMILAR ROCKS *Dolomite (p.34), which does not react vigorously with dilute acid.*

NOTE

Limestones are an excellent source of fossils in rocks of all ages. Reef-forming animals, such as corals and algae, and shelled animals such as bivalves, gastropods, brachiopods, ammonites, and echinoids are all common and sometimes form the entire rock.

Oolite

This is a type of limestone made of spherical grains of calcium carbonate. These are usually about 1–2mm in diameter and white or yellow in colour. The ooliths usually have a concentric structure and have been formed by a nucleus grain rolling around in lime-rich shallow sea water. Sometimes the ooliths are larger, and the rock is then known as pisolite.

WELL-BEDDED *yellow oolitic limestone is seen in these quarry walls.*

large oolith

PISOLITE

SECTION SHOWN

oolith

lime mud matrix

GRAIN SIZE *0.5–2mm.*
ESSENTIAL COMPONENTS *Calcite.*
ADDITIONAL COMPONENTS *Fossils, including bivalves.*
ORIGIN *Chemical precipitation in shallow water.*
SIMILAR ROCKS *Oolite is a type of limestone (p.32), containing ooliths.*

Chalk

A pure white fine-grained limestone, which formed in clean shallow-water marine conditions by the accumulation of the hard calcium carbonate-rich skeletons of very tiny organisms. Typical of the Cretaceous period, thick chalks are found in southern England. They contain layers of flint nodules. Common fossils include echinoids, bivalves, and ammonites.

WHITE *cliffs of chalk (here in East Sussex), are found along the English Channel coast.*

echinoid

CHALK WITH FOSSIL

very fine white grains

GRAIN SIZE *Less than 0.005mm.*
ESSENTIAL COMPONENTS *Calcite.*
ADDITIONAL COMPONENTS *Fossils common.*
ORIGIN *Accumulation of minute fossils in quiet marine conditions.*
SIMILAR ROCKS *Chalk is a type of limestone (p.32), recognized by its pure white colour.*

Dolomite

THE DOLOMITES, *a mountain range in south central Europe, give their name to the rock type.*

This rock is also known as dolostone to distinguish it from the mineral dolomite, which is a major constituent. It looks like limestone but contains more crystalline material, and does not react with dilute acid unless finely powdered. Dolomite is often yellow-grey or brown. It has formed by the reaction of magnesium-rich fluids passing through limestone before it has hardened into a rock.

dolomite crystal

MICROGRAPH

fine, even-sized grains

GRAIN SIZE *0.005–2mm.*
ESSENTIAL COMPONENTS *Dolomite.*
ADDITIONAL COMPONENTS *Calcite, quartz.*
ORIGIN *Chemical change of limestone, by magnesium-rich solutions.*
SIMILAR ROCKS *Limestone (p.32), but unlike dolomite, it reacts vigorously with dilute acid.*

brown colour

Marl

WEATHERED *outcrops of nodular grey marl are found in the Badlands, central USA.*

A mudstone or clay that reacts with dilute acid because of its high calcium carbonate content, marls are usually light coloured and may be grey, green, red, or variegated. They are often nodular with the nodules being better cemented than the surrounding rock. Marls are commonly found in lakes and other shallow water settings, such as lagoons.

red iron oxides

RED MARL

grey colour

fine grain size

GRAIN SIZE *Less than 0.1mm.*
ESSENTIAL COMPONENTS *Mud, calcite.*
ADDITIONAL COMPONENTS *Fossils, gypsum, iron oxide minerals.*
ORIGIN *Detrital, from lime mud.*
SIMILAR ROCKS *Limestone (p.32) is softer; mudstone (p.29) has less calcite.*

Ironstone

Sandstones and limestones that are very rich in hematite, goethite, siderite, chamosite, or other iron minerals, are known as ironstones. These minerals give the rock a dark red, brown, green, or yellow colour. They usually form by space-filling or replacement of previous minerals.

FORMED *by the oxidation of a sulphide deposit to iron oxides minerals, ironstone is found in Colorado, USA.*

iron on oolith

pore space

MICROGRAPH

red hematite

oolitic grains

GRAIN SIZE *0.1–2mm.*
ESSENTIAL COMPONENTS *Hematite, goethite, siderite.*
ADDITIONAL COMPONENTS *Quartz or calcite of host rock.*
ORIGIN *Chemical change of limestone or sandstone, by iron-rich solutions.*
SIMILAR ROCKS *Limestone (p.32).*

Bog Iron Ore

Marshes and shallow lakes in Scandinavia and Canada are the source of a rich ironstone forming at the present day. It is typically a brown-yellow mudstone with yellow, red, brown, or black concretions of iron oxides and hydroxides, and contains up to 70 per cent Fe_2O_3. It was formerly used as an ore, hence the name, but is rarely of suitable quality for modern iron production. Bog iron ore often contains carbonaceous plant material, sometimes preserved by iron minerals.

SWAMPS *in temperate climates can be the source of bog iron ore, where iron is concentrated by chemical and biological processes.*

oxides and hydroxides of iron

grey mudstone

GRAIN SIZE *Less than 0.1mm.*
ESSENTIAL COMPONENTS *Mud, iron minerals especially goethite.*
ADDITIONAL COMPONENTS *Plants.*
ORIGIN *Chemical and bacterial concentration of iron in swamps.*
SIMILAR ROCKS *Mudstone (p.29), but this has little iron-staining.*

Banded Ironstone

BANDED *ironstones are often interbedded with chert and other sedimentary rocks, as in this example from Zimbabwe.*

Also known as banded iron formation (BIF), this rock is made up of thin layers of alternating red, brown, or black iron oxides (hematite or magnetite), and grey or off-white chert. It is a very fine-grained rock that breaks into smooth splintery pieces. It is particularly abundant in Precambrian rocks (more than 500 million years old) and can form very thick sequences, such as in the Hammersley Range of Australia. It is as economically important as iron ore.

magnetite and chert layer

hematite-rich layer

GRAIN SIZE *Not granular or very fine.*
ESSENTIAL COMPONENTS *Hematite, magnetite, chalcedony.*
ADDITIONAL COMPONENTS *None.*
ORIGIN *Chemical precipitation of iron minerals and silica.*
SIMILAR ROCKS *Chert (right) does not have as much red-coloured banding.*

Laterite

LATERITE *is formed in tropical and desert areas where heat plays a major role in the weathering process.*

A hardened iron and aluminium-rich nodular soil, laterite is formed in tropical and desert climates. The nodules of laterite are red-brown or yellow, and contain grains of sand or hardened clay. In desert climates, it may have a shiny surface, polished by the wind. It is formed by evaporation and leaching of minerals from loose sediments and soil, leaving behind insoluble salts.

iron oxide minerals

sand grains

polished surface

DESERT-VARNISHED LATERITE

GRAIN SIZE *Not granular.*
ESSENTIAL COMPONENTS *Hematite, magnetite, chalcedony.*
ADDITIONAL COMPONENTS *Sand; clay.*
ORIGIN *Chemical precipitation of iron minerals and silica.*
SIMILAR ROCKS *Chert (above right) does not have as much red-coloured banding.*

Chert

Chert is a rock composed of the mineral chalcedony. It is most commonly grey, white, brown, or black. It breaks along flat to rounded, smooth surfaces and has a glassy appearance. It may occur as beds, or as nodules. Chert forms by precipitation from silica-rich fluids and colloids and may fill fractures in lavas.

BEDS *of chert in various shades of grey; the orange streak is iron-staining from surface water.*

grey-brown colour

chalcedony | microcrystals

MICROGRAPH

GRAIN SIZE *Not granular.*
ESSENTIAL COMPONENTS *Chalcedony.*
ADDITIONAL COMPONENTS *None.*
ORIGIN *Chemical precipitation of silica.*
SIMILAR ROCKS *Flint (below), which has a conchoidal fracture.*

vitreous lustre

flat fracture surface

Flint

Flint is a variety of chert that occurs in chalk as nodules, often in bands parallel to the bedding. These nodules are irregular but rounded. Flint breaks with a conchoidal fracture and is grey in colour and sometimes banded. It is more resistant to weathering than chalk, so can form thick beach pebble beds.

BLACK *flint nodules, coated with white chalk, stand out against a background of cream-coloured chalk.*

surface flaking

conchoidal fracture

SECTION SHOWN

GRAIN SIZE *Not granular.*
ESSENTIAL COMPONENTS *Chalcedony.*
ADDITIONAL COMPONENTS *Sometimes fossils, such as sponges.*
ORIGIN *Chemical precipitation of silica.*
SIMILAR ROCKS *Chert (above), which has a flat fracture. Chalk coating is a key feature.*

chalk

Diatomite

DEPOSITS *of diatomite found at Lough Neagh, Northern Ireland were formed when the lake covered a larger area.*

A low-density rock made out of opal, Diatomite is derived from the remains of the hard parts of minute animals called diatoms. It can form in quiet marine and non-marine conditions by the accumulation of millions of tiny spiky exoskeletons, usually too small to be seen even with a hand lens. The hardness, size, and shape of the particles make diatomite a useful abrasive. It is also used as a filter in water purification.

loose porous structure

rough texture

GRAIN SIZE	*Less than 0.1mm.*
ESSENTIAL COMPONENTS	*Opal.*
ADDITIONAL COMPONENTS	*None.*
ORIGIN	*Accumulation of silica-rich organisms.*
SIMILAR ROCKS	*Pumice (p.66), which is usually grey in colour, and associated with glassy volcanic rocks.*

Geyserite

GEYSERITE *deposits around Clepsydra, a geyser in Yellowstone National Park, USA.*

Geyserite is a hard white, cream, or pink rock that forms in active volcanic districts. It is also known as siliceous sinter and results from the evaporation of water from a silica-rich solution, leaving a precipitate of opal. It is common around geysers, hence its name, but also forms wherever water escapes from or comes into contact with hot lava.

banded structure

multicoloured layers

SECTION SHOWN

GRAIN SIZE	*Not granular.*
ESSENTIAL COMPONENTS	*Opal.*
ADDITIONAL COMPONENTS	*Metal oxide minerals, such as hematite.*
ORIGIN	*Precipitation from hot water in volcanic areas.*
SIMILAR ROCKS	*Travertine (p.39), but this reacts with acid.*

Tufa

Tufa is poorly-cemented, soft, porous, white calcium carbonate (usually calcite) that precipitates out of calcium-rich water by evaporation. It is not bedded and may be stained yellow or red by iron oxides. It occurs in limestone areas in temperate climates, but is ubiquitous in dry river beds and desert surfaces in hotter climes. Where it is associated with loose sediments, it is known as calcrete.

TUFA *forms spires of rock due to a reaction between underwater, spring water, and lake water in Mono Lake, California, USA.*

YELLOW TUFA

petrified plant stem

loosely cemented

soft, powdery texture

GRAIN SIZE *Less than 1mm.*
ESSENTIAL COMPONENTS *Calcite.*
ADDITIONAL COMPONENTS *None.*
ORIGIN *Precipitation from calcium-rich solutions.*
SIMILAR ROCKS *Travertine (below) is more solid and often banded.*

Travertine

A compact and crystalline variety of calcium carbonate, travertine is normally creamy-white but may be stained by metal salts. It often occurs in rounded, banded, or botryoidal structures. It can be a product of hot springs, but is more usually seen underground in caves, where it covers walls and forms stalagmites and stalactites, a variety known as flowstone.

FLOWSTONE *deposits in caves are made of travertine, as seen in this spectacular example.*

calcite crystals

STALACTITE

banding of iron-stained calcite

flowstone

GRAIN SIZE *Wide range.*
ESSENTIAL COMPONENTS *Calcite.*
ADDITIONAL COMPONENTS *None.*
ORIGIN *Precipitation from calcium-rich solutions.*
SIMILAR ROCKS *Tufa (above), which has a lighter density and is more porous; alabaster (gypsum rock, p.42), which is softer.*

Coal

SMALL *coal mines, like this, are rarer now that larger and more mechanized mines produce cheaper coal.*

This low-density black rock is formed by the compression of thick layers of plant material. Peat is an intermediate stage between vegetation and coal, in which the plant matter is still visible. In coal, the plant matter has been reduced to carbon, although traces of plant fossils may remain. Depending on the grade, coal may be sooty and powdery, or compact and shiny.

rectangular-shaped piece

black colour

plant material

PEAT

GRAIN SIZE *Less than 0.1mm.*
ESSENTIAL COMPONENTS *Carbon.*
ADDITIONAL COMPONENTS *Fossils are common.*
ORIGIN *Accumulation of organic debris.*
SIMILAR ROCKS *Black shale (p.31) is laminated; lignite (below) and anthracite (right) do not break into rectangular lumps.*

Lignite

MINING *of lignite occurs on a vast scale, as seen here in Germany.*

A low grade brown-coloured coal, lignite is a product of the stage between peat and black coal. Some plant material is still visible and, although consolidated, it easily crumbles. It has a lower density than other coals and a woody appearance. Most coal deposits are found in Carboniferous Age rocks, but lignites are usually much younger, though still economically important. This is partly because gas and liquid petroleum products are easily extracted from lignites.

salt deposits

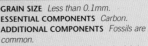

woody texture

SECTION SHOWN

GRAIN SIZE *Less than 0.1mm.*
ESSENTIAL COMPONENTS *Carbon, organic material.*
ADDITIONAL COMPONENTS *None.*
ORIGIN *Accumulation of organic debris.*
SIMILAR ROCKS *Other coals (above) are black, rather than brown, and contain less plant materials.*

Anthracite

A high grade black and shiny coal, anthracite does not dirty the fingers and breaks with a conchoidal fracture. It has a higher carbon content than other coals, and so lights and burns at a higher temperature. Jet is a similar rock, hard and black, and with a conchoidal fracture, but with a brown streak. Jet occurs in layers in bituminous shales, notably at Whitby, England.

BIG PIT, *Blaenafon, part of the South Wales coalfield, is famous for its high grade anthracite deposits.*

shiny, black colour

JET LAYER IN SHALE

hard surface

conchoidal fracture

> **GRAIN SIZE** *Less than 0.1mm.*
> **ESSENTIAL COMPONENTS** *Carbon.*
> **ADDITIONAL COMPONENTS** *None.*
> **ORIGIN** *Accumulation of organic debris.*
> **SIMILAR ROCKS** *Coal (left), but this is powdery.*

Amber

Another organic 'rock', amber is the fossilized resin of pine trees. It is a soft, transparent to translucent yellow-orange substance that has a density similar to water and may in fact float. Sometimes fossil insects, and other animals, and plants, are preserved in amber. It is found worldwide, but much amber comes from the Baltic Sea.

THE BALTIC SEA *coast, is a source of the world's largest and highest quality amber deposits.*

orange colour

trapped spider

resinous lustre

> **GRAIN SIZE** *Not granular.*
> **ESSENTIAL COMPONENTS** *Amber.*
> **ADDITIONAL COMPONENTS** *Trapped animals.*
> **ORIGIN** *Solidification of fossil resin.*
> **SIMILAR ROCKS** *Amber, unlike similar substances, softens and then burns with a pine smell when heated.*

Evaporites

EVAPORITES, *including rock salt, potash, and gypsum rock, are forming along the coasts of the Dead Sea – the world's saltiest sea.*

The commonest of the evaporite rocks is rock salt, which like the other evaporites, results from the evaporation of sea water. Rock salt (formed of the mineral halite) is colourless to orange, or rarely blue, and is soluble in water. The evaporite rock gypsum occurs as massive white layers, often in marl, or banded in light colours and is sometimes known as alabaster. Potash rock is formed of soluble potassium salts, such as sylvite and carnallite often mixed with halite. It is granular, pink to brown in colour and has a greasy feel.

orange colour from iron-rich clays

blue and white halite

cubic crystals

sylvite crystals

RARE BLUE ROCK SALT

POTASH ROCK

GYPSUM ROCK

GRAIN SIZE *Not granular to more than 1cm.*
ESSENTIAL COMPONENTS *Halite, gypsum, or potassium minerals.*
ADDITIONAL COMPONENTS *Clay.*
ORIGIN *Evaporation of sea water.*
SIMILAR ROCKS *Travertine (p.39), marble (p.77) but these are harder, have no taste, and are insoluble.*

NOTE

The minerals found in evaporite rocks can be seen on pages 171–75. Many of these occur together. Some continue to form in arid climates, such as the Dead Sea area today, but others are only found in ancient evaporites, such as the 270 million year old deposits at Stassfurt in Germany.

Igneous Rocks

In the pages that follow, igneous rocks are arranged in the order: intrusive, extrusive, and pyroclastic. Intrusive igneous rocks are those that have crystallized beneath the Earth's surface and are coarse-grained. Extrusive rocks, such as those of the Giant's Causeway, Northern Ireland (below), are solidified lava and have a fine grain size. Each rock type is listed by decreasing silicon dioxide content: high (acid), intermediate, and low (basic), followed by more unusual compositions. Pyroclastic rocks are formed from volcanic ejecta.

ORPHYRITIC
GRANITE

PERIDOTITE

PUMICE

SNOWFLAKE
OBSIDIAN

Granite

THESE TORS *were formed by the weathering of a granite outcrop along vertical and horizontal joints.*

Granite is a common and familiar rock. Like other coarse-grained igneous rocks, its essential minerals can be identified with the naked eye or a hand lens. For granite, these are quartz – usually in rounded glassy grains – and feldspars. Feldspars are more or less rectangular, plagioclase, usually white, and alkali feldspars pink. Black grains of hornblende and/or biotite are the most common dark-coloured minerals. In porphyritic granite some of the feldspars, known as phenocrysts, are much larger than other grains. Granite forms by the cooling of magma below the earth's surface and is the commonest rock type of the continents.

granular texture

WHITE GRANITE

HORNBLENDE GRANITE

phenocryst

PORPHYRITIC GRANITE

hornblende

quartz

feldspar

SECTION SHOWN

NOTE

Granite is a hard-wearing rock and is used as a building stone, both in blocks and in polished slabs. Some especially attractive examples are porphyritic ones from Shap and from Dartmoor, in England, or the ones with red feldspars from Bushveld, South Africa, and Aberdeen, Scotland.

GRAIN SIZE *2–5mm, phenocrysts to 10cm.*
ESSENTIAL COMPONENTS *Quartz, alkali feldspar, plagioclase.*
ADDITIONAL COMPONENTS *Biotite, muscovite, hornblende, apatite.*
ORIGIN *Crystallization of an acid magma in a major intrusion.*
SIMILAR ROCKS *Diorite (p.48).*

Orbicular Granite

This is an unusual but spectacular rock, characterized by spheres of concentric layers of granitic minerals within granite. The orbicules are typically about 5–10cm in diameter and often richer than granite in darker minerals. Excellent examples are found in Finland. An example from Australia has been quarried to provide polished stone. Orbicular diorites are also found.

ORBICULES *are usually restricted to a small area within a larger granite mass.*

orbicule

ORBICULAR DIORITE

biotite

granite

feldspar and hornblende

GRAIN SIZE *2–5mm, orbicules 2–20cm.*
ESSENTIAL COMPONENTS *Quartz, plagioclase, alkali feldspar, biotite.*
ADDITIONAL COMPONENTS *Hornblende.*
ORIGIN *Concentric growth within a granite magma.*
SIMILAR ROCKS *This is a type of granite (left); orbicular diorite has no quartz (p.143).*

Graphic Granite

In some granites, and also pegmatites, the minerals are intergrown in such a way that straight-sided quartz crystals, which look like hieroglyphic characters, are set in a background of feldspar. The composition is roughly 30 per cent quartz and 70 per cent feldspar, with few other minerals. The texture forms when both main minerals crystallize from the magma at the same time.

PEGMATITE *veins with graphic granite and graphic amazonite have been found at Pikes Peak, Colorado, USA.*

quartz

feldspar

GRAIN SIZE *2–10mm, or larger.*
ESSENTIAL COMPONENTS *Quartz, feldspar.*
ADDITIONAL COMPONENTS *None.*
ORIGIN *Simultaneous crystallization of quartz and alkali feldspar.*
SIMILAR ROCKS *Granophyre (see microgranite, p.47).*

Pegmatite

DARK *gray amphibolite gneiss is cut by a series of minor intrusions of pegmatite. The irregular shapes are typical.*

Pegmatites are very coarse-grained rocks, mostly of a granitic composition, with individual crystals that range from smaller than one centimetre to several metres in size. They are light-coloured rocks and occur in small igneous bodies, such as veins and dykes, or as patches in larger masses of granite. Quartz and feldspar dominate but many other minerals can form large beautiful crystals. Muscovite and other micas are commonly seen and occur in large flat sheets known as books. Some gemstones are mined from pegmatites, such as emerald, aquamarine, tourmaline group minerals, and topaz. Other pegmatites contain important ore minerals that are the source of industrial metals, such as lithium, tin, tantalum, and tungsten.

feldspar (microcline)

tourmaline

muscovite

GRANITE PEGMATITE

TOURMALINE PEGMATITE

MICA PEGMATITE

quartz

feldspar

mica

GRAIN SIZE *More than 5mm to many metres.*
ESSENTIAL COMPONENTS *Quartz, alkali feldspar, plagioclase.*
ADDITIONAL COMPONENTS *Mica, apatite, fluorite, beryl, tourmaline, cassiterite, etc.*
ORIGIN *Fluid-rich crystallization in the final stages of the formation of a granite.*
SIMILAR ROCKS *Granite (p.44).*

NOTE

Pegmatites are sometimes associated with an even, medium- to fine-grained sugary-textured rock called aplite. It has a similar composition to granite (p.44), but little or no biotite (p.161), hornblende (p.163), or other dark-coloured minerals. Like pegmatite, it may contain topaz (p.178) or tourmaline (pp.180–81).

Microgranite

Microgranite is identical to granite in all but grain size and its occurrence in minor intrusions, such as sills and dykes. As with granites, porphyritic varieties are common. In microgranite, granophyre, quartz, and feldspar are intergrown in the same way as in graphic granite, but this is only visible under a hand lens.

WELL-JOINTED *microgranite in a quarry at Threlkeld mining museum, Cumbria, England.*

fine graphic texture

GRANOPHYRE

medium grained

pink feldspar

GRAIN SIZE *0.1–2mm.*
ESSENTIAL COMPONENTS *Quartz, alkali feldspar, plagioclase.*
ADDITIONAL COMPONENTS *Biotite, muscovite, hornblende, apatite.*
ORIGIN *Crystallization of an acid magma in a minor intrusion.*
SIMILAR ROCKS *Granite (p.44).*

Greisen

This rock is produced by fluids altering a granite in the final stages of crystallization. It is a coarse- to medium-grained mixture of muscovite and quartz, often with fluorite and minerals found in pegmatites. Similar rocks can be mixtures of quartz and tourmaline. All of these types are common in dykes, veins, and marginal areas of the granites of south-west England, and elsewhere.

IRREGULAR *quartz veins often cut through greisen rocks and these may carry ore minerals.*

muscovite

pegmatite

aplite

greisen

GRAIN SIZE *2–5mm.*
ESSENTIAL COMPONENTS *Muscovite, quartz.*
ADDITIONAL COMPONENTS *Fluorite, tourmaline, topaz.*
ORIGIN *Alteration of granite by hot fluids.*
SIMILAR ROCKS *Mica schist (p.78), occurs on a regional scale; aplite (see note, left).*

Felsite

Felsite is a general term for medium- to fine-grained, light-coloured, pink, beige, or grey igneous rocks from small intrusions, such as sills and dykes. Blocky jointing is common, and occurs perpendicular and parallel to the walls of the intrusion. Felsite may be slightly porphyritic, with small phenocrysts, often of quartz, or it may contain spherical structures.

light beige matrix

darker weathered surface

quartz phenocryst

GRAIN SIZE *Less than 2mm.*
ESSENTIAL COMPONENTS *Quartz, feldspars.*
ADDITIONAL COMPONENTS *None.*
ORIGIN *Crystallization of an acid or intermediate magma in a minor intrusion.*
SIMILAR ROCKS *Rhyolite (p.56), dacite (p.59), and porphyry (p.60).*

Diorite

An intermediate, coarse-grained igneous rock, diorite consists of white plagioclase and dark hornblende in roughly equal proportions, but other dark minerals may include biotite and augite. With the addition of small amounts of quartz and alkali feldspar it becomes a granodiorite; with larger amounts, a granite. These three rock types often occur together in large intrusions.

SECTION SHOWN

minerals in equal proportion

plagioclase

hornblende

MICROGRAPH

GRAIN SIZE *2–5mm.*
ESSENTIAL COMPONENTS *Plagioclase, hornblende.*
ADDITIONAL COMPONENTS *None.*
ORIGIN *Crystallization of an intermediate magma in a major intrusion.*
SIMILAR ROCKS *Syenite (top right), which has more alkali feldspar.*

Syenite

Syenites are attractive, multi-coloured rocks, which may be polished and used as a decorative stone, as in the case of Norwegian larvikite. Alkali feldspar is the main component. Many other minerals, such as plagioclase, biotite, pyroxene, and amphibole group minerals, minor quartz, or nepheline, can accompany it.

DIFFERENCES *in grain size and composition are typical across an outcrop of syenite.*

attractive polished surface

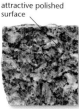

LARVIKITE

hornblende

alkali feldspar

> **GRAIN SIZE** *2–5mm.*
> **ESSENTIAL COMPONENTS** *Alkali feldspar, pyroxene/amphibole.*
> **ADDITIONAL COMPONENTS** *Plagioclase, biotite.*
> **ORIGIN** *Crystallization of an alkaline intermediate magma in a major intrusion.*
> **SIMILAR ROCKS** *Diorite (below left).*

Nepheline Syenite

Both nepheline and alkali feldspar are essential minerals in nepheline syenite, but this intermediate rock can contain many others, including unusual and attractive ones, such as eudialyte. Nepheline is typically brownish white with square crystals; alkali feldspar is white and rectangular. If the nepheline syenite includes a pyroxene, it is usually aegirine and if an amphibole, it is commonly arfvedsonite; both of which are rich in sodium.

IN ADDITION *to nepheline, this example contains alkali feldspar, pyroxene, sodalite, and andradite.*

aegirine

nepheline

alkali feldspar

SECTION SHOWN

> **GRAIN SIZE** *2–5mm.*
> **ESSENTIAL COMPONENTS** *Alkali feldspar, nepheline.*
> **ADDITIONAL COMPONENTS** *Aegirine, biotite.*
> **ORIGIN** *Crystallization of a low silica intermediate magma in a major intrusion.*
> **SIMILAR ROCKS** *Syenite (above).*

Gabbro

GABBRO *is found in the Cuillins layered intrusion, Skye, Scotland, in rugged topography.*

A dark-coloured rock composed of coarse grains of dark green pyroxene (augite and lesser amounts of orthopyroxene), plus white- or green-coloured plagioclase and black millimetre-sized grains of magnetite and/or ilmenite. Gabbros occur in thick sills, in uplifted sections of oceanic crust called ophiolites, and with cumulate rocks in layered igneous intrusions.

plagioclase

plagioclase

SECTION SHOWN   **LEUCOGABBRO**

pyroxene

GRAIN SIZE *2–5mm.*
ESSENTIAL COMPONENTS *Plagioclase, augite, magnetite.*
ADDITIONAL COMPONENTS *Olivine.*
ORIGIN *Crystallization of a basic magma in a major intrusion.*
SIMILAR ROCKS *Diorite (p.48), which contains hornblende (p.163), its main mineral.*

Dolerite

ALTERED *dolerite, or diabase, can be seen in this irregular dyke with darker-coloured chilled margins.*

A medium-grained rock with the same composition as gabbro. It is found in minor intrusions, sills, and dykes. Plagioclase crystals are usually tiny rectangles within larger pyroxene grains. Olivine is a common constituent, in rounded grains often weathered to an orange-brown colour. It is a hard and heavy rock, and used polished as a decorative stone, rough for paving, and crushed for roadstone.

plagioclase

brown weathered edge

pyroxene

GRAIN SIZE *0.1–2mm.*
ESSENTIAL COMPONENTS *Plagioclase, augite, magnetite.*
ADDITIONAL COMPONENTS *Olivine.*
ORIGIN *Crystallization of a basic magma in a minor intrusion.*
SIMILAR ROCKS *Basalt (p.61), occurs in lava flows and contains gas bubble holes.*

Cumulate Rocks

This is the name given to a number of different rock types that form in layered igneous intrusions, which are usually basic in composition. Each rock type consists of one or two or more coarse-grained minerals, which occur in layers. Each layer can range in size from millimetres to hundreds of metres thick. The usual minerals are olivine, augite, orthopyroxenes, plagioclase, chromite, and magnetite, but many others, such as apatite and alkali feldspar, may be present. To identify the combinations of minerals present, rock names, such as norite and troctolite, are given.

LAYERED *magnetite and anorthosite form cumulate rock in the Bushveld Complex, South Africa.*

SECTION SHOWN

orthopyroxene

chromite

NORITE

olivine

TROCTOLITE

serpentine

CHROMITE-SERPENTINITE

mottled anorthosite

GRAIN SIZE 2–5mm.
ESSENTIAL COMPONENTS *Any of olivine, plagioclase, orthopyroxene, clinopyroxene, magnetite.*
ADDITIONAL COMPONENTS *Chromite, sulphide minerals, platinum group minerals.*
ORIGIN *Crystallization in a layered intrusion.*
SIMILAR ROCKS *Gabbro (left) is not layered.*

NOTE

Other cumulates include: troctolite (plagioclase, pp.166–67, and olivine, p.159), norite (plagioclase and orthopyroxene, p.162), chromitite (chromite, p.141) and magnetite (magnetite, p.126). Other rocks that form cumulates include gabbro (above left), dunite (p.52), anorthosite and pyroxenite (p.53).

Dunite

THIS OUTCROP *in Cyprus, shows chrysotile veining and the contrast between fresh green and altered brown dunite.*

A green or brown coarse-grained rock consisting almost entirely of the mineral olivine, dunite also contains small black chromite or magnetite grains. In some countries, if it contains magnetite, it is known as olivinite. Dunites are found as cumulate rocks in layered intrusions and also as pipes and irregular bodies. Alteration of a dunite by the addition of water produces a serpentinite.

green olivine

brown weathered olivine

SECTION SHOWN

GRAIN SIZE *2–5mm.*
ESSENTIAL COMPONENTS *Olivine.*
ADDITIONAL COMPONENTS *Serpentine.*
ORIGIN *Crystallization of an ultrabasic magma in a major intrusion.*
SIMILAR ROCKS *Peridotite (below), contains less olivine (p.159).*

Peridotite

DARK BROWN *hills of peridotite stand out above the surrounding land in Oman.*

Peridotite contains 50–90 per cent olivine. It is a coarse-grained light to dark green rock, which usually contains pyroxene. Unlike olivine, pyroxene grains have a visible cleavage when viewed under a hand lens. It forms much of the Earth's mantle, and can occur as nodules brought up from the mantle by basalt or kimberlite magmas. Peridotite also occurs as a cumulate rock.

red pyrope

dark olivine and pyroxene crystals

GARNET PERIDOTITE

GRAIN SIZE *2–5mm.*
ESSENTIAL COMPONENTS *Olivine, pyroxene.*
ADDITIONAL COMPONENTS *Chromite, serpentine, spinel, amphibole, garnet.*
ORIGIN *Crystallization of an ultrabasic magma in a major intrusion, or the Earth's mantle.*
SIMILAR ROCKS *Pyroxenite (right) but this major mineral has a cleavage.*

Anorthosite

A coarse-grained rock composed of more than 90 per cent feldspar, while pyroxene often forms most of the rest of the rock. Anorthosite is white or grey but it can be green coloured and has a granular texture. It occurs in layered igneous intrusions as a cumulate rock, but also in large metamorphic gabbro-anorthosite complexes of the Precambrian Era.

A LAYER of white anorthosite sits above a weathered gabbro from the Bushveld Complex, South Africa.

plagioclase feldspar

mottled orthopyroxene

GRAIN SIZE 2–5mm.
ESSENTIAL COMPONENTS Plagioclase.
ADDITIONAL COMPONENTS Pyroxene, magnetite.
ORIGIN Crystallization of a basic magma in a major intrusion.
SIMILAR ROCKS Marble (p.77), is softer and reacts with dilute acid.

Pyroxenite

This is a coarse-grained, granular rock that contains at least 90 per cent orthopyroxene, clinopyroxene or both. It is a hard and heavy rock, which is light green, dark green, or black, and the surface often weathers to rusty brown. Pyroxenites may also contain olivine and oxide minerals when they occur as cumulate rocks in layered intrusions, or nepheline in alkaline intrusions.

RUM intrusion in Scotland, is an example of where pyroxenites form prominent resistant layers.

plagioclase

pyroxene

sulphide

GRAIN SIZE 2–5mm.
ESSENTIAL COMPONENTS Pyroxene.
ADDITIONAL COMPONENTS Plagioclase, sulphides, and platinum minerals.
ORIGIN Crystallization of a basic magma in a major intrusion.
SIMILAR ROCKS Serpentinite (p.72), is softer and fine-grained.

Lamprophyre

Usually black when fresh, lamprophyre is hydrothermally altered and then weathers to a brown, green, or yellow colour. It is a porphyritic rock with black or dark brown phenocrysts of mica and/or amphibole, but never with feldspar phenocrysts like most other porphyries. It occurs in minor intrusions, especially dykes. Common varieties are alnöite (phlogopite, augite, and olivine phenocrysts) and minette (phlogopite only).

mica flake

brown weathered surface

WEATHERED ROCK

brown colour

GRAIN SIZE *0.1–2mm.*
ESSENTIAL COMPONENTS *Hornblende/ Biotite.*
ADDITIONAL COMPONENTS *Titanite.*
ORIGIN *Crystallization of an alkaline magma in a minor intrusion.*
SIMILAR ROCKS *Dolerite (p.50), does not contain biotite (p.161) or hornblende (p.163).*

Kimberlite

Kimberlite is a rare rock, best known for being the major source of diamonds. It is found in dykes and carrot-shaped pipes called diatremes, up to a kilometre in diameter. When fresh, it is a blue-green colour but it weathers to yellow. It is coarse to fine-grained and contains clasts, or is brecciated. Common minerals as phenocrysts include purple pyrope, bright green chromium-rich diopside, chromite, calcite, and phlogopite.

megacryst in finer matrix

yellow colour

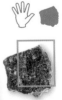

SECTION SHOWN

WEATHERED KIMBERLITE

GRAIN SIZE *Wide range.*
ESSENTIAL COMPONENTS *Serpentine, phlogopite, calcite, chromite.*
ADDITIONAL COMPONENTS *Chrome-rich diopside, almandine, diamond.*
ORIGIN *Extrusion of a fluid part of the Earth's mantle.*
SIMILAR ROCKS *Tuff (p.65).*

Carbonatite

Carbonatite is an unusual rock type – an igneous rock comprising over 50 per cent carbonate minerals – usually calcite, dolomite, or siderite. It looks like marble, and may be coarse-grained, if intrusive, or fine-grained if volcanic. Typically cream-coloured, yellow or brown, it may contain phlogopite, magnetite (often as octahedral crystals) and rare-earth minerals, such as pyrochlore. It is usually found in areas of continental rifting.

CARBONATITES *are often economically important, such as here at Phalaborwa copper mine, South Africa.*

magnetite

carbonate mineral

GRAIN SIZE *Wide range.*	
ESSENTIAL COMPONENTS *Calcite and/or dolomite.*	
ADDITIONAL COMPONENTS *Magnetite, apatite, phlogopite, rare earth minerals.*	
ORIGIN *Crystallization of a carbonate magma derived from the Earth's mantle.*	
SIMILAR ROCKS *Limestone (p.32).*	

Xenoliths

Magma often incorporates fragments of the country rock through which it passes during intrusion. These often remain within the igneous rock that forms when the magma cools and solidifies, and are known as xenoliths. Xenoliths are often rounded, may be any size, and may have been metamorphosed.

ROUNDED *dark-coloured xenoliths are seen here in an outcrop of light-coloured diorite.*

xenolith

granite

peridotite

basalt

PERIDOTITE XENOLITH

GRAIN SIZE *Any size.*	
ESSENTIAL COMPONENTS *Country rock.*	
ADDITIONAL COMPONENTS *Thermal metamorphic minerals.*	
ORIGIN *Incorporation of country rocks into a magma without melting.*	
SIMILAR ROCKS *Volcanic breccia (p.62), clasts are angular.*	

Rhyolite

SNOWDON, *the highest mountain in Wales, is built of ancient rhyolite flows, each of limited extent.*

Rhyolite is a fine-grained, light-coloured rock. It is often composed largely of volcanic glass. Individual grains of quartz, feldspar, and mica may be present, but are too small to be visible. Sometimes rhyolites are porphyritic with millimetre-scale phenocrysts of quartz and/or feldspar. The granitic magma from which rhyolite crystallizes is very viscous, and so, flow-banding is often preserved and can be seen on weathered surfaces. Devitrification of glassy rhyolite produces tiny crystals arranged in radiating spheres, usually of a centimetre or so in size: a variety known as spherulitic rhyolite.

banding

BANDED RHYOLITE

phenocryst

flow banding

MICROGRAPH

quartz phenocryst

dark glass clast

pale-coloured rhyolite

GRAIN SIZE *Less than 0.1mm.*
ESSENTIAL COMPONENTS *Quartz, alkali feldspar, plagioclase.*
ADDITIONAL COMPONENTS *None.*
ORIGIN *Extrusion of an acid magma.*
SIMILAR ROCKS *Andesite (p.58) and dacite (p.59), are darker coloured.*

NOTE

The high viscosity of rhyolite magma has two other effects: the lava does not flow far from its source and forms domes; and gas pressure can build up in the magma leading to explosive volcanicity, so rhyolites are often associated with pyroclastic rocks, such as tuff (p.65).

Pitchstone

This acid volcanic glass, is usually green-coloured but yellow, red, brown, and black varieties are also seen. It may break with either a flat or a conchoidal fracture. Small phenocrysts of feldspar or pyroxene may be present. It occurs both as a volcanic rock, as small intrusions, and as the basal parts of rhyolite and dacite lava flows.

AN IRREGULAR *dyke of pitchstone, darker along its edges, is shown here cutting a brown-weathered basalt.*

smooth pitch-like surface

feldspar phenocryst

PORPHYRITIC PITCHSTONE

bottle-green colour

GRAIN SIZE *Not granular.*
ESSENTIAL COMPONENTS *Volcanic glass.*
ADDITIONAL COMPONENTS *Quartz phenocrysts.*
ORIGIN *Extrusion and rapid cooling of an acid magma.*
SIMILAR ROCKS *Obsidian (below).*

Obsidian

A black, acid volcanic glass with a well-developed conchoidal fracture, obsidian forms by the rapid cooling of an acid lava and is often found with grey pumice. The fragments of the rock are sharp and have been used as cutting implements. A variety with centimetre-scale spheres of tiny white radiating crystals is known as snowflake obsidian.

THIS OBSIDIAN *outcrop is in Iceland, an island where acid igneous rocks are rare.*

conchoidal fracture

glass

tiny crystals

SNOWFLAKE OBSIDIAN

sharp edge

GRAIN SIZE *Not granular.*
ESSENTIAL COMPONENTS *Volcanic glass.*
ADDITIONAL COMPONENTS *None.*
ORIGIN *Extrusion and rapid cooling of an acid magma.*
SIMILAR ROCKS *Industrial glass, which is softer.*

Andesite

An intermediate volcanic rock named after the Andes, andesite is usually grey coloured and porphyritic. Plagioclase, pyroxene, hornblende, and biotite may be present as phenocrysts, as well as, forming the finer groundmass. It occurs in the form of blocky or columnar jointed lava flows.

BLOCKY-JOINTED *andesites can be seen here in a lava field on the island of Lanzarote.*

small phenocrysts

feldspar phenocryst

PORPHYRITIC ANDESITE

dark grey colour

fine groundmass

GRAIN SIZE *Less than 0.1mm.*
ESSENTIAL COMPONENTS *Plagioclase.*
ADDITIONAL COMPONENTS *Pyroxene, amphibole.*
ORIGIN *Extrusion of an intermediate magma.*
SIMILAR ROCKS *Difficult to differentiate from dacite (right).*

Trachyte

The volcanic equivalent of syenite, trachyte's composition is dominated by alkali feldspar. This is a major component both of the fine groundmass and of abundant phenocrysts, which are usually flow-aligned. It is often a vesicular lava and may also occur as a pyroclastic rock. It is usually grey coloured and frequently banded or streaky.

DOME-SHAPED *outcrops of trachyte are seen in this volcano on the island of Tenerife.*

feldspar phenocryst

light-grey groundmass

alignment of feldspar crystals

MICROGRAPH

GRAIN SIZE *Less than 0.1mm.*
ESSENTIAL COMPONENTS *Alkali feldspar, plagioclase.*
ADDITIONAL COMPONENTS *Pyroxene, amphibole, biotite.*
ORIGIN *Extrusion of an alkaline intermediate magma.*
SIMILAR ROCKS *Other porphyritic lavas.*

Dacite

Dacite lies between rhyolite and andesite in composition. It is usually pink or a shade of grey and often flow-banded. Porphyritic varieties are common, with phenocrysts usually of plagioclase feldspar and/or quartz. It occurs with rhyolite in continental volcanic districts, and with andesite on continental margins.

EXTRUSIVE and pyroclastic dacite forms much of the volcano at Crater Lake, Oregon, USA.

feldspar phenocryst

hornblende

pink-grey colour

quartz phenocryst

GRAIN SIZE Less than 0.1mm.
ESSENTIAL COMPONENTS Plagioclase, quartz.
ADDITIONAL COMPONENTS Pyroxene, amphibole, biotite.
ORIGIN Extrusion of an intermediate magma.
SIMILAR ROCKS Difficult to differentiate from andesite (left).

Phonolite

Phonolite gets its name from a distinctive clinking sound that it makes when hit with a hammer. It is the volcanic equivalent of nepheline syenite, and, like that rock, it may contain unusual minerals. Porphyritic examples with well-developed crystals of sodalite, haüyne, and leucite are known. It occurs in lava flows, minor intrusions, and as a pyroclastic rock. It is largely restricted to areas of the Earth's crust that have rifted apart, or to oceanic islands.

DEVIL'S TOWER, Wyoming, USA is a small intrusion or 'plug' of phonolite that has been exposed by erosion.

alkali feldspar

grey groundmass

SECTION SHOWN

GRAIN SIZE Less than 0.1mm.
ESSENTIAL COMPONENTS Alkali feldspar, nepheline.
ADDITIONAL COMPONENTS Leucite.
ORIGIN Extrusion of a low-silica intermediate magma.
SIMILAR ROCKS Similar to intermediate and basic lavas, but rarer.

Porphyry

THESE PHENOCRYSTS *of feldspar in a granite porphyry have been aligned by magmatic flow.*

Porphyry is a general name for igneous rocks that contain phenocrysts, especially if the phenocryst mineral is also found in the smaller crystals of the groundmass. It is most often used for rocks with a fine- to medium-grained groundmass, that have formed in minor intrusions or lava flows. The term porphyry is often prefixed. This can be a reference to the minerals it contains, such as quartz-feldspar-porphyry, which contains those two minerals as phenocrysts. Alternatively, it can refer to the composition, such as rhyolite porphyry, or texture, such as rhomb porphyry. The latter contains feldspars with rhombic cross-sections.

SECTION SHOWN

fine dark groundmass

white phenocryst

rectangular feldspar

GREEN PORPHYRY

rhombic feldspar

RHOMB PORPHYRY

NOTE

Porphyries have been used as decorative rocks for several millennia because of their hardness and beauty. A purple example from Egypt, Imperial Porphyry, was much prized by Roman Emperors, to whom the colour signified authority. The green porphyry (above) was also used in Ancient Rome, sourced from Greece.

GRAIN SIZE *Less than 0.1mm, phenocrysts to 2cm.*
ESSENTIAL COMPONENTS *Phenocrysts.*
ADDITIONAL COMPONENTS *None.*
ORIGIN *Two-stage crystallization of an igneous rock.*
SIMILAR ROCKS *Any lava or minor intrusive rock.*

Basalt

Basalt is the most common lava in the Earth's crust, forming almost all of the ocean floor and also large areas on land. It is a fine-grained rock and, when fresh it is black in colour, weathering to dark green, or brown. Some basalts are porphyritic with feldspar, augite, and olivine phenocrysts being common. Gas bubble holes give a vesicular texture, and these may be filled with later minerals, known as amygdales. The surface of basalt lava may be ropy and smooth, or blocky and rough.

EXCEPTIONAL *columnar-jointed basalt can be seen at Fingal's cave, Staffa, Scotland.*

SECTION SHOWN

vesicle

VESICULAR BASALT

columnar-jointed massive basalt

phenocryst

PORPHYRITIC BASALT

amygdale

AMYGDALOIDAL BASALT

fine grain size

GRAIN SIZE Less than 0.1mm.
ESSENTIAL COMPONENTS Plagioclase, augite, magnetite.
ADDITIONAL COMPONENTS Olivine, zeolites.
ORIGIN Extrusion of a basic magma.
SIMILAR ROCKS Dolerite (p.50) is coarser and occurs in minor intrusions.

NOTE

Basalt lava flows can cover huge areas and form great thicknesses of rock. Amongst the largest masses of basalt seen on land is the Deccan Traps of India, today covering more than half a million square kilometres. These volcanic rocks contain many of the beautiful zeolite group and related minerals.

Scoria

CINDER *cones can produce large quantities of scoriaceous lava.*

The top of a lava flow is made up of a highly vesicular, rubbly material called scoria. It has the appearance of vesicular lava but is usually weathered to a brown colour, and forms piles of loose rubble with small pieces. It is common in areas of recent volcanism, such as the Canary Islands and the Italian volcanoes, and is usually basaltic or intermediate in composition. High drainage means that areas of scoria often lack vegetation.

vesicle

many loose pieces

SECTION SHOWN

GRAIN SIZE *Less than 0.1mm.*
ESSENTIAL COMPONENTS *Basalt.*
ADDITIONAL COMPONENTS *None.*
ORIGIN *Rubbly top of an extruded basic magma.*
SIMILAR ROCKS *This rock is a type of basalt (p.61), but differs in being unconsolidated.*

Volcanic Breccia

DARK *red vesicular and non-vesicular purple lava with flow lines, make up this volcanic breccia.*

A brecciated rock formed by the interaction of lava and scoria, or by the mixture of cooled lava and flowing lava. It takes the form of centimetre-scale angular clasts of often vesicular lava in a more compact matrix. It commonly forms at the top of a lava flow, and is then known as flow-top breccia. It is especially common between basaltic lava flows.

vesicular lava

SECTION SHOWN

oxidised lava

GRAIN SIZE *Less than 0.1 mm, clasts 0.5–20cm.*
ESSENTIAL COMPONENTS *Basalt.*
ADDITIONAL COMPONENTS *Volcanic glass, spilite.*
ORIGIN *Mixing of liquid and solid material during crystallization of a basic magma.*
SIMILAR ROCKS *Agglomerate (p.64).*

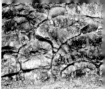

Pillow Lava

When basalt is extruded under water it forms a ball of lava with a thin solid skin. The 'balls' are typically 0.2–1m in diameter, and settle on top of one another, becoming pillow-shaped. They have basalt interiors with chilled edges of finer grained basalt, often altered. Sometimes they have radially-oriented vesicles. Rubbly material or quartz fills the small spaces between pillows.

POINTED *bottoms and rounded tops of this pillow lava, show it has the same orientation as when the lava was extruded.*

quartz veining

WHOLE PILLOW

altered edge

veining

GRAIN SIZE	Less than 0.1mm, pillows 0.1–1m.
ESSENTIAL COMPONENTS	Basalt.
ADDITIONAL COMPONENTS	Spilite.
ORIGIN	Underwater extrusion of a basic magma.
SIMILAR ROCKS	This rock is a mixture of basalt (p.61) and spilite (below).

Spilite

A spilite is an altered basalt, usually by reaction with sea water. Calcium-rich plagioclase is converted to albite. The edges of pillow lavas are often spilite, or it may result from hydrothermal alteration by seawater circulating through hot volcanic rocks. Spilite is lighter in colour than basalt, veined by calcite or chalcedony, and vesicles and cavities are filled with secondary minerals.

A REACTION *between molten lava and sea water, seen here in Hawaii, produces spilite.*

flow structure

altered basalt

IRON-RICH SPILITE

GRAIN SIZE	Less than 0.1mm.
ESSENTIAL COMPONENTS	Plagioclase (albite), augite, magnetite.
ADDITIONAL COMPONENTS	None.
ORIGIN	Alteration of basalt by sea water.
SIMILAR ROCKS	Basalt (p.61) but is darker and harder.

filled vesicles and vein

Agglomerate

COARSE *angular fragments from several sources can make up an agglomerate.*

An agglomerate is a pyroclastic rock in which coarse, centimetre-scale, rounded to sub-rounded clasts lie in a matrix of lava or ash. The clasts themselves may be lava or pyroclastic rocks, or they may be the country rocks, which surround and lie beneath the volcano. Rounding of the clasts may have occurred in the magma, during eruption, or by later sedimentary re-working.

carbonatite lava

CARBONATITE AGGLOMERATE

red dolomite clast

small igneous clasts

fine-grained ash

GRAIN SIZE *Less than 0.1mm, clasts 0.5–20cm.*
ESSENTIAL COMPONENTS *Igneous rock fragments.*
ADDITIONAL COMPONENTS *Country rock.*
ORIGIN *Pyroclastic accumulation of coarse material.*
SIMILAR ROCKS *Vent agglomerate (below).*

Vent Agglomerate

BOTH *the main and parasitic side vents can be filled with vent agglomerate.*

This is the rock which plugs the main or a satellite vent of a volcano. The outcrop of this rock is circular on a geological map and of limited extent. The rock itself, like other agglomerates, contains a variety of clasts of different sizes, shapes, and compositions from the lava, other volcanic rocks, and country rocks. The matrix will be a fine-grained igneous rock.

mixed country rock and igneous clasts

lava matrix

SECTION SHOWN

GRAIN SIZE *Less than 0.1mm, clasts 5mm–several metres.*
ESSENTIAL COMPONENTS *Igneous and country rock fragments in lava.*
ADDITIONAL COMPONENTS *None.*
ORIGIN *Accumulation of material in a volcanic vent.*
SIMILAR ROCKS *Type of agglomerate (above).*

Tuff

Acid and intermediate magmas are more viscous than basic ones, and this means that the volcanicity associated with these magmas is more explosive, as greater pressures can build up. The major product of explosive volcanism is volcanic ash which, when settled, forms a rock called tuff. The material comprises a mixture of crystal fragments, bits of lava and pyroclastic rock, and volcanic glass. If any of these are dominant, the rock can be called crystal tuff, lithic tuff, or vitric tuff. Tuffs are usually light grey rocks and often exhibit graded bedding, either as a primary feature from settling ash, or as a secondary feature from deposition of ash in water or reworking of sedimented ash in the water.

STEEP *cliffs develop in layered tuffs because it is an easily eroded rock.*

SECTION SHOWN

mineral fragments

fragments of rock and glass

CRYSTAL TUFF

small rock fragments

LITHIC TUFF

graded bedding

GRAIN SIZE *0.0625–2mm.*

GRAIN SIZE *0.0625–2mm.*
ESSENTIAL COMPONENTS *Igneous rock, volcanic glass, and crystal fragments.*
ADDITIONAL COMPONENTS *None.*
ORIGIN *Pyroclastic accumulation of fine material.*
SIMILAR ROCKS *Turbidite (p.27), where the clasts are sedimentary grains.*

NOTE

Some tuffs contain fossils of animals and plants trapped in the volcanic ash. Tuffs from Mount Vesuvius, Italy, contain casts of humans killed during the eruption of 79CE. At Pompeii the tuff layer is up to 3m thick, but at nearby Herculaneum where the ash built up in pyroclastic flows and mud slides, it is 20m thick.

Ignimbrite

NOVARUPTA, *an Alaskan volcano, produced the largest historical quantity of ignimbrite in June 1912.*

Ignimbrite is a particular type of tuff formed when the ash was so hot that any volcanic glass was re-melted, and so fused or welded the rock. The glass appears as deformed, curved shards surrounded by crystal and rock fragments. Ignimbrite is deposited by an ash flow – a mixture of hot gases and pyroclastic material that travels at fast speeds. Ash flows are responsible for many casualties during volcanic eruptions.

SECTION SHOWN

deformed glass shard

pale tuff matrix

GRAIN SIZE *0.0625–2mm.*
ESSENTIAL COMPONENTS *Igneous rock and crystal fragments, welded volcanic glass.*
ADDITIONAL COMPONENTS *None.*
ORIGIN *Pyroclastic flow of lava and hot gas.*
SIMILAR ROCKS *Ignimbrite differs from other tuffs (p.65) in having deformed glass shards.*

Pumice

THE WHITE *pumice landscape of Sarakiniko in Greece has heavily dissected valleys.*

Pumice is a light grey or white, glassy volcanic rock, full of gas bubble holes, which may be spherical or compressed. These holes make it an extremely light rock which can usually float on water. It results from frothy acid lava and may be associated with rhyolite and obsidian. Pumice can be carried long distances from its source volcano by water or even wind.

gas bubble hole

spiky rock

glass fragments

SECTION SHOWN

GRAIN SIZE *Less than 0.1mm.*
ESSENTIAL COMPONENTS *Vesicular acid lava.*
ADDITIONAL COMPONENTS *None.*
ORIGIN *Solidification of acid lava with trapped gas bubbles.*
SIMILAR ROCKS *Vesicular rhyolite, dacite, and andesite can have the same chemical composition but are much denser rocks.*

Pélé's hair

Named after the Hawaiian goddess of fire, Pélé's hair is very long and thin basaltic glass. It is formed by fountaining and rapid mid-air cooling of a very liquid magma. It is pale yellow-brown to black and brittle. Similar tear-drop shaped glasses are known as Pélé's tears. Other rock shapes are generally known as achneliths and include small spheres and dumb-bells.

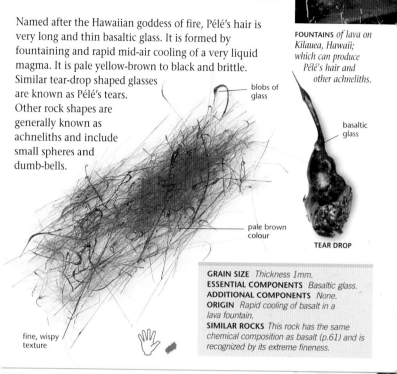

FOUNTAINS *of lava on Kilauea, Hawaii; which can produce Pélé's hair and other achneliths.*

blobs of glass

basaltic glass

pale brown colour

TEAR DROP

fine, wispy texture

GRAIN SIZE *Thickness 1mm.*
ESSENTIAL COMPONENTS *Basaltic glass.*
ADDITIONAL COMPONENTS *None.*
ORIGIN *Rapid cooling of basalt in a lava fountain.*
SIMILAR ROCKS *This rock has the same chemical composition as basalt (p.61) and is recognized by its extreme fineness.*

Volcanic Bomb

A pyroclastic rock that has formed by the cooling of a batch of lava while flying through the air after eruption. During transport it becomes rounded and may be twisted and pointed, then called a spindle bomb. It is usually brown or red, weathering to yellow-brown and may have a cracked, fine-grained, or glassy surface, then called a breadcrust bomb.

VOLCANIC BOMBS *are seen in a layer of ash beneath a brown lava flow in this road-cut.*

weathered surface

twisted shape

loaf shape

GRAIN SIZE *Bombs 0.02–1m.*
ESSENTIAL COMPONENTS *Basalt.*
ADDITIONAL COMPONENTS *None.*
ORIGIN *Mid-air cooling of batches of basic magma.*
SIMILAR ROCKS *This type of basalt (p.61) can be recognised by its round shape, and by its size.*

ROUNDED SPINDLE BOMB

Metamorphic Rocks

Metamorphism is the transformation of rocks by heat and pressure. High-grade metamorphic rocks form deep in the Earth's crust, where temperatures and pressures are high; low-grade rocks, such as slate (below), form at shallower depths. Metamorphic rocks are grouped here by their precursor rock: firstly those that were basic igneous rocks, then acid igneous and sedimentary. Next are contact metamorphic rocks, formed by close proximity to igneous intrusions; deformation rocks, which show features of stretching, squashing, or fracture; and meteorites and rocks formed by their impacts on Earth.

BASALT   PEGMATITE   GRANITE   OBSIDIAN

Metabasalt

This is a metamorphosed basalt which retains some of its original igneous features, such as gas bubble holes, or flow top breccia. It differs from basalt in being dark green coloured due to the presence of the mineral chlorite, and is sometimes known as "greenstone". Greenstones are common in long, narrow outcrops of the Precambrian age, between granites or orthogneisses. Like the rock it is derived from, metabasalt has a very fine grain size and individual crystals are too small to be identified without a microscope.

GREEN *metabasalt with white quartz veins in a typical fractured and weathered outcrop.*

brown weathered surface

SECTION SHOWN

fine grain size

green colour

spinifex texture

fold

schistosity

GREENSCHIST

KOMATIITIC METABASALT

GRAIN SIZE *Less than 0.1mm.*
ESSENTIAL COMPONENTS *Chlorite, albite, actinolite.*
ADDITIONAL COMPONENTS *None.*
ORIGIN *Low grade metamorphism of basalt.*
SIMILAR ROCKS *Basalt (p.61) is black when fresh, and harder and less altered than metabasalt.*

NOTE

One type of metabasalt is called komatiitic metabasalt. It is rich in magnesium and recognized by spiky crystals, called spinifex texture. These crystals were formed by rapid growth of olivine or pyroxene. If a metabasalt is deformed it can form greenschist, a chlorite-rich schist (p.78).

Amphibolite

BODIES of dark-coloured amphibolite contrast with grey schists in these Alpine hills.

These are dark-coloured, coarse-grained rocks dominated by black or dark green hornblende, or alternatively, by green tremolite-actinolite. They usually contain plagioclase, and may contain epidote or garnet. The mineral grains, except for garnet, are aligned and sometimes the rock is banded. Amphibolites form deep in the Earth's crust by high grade metamorphism of basic igneous rocks.

SECTION SHOWN

plagioclase

green hornblende

GRAIN SIZE *2–5mm.*
ESSENTIAL COMPONENTS *Plagioclase, hornblende.*
ADDITIONAL COMPONENTS *Epidote, garnet.*
ORIGIN *High grade metamorphism of basic igneous rocks.*
SIMILAR ROCKS *Gabbro (p.50).*

Granulite

Granulite is a coarse-grained metamorphic rock formed at high temperatures and pressures deep in the Earth's crust. Its name derives from its even-grained granular texture.

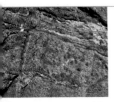

COARSE *pyroxene-rich aggregates form the brown spots in this granulite from Scotland.*

Some mineral groups, such as amphiboles and micas, cannot survive at the high metamorphic grade under which granulites form, and they are converted into pyroxenes and garnets, by losing water. Most granulites are of the Precambrian age.

red garnet

even grain size

SECTION SHOWN

GRAIN SIZE *2–5mm.*
ESSENTIAL COMPONENTS *Quartz, feldspar, pyroxene.*
ADDITIONAL COMPONENTS *Garnet.*
ORIGIN *Very high grade metamorphism of basic igneous rocks.*
SIMILAR ROCKS *Amphibolite (p.70) has elongated grains.*

Blueschist

Glaucophane is the mineral responsible for the blue colour of this rock, but it is often so fine grained that individual grains cannot be seen. The colour is a dark purple-blue, but this colouring may not be particularly strong and, at first glance, the rock may appear grey or black. Outcrops of blueschist are typically small areas within strongly folded and faulted rocks.

BLUESCHIST *can be found on the Argentario coast of Tuscany, Italy.*

aligned glaucophane crystals

wavy surface

GRAIN SIZE *2mm.*
ESSENTIAL COMPONENTS *Glaucophane, chlorite, epidote.*
ADDITIONAL COMPONENTS *Lawsonite, jadeite.*
ORIGIN *Low temperature, high pressure metamorphism of basalt.*
SIMILAR ROCKS *Greenschist (p.69).*

Eclogite

A beautiful coarse-grained, dense rock of bright red garnet and contrasting green omphacite, eclogite grains may be evenly distributed or banded. It may occur as nodules in basalts and kimberlites, or as larger bodies of rock. It forms at very high temperatures and pressures from basic igneous rocks, deep in the Earth's crust and in the mantle.

ECLOGITE *forms the dark rock below light brown schists in this cliff at As Sifah, Oman.*

red pyrope garnet

green omphacite

GRAIN SIZE *2-5mm.*
ESSENTIAL COMPONENTS *Garnet, omphacite.*
ADDITIONAL COMPONENTS *Kyanite, quartz.*
ORIGIN *Very high pressure metamorphism of basic igneous rocks.*
SIMILAR ROCKS *Garnet-bearing peridotite (p.52).*

banding

DARKER EXAMPLE

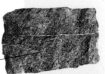

Serpentinite

An attractive rock with flowing bands of various colours, especially greens and yellow, largely made of serpentine. It is a soft rock, which is easily cut and polished to make a decorative stone. It forms from the metamorphism of olivine and pyroxene-rich ultrabasic igneous rocks. Chrysotile asbestos develops in sheared serpentinites.

ROUGH *columnar jointing is visible in this serpentinite. The wrinkled brown-grey surface is known as "elephant skin" texture.*

green colour

mottled, patchy texture

SECTION SHOWN

GRAIN SIZE *Less than 0.1mm.*
ESSENTIAL COMPONENTS *Serpentine.*
ADDITIONAL COMPONENTS *Chromite, magnetite, talc.*
ORIGIN *Water-rich low grade metamorphism of olivine-rich rocks.*
SIMILAR ROCKS *Marble (p.77), which reacts with dilute acid.*

Soapstone

A massive fine-grained rock easily recognized by its softness – it has a greasy feel and can be scratched with a fingernail. This is because talc, one of the softest minerals, is its principal component. It may be green, brown, or black, especially when polished but on scratching becomes white. It is associated with other metamorphosed ultrabasic igneous rocks like serpentinite.

SOAPSTONE *quarries of the Great Dyke, Zimbabwe provide material for sculpture.*

soft, flaky surface

easily scratched

GRAIN SIZE *Less than 0.1mm.*
ESSENTIAL COMPONENTS *Talc.*
ADDITIONAL COMPONENTS *Chlorite, magnesite.*
ORIGIN *Water-rich metamorphism of serpentine.*
SIMILAR ROCKS *Serpentinite (above) is harder; clay (p.29) does not have a greasy feel.*

SECTION SHOWN

Metatuff

An interesting rock in that it has igneous, sedimentary, and metamorphic features. Metatuff is a low grade metamorphosed volcanic ash that preserves its original features, such as graded bedding. The fine grain size means that metatuffs often form slates. Sometimes, a detailed section of the preserved sedimentary features can be seen on cleaved surfaces.

SECTION SHOWN

METATUFF *slates from the Honister quarries in Cumbria, England, frequently show graded bedding.*

graded bedding

slaty cleavage

beds of varying thickness

BANDED METATUFF

> **GRAIN SIZE** *Less than 2mm.*
> **ESSENTIAL COMPONENTS** *Quartz, feldspar, chlorite.*
> **ADDITIONAL COMPONENTS** *None.*
> **ORIGIN** *Low grade metamorphism of tuff.*
> **SIMILAR ROCKS** *Tuff (p.65), which is loosely compacted; greywacke and turbidite (p.27), which have sedimentary grains.*

Gneiss

This is a general term used for rocks that show "gneissic texture". This refers to a medium- to coarse-grained rock with oriented minerals. It is made of layers of contrasting mineral composition, grain size, or texture. Most gneisses contain quartz and feldspar as the main constituents but neither mineral is necessary for a rock to be called gneiss.

THIS QUARRY *face in the Sand River, South Africa, shows gneiss that was formed over three billion years ago.*

pale quartz and feldspar

biotite

stretched crystal

> **GRAIN SIZE** *2–5mm.*
> **ESSENTIAL COMPONENTS** *Quartz, feldspar.*
> **ADDITIONAL COMPONENTS** *Mica, garnet.*
> **ORIGIN** *High grade metamorphism of rocks containing quartz and feldspar.*
> **SIMILAR ROCKS** *In granite (p.44), the grains are evenly distributed. See also orthogneiss, augen gneiss (p.74), and paragneiss (p.76).*

gneissic banding

FOLDED GNEISS

Orthogneiss

DOME-SHAPED *outcrops of granitic gneiss form bare hillsides in a shape similar to that of a whale's back.*

This is a type of gneiss, which before metamorphism was an igneous rock, commonly a granite. This fact gives orthogneiss its other name, granitic gneiss. It can also be called quartzo-feldspathic gneiss because its principal constituents are quartz and feldspar, usually accompanied by biotite, and/or hornblende. It is an overall light grey rock in outcrop and is typical of the Precambrian era.

rich in quartz and feldspar

fold

MIGMATITIC ORTHOGNEISS

rich in hornblende and biotite

GRAIN SIZE *2–5mm.*
ESSENTIAL COMPONENTS *Quartz, feldspar.*
ADDITIONAL COMPONENTS *Mica.*
ORIGIN *High grade metamorphism of acid igneous rocks.*
SIMILAR ROCKS *Paragneiss (p.76), which contains a greater variety of minerals and textures.*

Augen Gneiss

AUGEN GNEISS *is accompanied by quartzite, eclogite, and other high grade rocks at Sognefjord, Norway.*

Augen are single-mineral, eye-shaped grains of a larger size than other grains in a rock. They are usually porphyroblasts: large crystals that have grown during metamorphism. Most common are pink alkali feldspars (microcline or perthite), 1–5cm in length, in a quartz, feldspar, and mica matrix. They are typical of high grade gneiss terrains of the Precambrian age.

hornblende, garnet, and quartz

augen of feldspar

SECTION SHOWN

GRAIN SIZE *2–5mm, augen 1–2cm.*
ESSENTIAL COMPONENTS *Alkali feldspar, quartz, plagioclase.*
ADDITIONAL COMPONENTS *Mica.*
ORIGIN *Unknown.*
SIMILAR ROCKS *Tectonite (p.83), when augen are formed by deformation, but they also form by other processes.*

Migmatite

A migmatite is a mixed rock: a mix of igneous granite and metamorphic gneiss. It represents the highest grade of gneiss, which has partially melted to form pockets of granite. The granitic parts consist of granular patches of quartz and feldspar; the gneissic parts of quartz, feldspar, and dark-coloured minerals. It is a common Precambrian-aged rock.

LIGHT-COLOURED *granite veins, grey gneiss, and dark grey amphibolite can be seen in this South African amphibolite.*

dark gneiss

folded granite layer

granite

GRAIN SIZE *2–5mm.*
ESSENTIAL COMPONENTS *Quartz, feldspar.*
ADDITIONAL COMPONENTS *None.*
ORIGIN *Partial melting of rocks containing quartz and feldspar.*
SIMILAR ROCKS *Gneiss (p.73), which has no granitic parts, and granite (p.44), which has no foliated parts.*

Charnockite

A high grade metamorphic rock, charnockite is similar to granulite with which it occurs. It has a granular texture and an overall composition and appearance of granite, except it is darker coloured. It does not contain amphiboles as these have been converted to pyroxenes under extreme metamorphism. Mostly occurring in Precambrian terrains, the best known examples are from India.

greenish colour

KABBAL DURGA, *a hill near Bangalore, India, is made of amphibole gneiss with charnockite.*

garnet gneiss

granite-like texture

lighter colour

GRAIN SIZE *2–5mm.*
ESSENTIAL COMPONENTS *Quartz, feldspar, pyroxene (enstatite).*
ADDITIONAL COMPONENTS *Garnet.*
ORIGIN *High grade metamorphism of granite or gneiss.*
SIMILAR ROCKS *Granite (p.44), is paler and does not contain pyroxene.*

Paragneiss

ALMANDINE *and kyanite are the knobbly-weathering minerals in this rock.*

A paragneiss is a gneissic rock, which was a sediment before metamorphism. Paragneiss can contain many different minerals, depending on the sedimentary precursors. Changes in mineralogy and texture occur across an outcrop or on the scale of a few hundred metres. Typical minerals in paragneiss are quartz and feldspar, plus kyanite, staurolite, garnet, and muscovite.

SECTION SHOWN

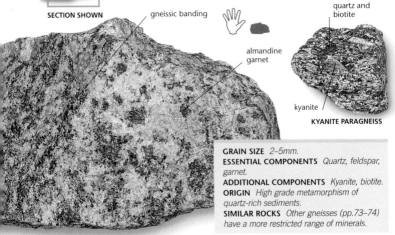

gneissic banding

almandine garnet

quartz and biotite

kyanite

KYANITE PARAGNEISS

> **GRAIN SIZE** 2–5mm.
> **ESSENTIAL COMPONENTS** *Quartz, feldspar, garnet.*
> **ADDITIONAL COMPONENTS** *Kyanite, biotite.*
> **ORIGIN** *High grade metamorphism of quartz-rich sediments.*
> **SIMILAR ROCKS** *Other gneisses (pp.73–74) have a more restricted range of minerals.*

Quartzite

QUARTZITES, *being resistant, often form white vegetation-free hilltops and ridges.*

Quartzite, or metaquartzite, is a hard, sugary-textured rock, usually white, cream, or pink. It has a medium grain size, and under a hand lens the grains appear to be fused together. It can form by contact metamorphism of sandstones a few metres around the edge of an igneous intrusion, but is usually found as a laterally extensive regional metamorphic rock.

very quartz-rich

hard and resistant

rounded grains

> **GRAIN SIZE** 2–5mm.
> **ESSENTIAL COMPONENTS** *Quartz.*
> **ADDITIONAL COMPONENTS** *Heavy minerals, such as zircon, rutile, and titanite.*
> **ORIGIN** *Regional metamorphism of orthoquartzite.*
> **SIMILAR ROCKS** *Orthoquartzite (p.25), which has more pore spaces.*

Marble

Marble is metamorphosed limestone and, when pure, is a white granular crystalline, fine- to medium-grained rock. Marble can easily be identified by its softness and vigorous reaction to dilute acid. The best examples are valuable decorative rocks that can be carved or worked into tiling and facing stone. Many impure marbles are desirable because of their colour variation or texture of folding and banding. Marble can be formed by contact metamorphism of limestone next to igneous intrusions, in which case, it is often associated with skarn. Mostly, it is a regional metamorphic rock that occurs over large areas.

CALC-SILICATE *minerals form the green and grey parts of this marble, which is being worked as a decorative stone.*

granular texture

forsterite, tremolite, or serpentine

fine crystals of diopside

WHITE MARBLE

CALC-SILICATE ROCK

BLUE-GREY MARBLE

fine-grained metamorphic rock

iron-stained veinlet

cream-white marble

brecciated texture

NOTE

If silicate minerals form a considerable portion of the marble, then it is known as a calc-silicate rock and can contain metamorphic calcium-rich silicate minerals, such as green-coloured tremolite (p.198) and diopside (p.213), in patches or bands. Others include dolomite (p.152), and serpentine (p.202).

GRAIN SIZE Less than 0.01–2cm.
ESSENTIAL COMPONENTS Calcite.
ADDITIONAL COMPONENTS Dolomite, tremolite, diopside, serpentine.
ORIGIN Contact or regional metamorphism of limestone.
SIMILAR ROCKS Limestone (p.32) and dolomite (p.34), which are not crystalline.

Schist

TIGHTLY-FOLDED *silver-grey schist, can be seen in this outcrop in the European Alps.*

Schist is a metamorphic rock with a schistose texture, that is, sheets that are wrinkled, wavy, or irregular on a small scale. Many different mineral compositions can occur, but it usually includes a mica. The rock colour will depend on the constituent minerals and the grain size is usually medium. Larger crystals of garnet, staurolite, kyanite, or other metamorphic minerals may be present. Schist is a medium-grade rock resulting from the metamorphism of fine-grained sediments, and often occurs on a regional scale in mountain belts.

SECTION SHOWN

sheen on mica-rich surface

crenulations or wavy folds

dark mineral

kyanite

KYANITE SCHIST

garnet

GARNET SCHIST

muscovite

MUSCOVITE SCHIST

GRAIN SIZE *0.1–2mm.*
ESSENTIAL COMPONENTS *Mica.*
ADDITIONAL COMPONENTS *Quartz, feldspar, garnet, staurolite, cordierite, kyanite, sillimanite.*
ORIGIN *Regional metamorphism of fine-grained sediments.*
SIMILAR ROCKS *Phyllite (p.80).*

NOTE

To provide a more detailed rock name, the major minerals present in schist are hyphenated and used as a prefix, for example, talc-tremolite-magnesite schist or quartz-sericite schist. Garnet-mica schist is a particularly common variety, and it occurs across wide areas.

Slate

Slate is a familiar rock type as it is used as a roofing material. It is characterized by a strong and flat cleavage, enabling the rock to be easily split into sheets. The colour is usually dark: possibly grey, black, green, purple, or red. It is a very fine-grained rock, but may contain well-developed coarser crystals, such as pyrite. Slates are frequently quarried and being regional metamorphic rocks, these workings may extend over large areas, such as the slate quarries in north Wales. Welsh slate, like other examples worldwide, is a Lower Palaeozoic rock.

NORTH WALES *has many large scale quarries of slate with vast waste tips.*

raised notches

BLACK SLATE

brachiopod shell

SLATE WITH DISTORTED FOSSIL

cubic crystal of pyrite

SLATE WITH PYRITE

flat surface

dark purple colour

NOTE

Being low-grade metamorphic rocks, some slates retain sedimentary or igneous features, such as graded bedding or fossils.

GRAIN SIZE *Less than 0.1mm.*
ESSENTIAL COMPONENTS *Quartz, mica.*
ADDITIONAL COMPONENTS *Pyrite.*
ORIGIN *Low-grade regional metamorphism of fine-grained sediments.*
SIMILAR ROCKS *Shale (p.31), which is crumbly; phyllite (p.80), which is rougher and will not cleave into very thin sheets.*

Spotted Slate

PRISMATIC *andalusite crystals can be seen in this purple spotted slate from the Skiddaw granite aureole, England.*

The spots in a spotted slate are coarser-grained minerals that are scattered throughout the finer groundmass of the slate. Typical minerals that form the spots are cordierite and andalusite, the former as darker diffuse areas and the latter as distinct square-ended long prismatic crystals, often of the variety chiastolite. Spotted slates are produced by close proximity to an igneous intrusion, in a narrow zone known as an aureole.

dark spot
of cordierite

rough, slaty
cleavage

SECTION SHOWN

GRAIN SIZE *Less than 0.1mm, spots 1–5mm.*
ESSENTIAL COMPONENTS *Quartz, mica.*
ADDITIONAL COMPONENTS *Cordierite, andalusite, staurolite.*
ORIGIN *Low-grade regional metamorphism followed by contact metamorphism.*
SIMILAR ROCKS *Slate (p.79).*

Phyllite

LIGHT *reflected off the cleavage surfaces gives a characteristic sheen in this folded phyllite.*

Phyllite is a dark coloured metamorphic rock, usually grey or dark green, with a fine grain size. It has a strong foliation of aligned mica, which is often visible as a sheen on cleavage surfaces. These surfaces are more irregular than slate but less than schist, so it splits into slabs. Phyllite is often deformed into folds a few centimetres across, and veined with quartz.

fine
grain

mica
sheen

fairly flat
surface

dark
colour

GRAIN SIZE *Less than 0.1mm.*
ESSENTIAL COMPONENTS *Quartz, muscovite.*
ADDITIONAL COMPONENTS *None.*
ORIGIN *Regional metamorphism of fine-grained sediments.*
SIMILAR ROCKS *Slate (p.79), which has flat, smooth cleavage surfaces; and schist (p.78), which is more crumpled.*

Hornfels

Hornfels is a hard-to-break, fine-grained or glassy rock with a splintery fracture. It is formed by the metamorphism of fine sediments in contact with an igneous intrusion. The colour is usually even throughout, but varies depending on the composition of the original rock. An outcrop of hornfels rarely extends more than a few metres from the contact and may pass outwards into spotted slate.

MARBLE, *in the top left corner, has been converted to darker striped calc-hornfels.*

dark and fine-grained

CORDIERITE HORNFELS

garnet crystals

black, hackly matrix

GRAIN SIZE *Less than 0.1mm.*
ESSENTIAL COMPONENTS *Many different compositions.*
ADDITIONAL COMPONENTS *Calcite, cordierite, pyroxene.*
ORIGIN *Contact metamorphism of fine-grained sediment.*
SIMILAR ROCKS *Lavas (are of greater extent).*

Skarn

This is a product of contact metamorphism of a limestone or dolomite by an intermediate or acid igneous intrusion. Skarn is rich in carbonate minerals, as well as, in calcium, iron, and magnesium silicates, which may be fine to medium-grained, but often occur as coarse radiating crystals or bands. Some skarns are rich in metallic ores and can form valuable deposits of metals such as gold, copper, iron, tin, tungsten, lead, and zinc.

MONTICELLITE *forms the darker layers in this South African skarn. Calcite forms the lighter layers.*

diopside and tremolite

brown calcite

GRAIN SIZE *0.01–2cm.*
ESSENTIAL COMPONENTS *Calcite.*
ADDITIONAL COMPONENTS *Garnet, serpentine, forsterite, vesuvianite.*
ORIGIN *Contact metamorphism of limestone.*
SIMILAR ROCKS *Calc-silicate rocks (p.77), which occur over larger areas.*

Fault Breccia

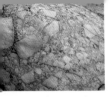

FAULT *breccia with variably sized clasts in a matrix of ground rock fragments.*

In some faults, pieces of rock can be broken up by crushing within the fault zone. When cemented, usually by a mineral, such as quartz or calcite, this crushed material becomes a fault breccia. Fragments within the breccia are of the rocks found on either side of the fault plane and may be of any dimension, depending on the size and nature of the fault itself.

SECTION SHOWN

angular slate clasts

orange quartz matrix

> **GRAIN SIZE** *Clasts of any size in a fine or crystalline matrix.*
> **ESSENTIAL COMPONENTS** *Surrounding rocks.*
> **ADDITIONAL COMPONENTS** *Quartz and calcite are common cements.*
> **ORIGIN** *Crushing of rock in a fault.*
> **SIMILAR ROCKS** *Sedimentary breccia (p.21), volcanic breccia (p.62).*

Mylonite

LINEATIONS, *produced by stretching, in a mylonitic gneiss with a much-reduced grain size.*

A mylonite is a fine-grained rock with streaks or rod-like structures that are evidence of the ductile deformation (stretching) of mineral grains. It is typically produced in a zone of thrusts, or low-angle faults. The fine grain size may have been produced by recrystallization under pressure. In some cases, the rock is so fine it has the appearance of streaky flint.

fine grain size

stretched mineral grains

> **GRAIN SIZE** *Less than 2mm.*
> **ESSENTIAL COMPONENTS** *Surrounding rocks, but usually the mylonite is a finer grain size.*
> **ADDITIONAL COMPONENTS** *None.*
> **ORIGIN** *Stretching of a rock in a large fault.*
> **SIMILAR ROCKS** *Hornfels (p.81), has randomly oriented grains.*

Tectonite

This rock has a well-developed deformation texture. It has elongated or flattened mineral grains or other components, such as pebbles. If flattening (foliation) is dominant, it is called an S-tectonite; if stretching (lineation), an L-tectonite, if neither, an L-S tectonite. Tectonites are found in shear zones, where a body of rock has been highly strained within a narrow planar area. Many examples are coarse-grained rocks, such as gneiss.

TECTONITES *can be found in shear zones, such as this one within gneiss.*

banded layers

GRAIN SIZE *0.2–2cm.*
ESSENTIAL COMPONENTS *Any rock type, which shows evidence of deformation.*
ADDITIONAL COMPONENTS *None.*
ORIGIN *Stretching or squashing of a rock.*
SIMILAR ROCKS *Mylonite (bottom left), which is finer grained. The term can be added to, such as "gneissic tectonite".*

Pseudotachylite

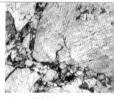

Pseudotachylite is a dark-coloured glassy substance found in rocks that have experienced very severe stress or friction. This happens within large faults and thrusts, and beneath meteorite impacts. It is usually seen in gneiss, as a series of discontinuous veins, up to several centimetres wide, or as the matrix of a breccia.

VEINS *of black pseudotachylite with light grey gneiss fragments, found on the Isle of Barra, Scotland.*

black pseudotachylite

gneiss

filling extension vein

PSEUDOTACHYLITE IN GNEISS

GRAIN SIZE *Not granular.*
ESSENTIAL COMPONENTS *Metamorphic glass.*
ADDITIONAL COMPONENTS *Often contains gneiss fragments.*
ORIGIN *Frictional melting in a fault zone.*
SIMILAR ROCKS *Volcanic glass, such as obsidian (p.57), which is associated with lava.*

Meteorites

METEOR *crater, in Arizona, USA, was formed by the impact of the Canyon Diablo meteorite.*

Meteorites are rocks from space, and can be divided into three groups: irons, stony irons, and stony meteorites. Irons are made of nickel-iron and readily rust in the Earth's atmosphere. If sliced, the inner surface may reveal metal crystals. Stony irons consist of roughly equal amounts of nickel-iron and silicate material; either igneous rock or single minerals, such as olivine. Stony meteorites may have the appearance of igneous rocks, such as gabbro or anorthosite, but frequently contain small metallic patches too. One type, known as chondrites contain spheroidal structures and graphite crystals.

black fusion crust

thumb-shaped depression

stony interior

fusion crust

nickel-iron crystals

IRON METEORITE SLICE

pointed metal

hollow

IRON METEORITE

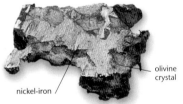

olivine crystal

nickel-iron

STONY IRON METEORITE

GRAIN SIZE *Typically 2mm–1cm.*
ESSENTIAL COMPONENTS *Iron, nickel.*
ADDITIONAL COMPONENTS *Pyroxene, plagioclase, olivine, graphite.*
ORIGIN *As asteroids in space.*
SIMILAR ROCKS *Basic and ultrabasic igneous rocks; man-made iron objects.*

NOTE

All meteorites may show thumb-like depressions on the surface, known as regmaglypts, or they may have a layer of black, burnt material on the outside, known as a fusion crust. Constant weathering, over thousands of years, may again affect the surface appearance.

Impact Rocks

When a large meteorite hits the Earth's surface, the rocks beneath suffer great heat and pressure. This produces impact breccia from shattering, and impact glass from melting. If the molten material is thrown into the air, it can form interestingly-shaped glass objects, known as tektites. Impact glass mixed with impact breccia is known as suevite. Shatter cones are rocks with radiating cone-shaped fractures produced on impact. Meteorite impact sites can be recognized by their circular shape, and rock and mineral products of impact. Meteorites themselves are rarely found at sites, because some vapourize on impact, and others weather away quickly.

SUEVITE, *a type of impact breccia with some glass clasts, is seen here at the Ries impact site, southern Germany.*

NOTE

Bottle-green tektites, from a large area of the southern Czech Republic, are known as moldavites. These tektites probably represent ejecta from the 215 million year old Ries meteorite impact site in Bavaria, Germany.

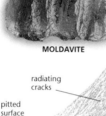

green glass

flow effects

MOLDAVITE

black glass

TEKTITE

pitted surface

radiating cracks

shatter cone

GRAIN SIZE *Breccia has clasts of about 1–10cm.*
ESSENTIAL COMPONENTS *Usually glass, or shatter effects.*
ADDITIONAL COMPONENTS *None.*
ORIGIN *Impacts of meteorites on Earth.*
SIMILAR ROCKS *Other breccias (pp.21, 62, 82) and glasses (pp.57, 83).*

Ore Minerals

Ore minerals are those which we mine to obtain the metals we use in our everyday lives. Chalcopyrite, for example, is an ore of copper; it was extracted at the Welsh mine pictured below. Many ores are hydrothermal in origin, crystallizing out of hot chemical-rich water; others form in igneous rocks; others still in metamorphic skarn deposits. When exposed to water, primary ores may break down to form secondary minerals. In this chapter, ores and their secondary minerals are grouped by their principal metal. Those commonly found in hydrothermal veins precede those found in igneous rocks.

GALENA   HEMATITE   WULFENITE   CYANOTRICH

Gold

Au

Gold is normally found in nature in its elemental state because it does not bond with most chemical elements. It is opaque and metallic golden-yellow in colour, but it is paler when alloyed with silver in the variety electrum. Gold crystals are octahedral, rarely cubic or dodecahedral, and they usually occur as dendritic aggregates. Most gold is found as tiny grains, platy masses, and nuggets. It is very dense, soft, sectile, and easily bent, and it does not develop a tarnish. Gold is widespread in occurrence but it is usually found in minute quantities. It is most abundant in hydrothermal veins and placer deposits.

THE MINES *at Banská Štiavnica, Slovakia, were once one of the world's richest sources of gold and silver.*

grains of placer gold

NOTE

Gold deposits are cemented into sandstones, siltstones, and conglomerates, and may be subsequently metamorphosed. Much of the world's gold ore comes from an ancient placer deposit in South Africa. Recent placers are sands and gravels where gold can be extracted by panning.

octahedral crystals

fine-grained quartz

SECTION SHOWN

mass of soft pure gold

flakes of gold compressed into a single nugget

metallic golden-yellow

COMPOSITION	*Element.*
CRYSTAL SYSTEM	*Cubic.*
CLEAVAGE/FRACTURE	*None/Hackly.*
LUSTRE/STREAK	*Metallic/Metallic golden-yellow.*
HARDNESS/DENSITY	*2.5–3 / 19.30.*
KEY PROPERTIES	*Golden-yellow, dense, soft, sectile, and easily bent.*

Cinnabar

HgS

Cinnabar is bright scarlet to deep greyish red. It usually occurs as massive or granular aggregates and powdery coatings, but is also found as rhombohedral, tabular, or prismatic crystals. The principal ore of mercury, cinnabar forms in low-temperature hydrothermal veins. Bright red powdered cinnabar was used in the past as the artist's pigment vermillion.

CINNABAR *is often seen as a powdery red coating on the rock matrix. The best known locality for the mineral is Almadén, Spain.*

SECTION SHOWN

rich red crystalline mass

tabular crystals in cavity

COMPOSITION *Sulphide.*
CRYSTAL SYSTEM *Trigonal.*
CLEAVAGE/FRACTURE *Perfect/Subconchoidal.*
LUSTRE/STREAK *Adamantine to sub-metallic/Scarlet.*
HARDNESS/DENSITY *2–2.5 / 8.18.*
KEY PROPERTIES *More dense than realgar (below right).*

fine-grained rock matrix containing crystals of pyrite

Sulphur

S

Sulphur is normally bright yellow or orangish yellow, and forms pyramidal or tabular crystals, encrustations, powdery coatings, and granular or massive aggregates. Most sulphur forms in volcanic fumaroles, but it can also result from the breakdown of sulphide ore deposits and occur in some sedimentary rocks. Its low thermal conductivity means sulphur crystals may shatter in the warmth of a hand and should never be immersed in water.

DEPOSITS *of sulphur occur in fumaroles that formed in 1971 in the Kilauea Caldera of Hawaii, USA.*

yellow with resinous lustre

thick tabular crystals

pisolitic aragonite matrix

COMPOSITION *Element.*
CRYSTAL SYSTEM *Orthorhombic.*
CLEAVAGE/FRACTURE *Three, imperfect/Conchoidal to uneven.*
LUSTRE/STREAK *Resinous or greasy/White.*
HARDNESS/DENSITY *1.5–2.5 / 2.07.*
KEY PROPERTIES *A soft, low-density mineral with poor cleavage.*

Orpiment

As_2S_3

Orpiment is a soft yellow or orange mineral, once used as an artist's pigment. Typical orpiment is powdery or massive, or in foliated cleavable masses. It occurs in low-temperature hydrothermal veins, hot spring deposits, and volcanic fumeroles. It also results from the alteration of arsenic-bearing minerals like realgar.

ORPIMENT *forms around hot springs and vents in volcanic landscapes, such as this one in Japan.*

rare, stubby prismatic crystals

typical foliated habit

perfect cleavage into flexible yellow sheets

COMPOSITION *Sulphide.*
CRYSTAL SYSTEM *Monoclinic.*
CLEAVAGE/FRACTURE *Perfect, into flexible sheets/None.*
LUSTRE/STREAK *Pearly on cleavage faces/Pale yellow.*
HARDNESS/DENSITY *1.5–2 / 3.49.*
KEY PROPERTIES *Colour and cleavage.*

Realgar

As_4S_4

Bright red or orange-red, realgar is found as prismatic crystals striated along the length, or, as massive or granular aggregates and coatings. Realgar forms with other arsenic and antimony minerals in low-temperature hydrothermal veins. It is also deposited in volcanic fumeroles and hot spring deposits. When exposed to light, it disintegrates to form yellow powdery orpiment or pararealgar.

SECTION SHOWN

REALGAR *is found with other sulphides and sulphosalts in dolomite rock at the Lengenbach quarry, Switzerland.*

realgar altering to yellow orpiment

greasy lustre

rock matrix

conchoidal fracture

COMPOSITION *Sulphide.*
CRYSTAL SYSTEM *Monoclinic.*
CLEAVAGE/FRACTURE *Good/Conchoidal.*
LUSTRE/STREAK *Resinous or greasy/Orange-red to red.*
HARDNESS/DENSITY *1.5–2 / 3.56.*
KEY PROPERTIES *A soft, sectile, red mineral often found partially altered to yellow orpiment.*

Stibnite

Sb_2S_3

Stibnite is opaque silvery grey, but becomes tarnished and dull on exposure to light. It normally occurs as elongate, prismatic crystals with the curious property that they may be bent or twisted. Coarse irregular masses or radiating sprays of acicular crystals are typical, but it can also be granular or massive. It is found in hydrothermal antimony deposits.

CAVITIES *in this hydrothermal vein contain radiating sprays of stibnite crystals on white calcite.*

radiating prismatic crystals

dull and tarnished where exposed to light

calcite

bent crystals

COMPOSITION *Sulphide.*
CRYSTAL SYSTEM *Orthorhombic.*
CLEAVAGE/FRACTURE *Perfect/ Subconchoidal.*
LUSTRE/STREAK *Metallic/Lead grey.*
HARDNESS/DENSITY *2 / 4.63.*
KEY PROPERTIES *More common and less dense than bismuthinite (below).*

Bismuthinite

Bi_2S_3

Bismuthinite usually occurs as delicate acicular crystals and foliated or fibrous masses, but can form larger striated, prismatic crystals. It is opaque steel grey, often developing an iridescent or silvery yellow tarnish. It is found in hydrothermal veins, granite pegmatites, and in volcanic fumaroles. Bismuthinite occurs as large crystals at Tazna in Potosí, Bolivia.

WHEAL *coates and other mines in Cornwall, England, were once a source of bismuth as well as other metals.*

delicate fibrous crystals

metallic grey

SECTION SHOWN

COMPOSITION *Sulphide.*
CRYSTAL SYSTEM *Orthorhombic.*
CLEAVAGE/FRACTURE *Perfect/Brittle; slightly sectile.*
LUSTRE/STREAK *Metallic/Lead grey.*
HARDNESS/ DENSITY *2–2.5 / 6.78.*
KEY PROPERTIES *More dense and less common than stibnite (above).*

Cobaltite

CoAsS

Cobaltite crystals appear cubic, pyritohedral, octahedral, or combinations of these forms, and faces may be striated. Granular or massive aggregates occur. Although the shapes of crystals resemble pyrite, the colour is different. Cobaltite is opaque, pale silvery grey, often tinted pink. It is found in high-temperature hydrothermal veins or disseminated in metamorphic rocks.

COBALTITE *is found with other sulphides and quartz at Tunaberg, Sweden.*

combination of cube and octahedron

chalcopyrite and other sulphides

SECTION SHOWN

COMPOSITION *Sulphide.*
CRYSTAL SYSTEM *Orthorhombic.*
CLEAVAGE/FRACTURE *Perfect/Uneven.*
LUSTRE/STREAK *Metallic/Greyish black.*
HARDNESS/DENSITY *5.5 / 6.33.*
KEY PROPERTIES *Perfect cleavage, unlike cubic minerals skutterudite $CoAs_{2-3}$ and nickel-skutterudite $(Ni,Co)As_{2-3}$.*

Erythrite

$Co_3(AsO_4)_2 \cdot 8H_2O$

The bright purplish pink colour of erythrite in a rock indicates the presence of cobalt, and it was known to miners as 'cobalt bloom'. It typically occurs as flattened prismatic crystals and powdery coatings in the oxidized zones of cobalt-nickel-arsenic deposits. Widespread in occurence, fine crystals come from Mount Cobalt in Australia.

COBALT-NICKEL *mines in the Atlas Mountains, Morocco, are sources of exceptional erythrite.*

typically purplish pink

subadamantine lustre

COMPOSITION *Arsenate.*
CRYSTAL SYSTEM *Monoclinic.*
CLEAVAGE/FRACTURE *Perfect/Sectile and flexible.*
LUSTRE/STREAK *Subadamantine or pearly/Pale pink.*
HARDNESS/DENSITY *1.5–2.5 / 3.06.*
KEY PROPERTIES *Colour, sectility.*

flattened elongate crystals

Pentlandite

(Fe,Ni)$_9$S$_8$

PENTLANDITE *is mined underground at Sudbury, Ontario, Canada.*

Pentlandite is always massive or granular, so distinct crystals are not seen. It is opaque, metallic yellow in colour, tarnishes bronze, and is nearly always found mixed with pyrrhotite. Pentlandite typically occurs in basic and ultrabasic igneous intrusions. In the Sudbury region of Ontario, Canada, nickel from an ancient meteorite is thought to have enriched the ore. These deposits contain enough pentlandite to make this the most important ore of nickel.

bronze tarnish

granular, mixed with pyrrhotite

SECTION SHOWN

COMPOSITION	*Sulphide.*
CRYSTAL SYSTEM	*Cubic.*
CLEAVAGE/FRACTURE	*Parting/Conchoidal.*
LUSTRE/STREAK	*Metallic/Light bronze-brown.*
HARDNESS/DENSITY	*3.5–4 / 4.6–5.*
KEY PROPERTIES	*Bronze tarnish, not magnetic like pyrrhotite (p.125).*

Millerite

NiS

DELICATE *sprays of millerite crystals are found in hard concretions on coal mine dumps as here, in Limburg, Holland.*

Millerite's opaque golden crystals are fibrous or acicular and very delicate. They can be free-standing as single crystals, tufts, matted groups, or radiating sprays, or, are bedded within other sulphides and gangue minerals. This low-temperature hydrothermal mineral is found in cavities in limestones and carbonate veins, in nodules and other associated rocks with coal deposits, and in serpentinites.

crystals in rock cavity

golden crystals

acicular habit

COMPOSITION	*Sulphide.*
CRYSTAL SYSTEM	*Trigonal.*
CLEAVAGE/FRACTURE	*Perfect/Uneven.*
LUSTRE/STREAK	*Metallic/Greenish black.*
HARDNESS/DENSITY	*3–3.5 / 5.5.*
KEY PROPERTIES	*Golden acicular crystals may be coated with green annabergite (above right).*

Annabergite

$Ni_3(AsO_4)_2 \cdot 8H_2O$

Annabergite is normally bright apple-green, pale green, or, more rarely, grey. It is usually found as fibrous crusts, coatings, or earthy masses. Bladed or prismatic crystals come from only a few places, notably Lavrion (Laurium) in Greece. Annabergite forms by alteration of pentlandite, millerite, nickeline (niccolite), and other nickel-bearing sulphides and arsenides. It is the 'nickel bloom' that is seen coating the walls of nickel mines.

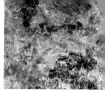

SILVERY *pink nickeline has altered to apple green annabergite in this sample from northern England.*

powdery green coating

rock matrix

SECTION SHOWN

COMPOSITION *Arsenate.*
CRYSTAL SYSTEM *Monoclinic.*
CLEAVAGE/FRACTURE *Perfect/Uneven.*
LUSTRE/STREAK *Subadamantine; pearly on cleavages; dull when earthy/Very pale green.*
HARDNESS/DENSITY *1.5–2.5 / 3.07.*
KEY PROPERTIES *Apple-green mineral that does not fizz in dilute HCl.*

Garnierite

Mixed nickel silicates

Garnierite is a general name for mixed nickel-bearing silicates, including népouite, a nickel serpentine. Crystals of this mineral are hexagonal, but garnierite normally occurs as soft foliated or earthy aggregates. The colour is pale to bright grass-green, typical of nickel secondary minerals. It has a waxy or dull lustre. Garnierite is an important ore of nickel, and results from tropical weathering of nickel-rich ultrabasic igneous rocks, to form laterite deposits.

GARNIERITE *is a major ore of nickel mined around Nouméa, on the tropical islands of New Caledonia.*

soft foliated mass

typical apple-green colour

COMPOSITION *Silicates.*
CRYSTAL SYSTEM *Various.*
CLEAVAGE/FRACTURE *Unknown/Splintery or uneven.*
LUSTRE/STREAK *Waxy, dull/White to light green.*
HARDNESS/DENSITY *2–4 / 2.3–2.8.*
KEY PROPERTIES *Apple-green; waxy lustre.*

Silver

Ag

Natural crystals of the element silver are cubic, octahedral, or dodecahedral, but usually, this mineral is found as grains and wiry, dendritic, lamellar, or scaly masses. Silver is opaque and bright silvery white with a slightly pink tint, but readily tarnishes grey or black on exposure to light and pollutants. A primary hydrothermal mineral, silver also forms by alteration of other silver-bearing minerals in the oxidized zone of ore deposits.

THE LARGEST *silver nugget in the world was extracted from the Smuggler mine in Aspen, Colorado, USA, in 1894.*

dendritic crystals

silvery white

wiry silver

COMPOSITION *Element.*
CRYSTAL SYSTEM *Cubic.*
CLEAVAGE/FRACTURE *None/Hackly.*
LUSTRE/STREAK *Metallic/Silvery white.*
HARDNESS/DENSITY *2.5–3 / 10.1–11.1.*
KEY PROPERTIES *A ductile and malleable silvery white mineral that tarnishes easily.*

Acanthite

Ag$_2$S

Acanthite usually crystallizes from argentite, the high-temperature form of silver sulphide, which has cubic or octahedral crystals. On cooling, acanthite develops internal monoclinic symmetry without altering crystal shape. It is opaque and greyish black. It occurs in hydrothermal veins and secondary veins of mineral deposits.

ACANTHITE *and silver were obtained from Bulldog mine near Creede, Colorado, USA, until it was closed in 1985.*

crystal appears to be cubic

opaque, metallic greyish black

uneven fracture

COMPOSITION *Sulphide.*
CRYSTAL SYSTEM *Monoclinic.*
CLEAVAGE/FRACTURE *Indistinct/Uneven.*
LUSTRE/STREAK *Metallic/Black.*
HARDNESS/DENSITY *2–2.5 / 7.22.*
KEY PROPERTIES *Distinguished from galena (p.96) by its imperfect cleavage and sectility.*

Pyrargyrite

Ag_3SbS_3

The silver sulphosalt pyrargyrite is typically massive or granular, or occurs as prismatic crystals with rhombohedral, scalenohedral, or flat terminations, different at each end. In colour, it is translucent dark red, but turns opaque dull grey on exposure to light, so should always be stored in the dark. Pyrargyrite forms in low-temperature hydrothermal deposits and by alteration of other silver-bearing minerals.

PYRARGYRITE *was once mined and processed at the historic works in Rammelsberg, Saxony, Germany.*

six-sided prismatic crystal

deep red colour

COMPOSITION	Sulphosalt.
CRYSTAL SYSTEM	Trigonal.
CLEAVAGE/FRACTURE	Distinct/Conchoidal to uneven.
LUSTRE/STREAK	Adamantine/Purplish red.
HARDNESS/DENSITY	2.5 / 5.82.
KEY PROPERTIES	Distinguished from cuprite (p.111) by crystal shape.

Proustite

Ag_3AsS_3

As its old name ruby silver suggests, proustite is translucent and red, but if it is exposed to light, it turns dull opaque grey. Red proustite should be stored in the dark. The striated crystals are typically prismatic with rhombohedral or scalenohedral terminations, or form massive or granular aggregates. Proustite occurs with other silver minerals in hydrothermal veins and in the secondary zone of silver deposits.

PROUSTITE *comes from Guanajuato, Mexico, one of four mining districts that make Mexico the world's largest producer of silver.*

adamantine lustre

striations on crystal face

translucent red

opaque grey after exposure to light

lustre becomes dull

COMPOSITION	Sulphosalt.
CRYSTAL SYSTEM	Trigonal.
CLEAVAGE/FRACTURE	Distinct/Conchoidal to uneven.
LUSTRE/STREAK	Adamantine/Scarlet.
HARDNESS/DENSITY	2–2.5 / 5.57.
KEY PROPERTIES	Lighter in colour and streak than pyrargyrite (above).

Galena

PbS

BANDS *of galena, purple fluorite, creamy dolomite, and white quartz are visible in this hydrothermal vein from the north Pennines, England.*

Composed of lead sulphide, galena is opaque and bright metallic grey when fresh, but it dulls on exposure to the environment. Its crystals are cubic, octahedral, dodecahedral, or combinations of these forms, and irregular, coarse, or fine crystalline masses are common. Galena is very common in lead-zinc-copper hydrothermal ore deposits worldwide, associated with sphalerite, chalcopyrite, and pyrite. It is also found in contact metamorphic rocks, but it is rarely found in pegmatites. Galena is both the principal ore of lead and the main source of silver; it often contains silver as an impurity.

NOTE

Lead was once widely used in the home and, also, in industry but, because it is toxic, it now has limited application. Galena is relatively insoluble and so it is not very toxic, but some other minerals are hazardous if ingested and should be kept away from children.

perfect cleavage in three directions at right angles

cubic crystal

bright metallic lustre

combination of cube and octahedron

granular pyrite

SECTION SHOWN

COMPOSITION *Sulphide.*
CRYSTAL SYSTEM *Cubic.*
CLEAVAGE/FRACTURE *Perfect, cubic/Subconchoidal.*
LUSTRE/STREAK *Metallic/Lead grey.*
HARDNESS/DENSITY *2.5–2.75 / 7.58.*
KEY PROPERTIES *A markedly heavy mineral with perfect cubic cleavage.*

Bournonite

PbCuSbS$_3$

Its popular name 'cog-wheel ore' alludes to the distinctive twinned crystals that are common to bournonite. Untwinned crystals of this opaque lead grey mineral are tabular or short prismatic, and granular or massive aggregates are also found. It forms in medium-temperature hydrothermal veins associated with galena, tetrahedrite, and other sulphide minerals.

COG-WHEEL *twins of bournonite with pyrite from a hydrothermal ore deposit at Baia Sprie, Romania.*

metallic lustre

short prismatic crystal

COMPOSITION *Sulphosalt.*
CRYSTAL SYSTEM *Orthorhombic.*
CLEAVAGE/FRACTURE *Imperfect/ Subconchoidal to uneven.*
LUSTRE/STREAK *Brilliant to dull/Steel grey to nearly black.*
HARDNESS/DENSITY *2.5–3 / 5.83.*
KEY PROPERTIES *Distinctive cog-wheel twins.*

Jamesonite

Pb$_4$FeSb$_6$S$_{14}$

Jamesonite is normally found as acicular or fibrous crystals forming columnar, radiating, plumose (feather-like), or felt-like masses. It is opaque dark grey but often develops an iridescent tarnish. Jamesonite forms in low- or medium-temperature hydrothermal veins with other lead and antimony sulphides and sulphosalts.

RICH *specimens of jamesonite come from the antimony-lead mine at Port Isaac, Cornwall, England.*

iron-stained weathered surface

slightly iridescent tarnish

feather-like aggregate of crystals

COMPOSITION *Sulphosalt.*
CRYSTAL SYSTEM *Monoclinic.*
CLEAVAGE/FRACTURE *Good/Brittle.*
LUSTRE/STREAK *Metallic/Grey to black.*
HARDNESS/DENSITY *2.5 / 5.63.*
KEY PROPERTIES *Crystals are usually more slender than stibnite (p.192); not flexible like boulangerite (Pb$_5$Sb$_4$S$_{11}$).*

Cerussite

PbCO₃

Cerussite is typically colourless, grey, or yellow. It forms tabular or pyramidal crystals or twins, which may be star-shaped or in reticulated (net-like) masses. Fragile aggregates of randomly grown prismatic crystals known as jack-straw cerussite are also common. A product of the weathering of galena, cerussite is found in the secondary zone of lead deposits. Sources of large crystals include Tsumeb, Namibia, and the Broken Hill mine in New South Wales, Australia.

THE KILLHOPE *museum preserves the history of northern England's lead mines, where cerussite is often found in altered galena.*

twinned crystal

adamantine lustre

tabular crystal

colourless crystal

star-shaped twin

jack-straw cerussite

COMPOSITION *Carbonate.*
CRYSTAL SYSTEM *Orthorhombic.*
CLEAVAGE/FRACTURE *Good/Conchoidal.*
LUSTRE/STREAK *Adamantine/White.*
HARDNESS/DENSITY *3–3.5 / 6.55.*
KEY PROPERTIES *Very dense; colourless or white with adamantine lustre; fizzes in dilute HNO₃.*

NOTE

The adamantine lustre – named after the Greek for diamond – is particularly bright. It is shown by certain transparent or translucent minerals, such as diamond (p.186) and cerussite (p.98), and gives an important clue to their identity. Opaque minerals with an equally bright appearance have a metallic lustre.

Anglesite

$PbSO_4$

Anglesite is colourless, white, grey, yellow, or pale shades of blue or green. It often occurs as well-formed crystals, but also as nodular, granular, or massive aggregates. Crystals can be prismatic, tabular, or equant, and striated along the length. This mineral forms by the alteration of galena and other lead minerals in the secondary zone of lead deposits.

ANGLESITE *takes its name from the Isle of Anglesey, Wales, site of the Parys Mountain copper mines.*

pointed blue crystal

adamantine lustre

COMPOSITION *Sulphate.*
CRYSTAL SYSTEM *Orthorhombic.*
CLEAVAGE/FRACTURE *Good/Conchoidal.*
LUSTRE/STREAK *Adamantine, resinous or vitreous/White.*
HARDNESS/DENSITY *2.5–3 / 6.38.*
KEY PROPERTIES *Very dense; colourless, yellow, white; does not fizz in dilute HNO_3.*

metallic grey galena

Linarite

$PbCu^{2+}(SO_4)(OH)_2$

Bright azure-blue linarite occurs as tabular or prismatic crystals, crystalline crusts, and massive aggregates. It forms by secondary alteration of lead and copper sulphides, and its association with lead minerals helps distinguish it from azurite. Although quite widespread in distribution, linarite is usually only found in small quantities.

EXCEPTIONALLY *large crystals of linarite come from the Mammoth-St Anthony and Grand Reef mines, Arizona, USA.*

blue crystals have vitreous lustre

grey galena

green and blue copper minerals

COMPOSITION *Sulphate.*
CRYSTAL SYSTEM *Monoclinic.*
CLEAVAGE/FRACTURE *Perfect/Conchoidal.*
LUSTRE/STREAK *Vitreous, subadamantine/ Pale blue.*
HARDNESS/DENSITY *2.5 / 5.35.*
KEY PROPERTIES *Turns white in dilute HCl.*

Pyromorphite

$Pb_5(PO_4)_3Cl$

PYROMORPHITE *and cerussite result from the weathering of galena at Leadhills, Lanarkshire, Scotland.*

Like mimetite, pyromorphite forms green, brown, yellow, or orange hexagonal prismatic crystals, drusy coatings, and globular or botryoidal masses. It is often found as a secondary mineral in lead deposits. Superb crystals come from Germany, France, England, and China, while the fine crystal groups of Bunkers Hill mine in Idaho, USA, make it a source of specimens for American collectors.

green, six-sided prismatic crystals

iron-rich matrix

COMPOSITION *Phosphate.*
CRYSTAL SYSTEM *Hexagonal.*
CLEAVAGE/FRACTURE *Poor/Subconchoidal.*
LUSTRE/STREAK *Subadamantine or vitreous/White.*
HARDNESS/DENSITY *3.5–4 / 7.04.*
KEY PROPERTIES *Dense hexagonal crystals, often yellow–green.*

resinous crystalline mass

Mimetite

$Pb_5(AsO_4)_3Cl$

THE VARIETY *campylite comes from Caldbeck Fells in Cumbria, England, and has rounded, barrel-shaped crystals.*

Mimetite is colourless, yellow, orange, brown, or, less commonly, green. It forms hexagonal prismatic crystals, drusy coatings, and globular or botryoidal masses, and is named after the Greek word for imitator because it looks like pyromorphite. A common secondary mineral of lead deposits, superb specimens come from Tsumeb, Namibia, and Santa Eulalia and San Pedro Corralitos, Chihuahua, Mexico.

barrel-shaped crystal

CAMPYLITE

hexagonal crystal

COMPOSITION *Arsenate.*
CRYSTAL SYSTEM *Hexagonal.*
CLEAVAGE/FRACTURE *Poor/Subconchoidal.*
LUSTRE/STREAK *Subadamantine or resinous/White.*
HARDNESS/DENSITY *3.5–4 / 7.24.*
KEY PROPERTIES *Dense hexagonal or barrel-shaped crystals.*

Vanadinite

$Pb_5(VO_4)_3Cl$

Vanadinite has orange-red, brown, or yellow hexagonal crystals. Curious hollow crystals and fibrous or globular masses may be found. It is a secondary mineral in lead deposits, vanadium being leached from surrounding rocks. Endlichite's composition is roughly midway between vanadinite and mimetite.

CRYSTALS *of vanadinite from the lead mine at Mibladen, Morocco, are of a particularly striking red colour.*

bright orangish red crystal

pale yellow prismatic crystals

ENDLICHITE

COMPOSITION *Vanadate.*
CRYSTAL SYSTEM *Hexagonal.*
CLEAVAGE/FRACTURE *None/Uneven to conchoidal.*
LUSTRE/STREAK *Resinous to subadamantine/White or yellow.*
HARDNESS/DENSITY *2.5–3 / 6.88.*
KEY PROPERTIES *Colour and crystal shape.*

rock matrix

resinous lustre

Descloizite

$PbZn(VO_4)(OH)$

The orange-red, brown, or nearly black colour, rather greasy lustre, and high density help distinguish descloizite from other minerals. Crystals may be equant, tabular, pyramidal, or prismatic, and often occur as coarse masses or drusy coatings. Descloizite can also be botryoidal, stalactitic, granular, or massive. It forms in the oxidized zone of deposits containing lead, zinc, and vanadium, where it occurs with other lead secondary minerals.

DESCLOIZITE *is one of many well-crystallized secondary minerals obtained from Tsumeb, Namibia.*

distinctly greasy lustre

mass of tabular crystals

SECTION SHOWN

COMPOSITION *Vanadate.*
CRYSTAL SYSTEM *Orthorhombic.*
CLEAVAGE/FRACTURE *None/Conchoidal to uneven.*
LUSTRE/STREAK *Vitreous to greasy/Orange to brownish red.*
HARDNESS/DENSITY *3–3.5 / 6.2.*
KEY PROPERTIES *Density, colour, and streak.*

Wulfenite

PbMoO$_4$

THE RED CLOUD mine, in a canyon in the Arizona hills, USA, is one of the world's most famous localities for wulfenite.

Small, platy, yellow, orange, or red crystals with a square cross-section that are found in the oxidized zone of a hydrothermal lead deposit are most likely to be wulfenite. It also forms massive or granular aggregates. Fine, large crystals come from Arizona, USA; other important localities are in Austria, Namibia, and Slovenia.

thin, square, tabular crystals

nearly adamantine lustre

red, tabular crystals

manganese-rich matrix

COMPOSITION	*Molybdate.*
CRYSTAL SYSTEM	*Tetragonal.*
CLEAVAGE/FRACTURE	*Distinct/ Subconchoidal to uneven.*
LUSTRE/STREAK	*Resinous or subadamantine/White.*
HARDNESS/DENSITY	*2.75–3 / 6.5–7.5.*
KEY PROPERTIES	*Shape and high density.*

Crocoite

PbCrO$_4$

CROCOITE mixes with green lead minerals in this specimen from Beresovsk, Russia.

One of the most eye-catching of minerals, crocoite is always bright orange to red. The prismatic or acicular crystals are nearly square in section, may be striated along the length, and rarely show distinct terminations. They usually occur in radiating or randomly intergrown clusters. Crocoite is found in the oxidized zones of lead deposits in chromium-bearing rocks, as at Dundas, Tasmania, Australia.

adamantine lustre

long, red, prismatic crystal

breaks with uneven surface

radiating acicular crystals

COMPOSITION	*Chromate.*
CRYSTAL SYSTEM	*Monoclinic.*
CLEAVAGE/FRACTURE	*Distinct/Conchoidal or uneven.*
LUSTRE/STREAK	*Adamantine/Yellow to orange.*
HARDNESS/DENSITY	*2.5–3 / 6.0–6.1.*
KEY PROPERTIES	*Dense, orange-red, prismatic crystals.*

Sphalerite

ZnS

Pure sphalerite is colourless and rather rare. Normally, iron is present and the colour varies from pale greenish yellow to brown and black, as the quantity of iron increases. It can also be red, a variety known as ruby blende; blende is the old name for sphalerite. Sphalerite crystals are normally complex, combining tetrahedral or dodecahedral forms with other faces. Often, sphalerite is coarsely crystalline or massive, or it forms banded, botryoidal, or stalactitic aggregates. Sphalerite is the main ore of zinc. It is a very common mineral, and it is found mainly in hydrothermal lead-zinc deposits in sedimentary rocks.

THE PRINCIPAL *ore of zinc, huge deposits of sphalerite are mined in Tennessee, USA.*

NOTE

Lustrous dark crystals of sphalerite are often mistaken for cassiterite (p.134). Sphalerite is less dense and has a perfect cleavage, and both minerals have different geological associations. Sphalerite is found in hydrothermal deposits with galena (p.96).

brown massive sphalerite

transparent, lustrous red crystals

massive sphalerite

bright adamantine lustre

RUBY BLENDE

crystal with cubic symmetry

transparent, pale yellow crystals

SECTION SHOWN

nearly black

COMPOSITION *Sulphides.*
CRYSTAL SYSTEM *Cubic.*
CLEAVAGE/FRACTURE *Perfect/Conchoidal.*
LUSTRE/STREAK *Resinous to adamantine/Brownish yellow to white.*
HARDNESS/DENSITY *3.5–4 / 3.9–4.1.*
KEY PROPERTIES *Perfect cleavage is not shown by yellow sulphur (p.88) nor red garnet.*

Zincite

$(Zn,Mn^{2+})O$

Rare natural crystals of zincite are pyramidal, pointed at one end and flat at the other. Mostly it occurs as cleavable or granular masses. It is orange, red, yellow, or green. Zincite forms by secondary alteration or metamorphism of zinc deposits. It is a rare constituent of volcanic ash. The chimneys of zinc smelters are sources of non-naturally occuring, large zincite crystals.

ZINCITE *was once extracted at Franklin and Sterling Hill, New Jersey, USA.*

SECTION SHOWN

granular zincite with franklinite

red, coarsely crystalline zincite

white calcite (fluoresces pink under UV light)

COMPOSITION *Oxide.*
CRYSTAL SYSTEM *Hexagonal.*
CLEAVAGE/FRACTURE *Perfect/Conchoidal.*
LUSTRE/STREAK *Resinous to subadamantine/Yellow to orange.*
HARDNESS/DENSITY *4 / 5.66.*
KEY PROPERTIES *Often associated with fluorescent minerals.*

Franklinite

$(Zn,Mn^{2+},Fe^{2+})(Fe^{3+},Mn^{3+})_2O_4$

Franklinite is nearly always opaque black, and its crystals are usually octahedral with rounded edges, or form granular or massive aggregates. It is strongly or weakly magnetic. It results from high-temperature metamorphism of sediments rich in manganese, iron, and zinc. In New Jersey, USA, fine crystals and beds of granular franklinite are rich enough to be an ore of zinc, but franklinite is rare elsewhere in the world.

FRANKLINITE *from Franklin, New Jersey, USA, is often associated with fluorescent minerals.*

submetallic black grains

octahedral crystal

COMPOSITION *Oxide.*
CRYSTAL SYSTEM *Cubic.*
CLEAVAGE/FRACTURE *Parting/Uneven to nearly conchoidal.*
LUSTRE/STREAK *Metallic, submetallic, or dull/Dark reddish brown.*
HARDNESS/DENSITY *6 / 5.05–5.22.*
KEY PROPERTIES *Streak, fracture, and magnetism.*

uneven fracture

large, single crystal

Gahnite

$ZnAl_2O_4$

Gahnite normally occurs as simple octahedral crystals and granular or massive aggregates. It is dark blue, blue-green, grey, yellow, or brown. Gahnite is a minor constituent in granites and granite pegmatites, and forms in medium- to high-grade metamorphic rocks, metamorphosed ore deposits, and skarns. It is also found in placer deposits.

SKARN *deposits at Falun, Dalarna, Sweden are a source of gahnite and other zinc minerals.*

very dark blue crystal, translucent with vitreous lustre

crystals show cubic symmetry

SECTION SHOWN

COMPOSITION *Oxide.*
CRYSTAL SYSTEM *Cubic.*
CLEAVAGE/FRACTURE *Parting/Conchoidal.*
LUSTRE/STREAK *Vitreous/Grey.*
HARDNESS/DENSITY *7.5–8 / 4.38–4.6.*
KEY PROPERTIES *Octahedral crystals can look like spinel (p.149) and hercynite ($Fe^{2+}Al_2O_4$).*

Smithsonite

$ZnCO_3$

Most smithsonite is spherular, botryoidal, stalactitic, massive, or earthy. Crystals are uncommon; they are prismatic, rhombohedral, or scalenohedral, and often have curved faces. Smithsonite can be of various colours including yellow, orange, brown, pink, lilac, white, grey, green, and blue. It forms in the oxidized zones of zinc deposits and in adjacent carbonate rocks. Like hermimorphite, it used to be known as calamine.

BRIGHTLY *coloured crystals and botryoidal masses come from Tsumeb, Namibia.*

botryoidal blue coating

earthy, white smithsonite

COMPOSITION *Carbonate.*
CRYSTAL SYSTEM *Trigonal.*
CLEAVAGE/FRACTURE *Nearly perfect, rhombohedral/Uneven to conchoidal.*
LUSTRE/STREAK *Vitreous or waxy/White.*
HARDNESS/DENSITY *4–4.5 / 4.43.*
KEY PROPERTIES *Does not fizz in cold, diluted HCl.*

Aurichalcite

$(Zn, Cu^{2+})_5(CO_3)_2(OH)_6$

Aurichalcite is found as delicate pale green, bluish green, or pale blue acicular or lath-like crystals. These form tufts, spherical aggregates, and coatings, and are found in the oxidized zones of copper-zinc deposits. Aurichalcite comes from many places, but rarely in large quantities.

HISTORIC *lead and zinc mines on the island of Sardinia, Italy, have yielded beautiful specimens of aurichalcite.*

SECTION SHOWN

iron-rich gossan matrix

soft crystals with pearly lustre

tufts of radiating, lathe-like crystals

COMPOSITION *Carbonate.*
CRYSTAL SYSTEM *Monoclinic.*
CLEAVAGE/FRACTURE *Perfect/Uneven.*
LUSTRE/STREAK *Silky or pearly/White or pale blue-green.*
HARDNESS/DENSITY *1–2 / 3.96.*
KEY PROPERTIES *Tufts softer than malachite (p.112) or rosasite (Cu,Zn)$_2$(Co$_3$)(OH)$_2$.*

Hydrozincite

$Zn_5(CO_3)_2(OH)_6$

Usually hydrozincite forms fibrous, stalactitic, or powdery coatings, and pisolitic, nodular, or massive aggregates. It is colourless or white, or tinted other colours by impurities. Under UV radiation, it fluoresces bluish white. Hydrozincite forms by the alteration of sphalerite or smithsonite in the oxidized zone of zinc deposits.

HYDROZINCITE *is seen encrusting the walls of the Andara zinc mine in the Picos de Europa, Spain.*

pea-like pisolitic crystal

dull lustre

rock matrix

COMPOSITION *Carbonate.*
CRYSTAL SYSTEM *Monoclinic.*
CLEAVAGE/FRACTURE *Perfect/None.*
LUSTRE/STREAK *Pearly, silky, dull or earthy/White.*
HARDNESS/DENSITY *2–2.5 / 4.00.*
KEY PROPERTIES *Fizzes in diluted HCl, fluoresces blue-white; associates with zinc ores.*

Adamite

Zn₂(As₄O)(OH)

Adamite forms honey-coloured, yellow, or yellowish green crystals and crystalline crusts, which may fluoresce lemon yellow under UV light. It is a secondary mineral found in the oxidized zone of zinc deposits. The most famous localities for adamite are Laurium in Greece, Tsumeb in Namibia, and Mapimí and elsewhere in Mexico.

THE MINERAL *is found in the ancient mines of Lavrion (Laurium), close to Cape Sounion in Greece.*

tufts of pale crystals in cavity

globular aggregate of small crystals

iron-rich orange matrix

COMPOSITION *Arsenate.*
CRYSTAL SYSTEM *Orthorhombic.*
CLEAVAGE/FRACTURE *Good/Uneven.*
LUSTRE/STREAK *Vitreous/White.*
HARDNESS/DENSITY *3.5 / 4.32.*
KEY PROPERTIES *Crystal shape and fluorescence distinguish it from hemimorphite (below) and smithsonite (p.105).*

Hemimorphite

Zn₄Si₂O₇(OH)₂·H₂O

Hemimorphite crystals are colourless, white, or yellow. They are thin, tabular, pointed at one end and straight at the other, and are usually grouped in fan-shaped clusters. Botryoidal or chalky hemimorphite is also common and is white, grey, brown, green, or greenish blue. Widely distributed in the oxidized zone of zinc deposits, hemimorphite used to be known as calamine, especially in the USA.

THE MINE *at Andara, Spain, is a source of hemimorphite, a secondary mineral of zinc deposits.*

botryoidal aggregates of tiny crystals

tabular crystals

vitreous lustre

rock matrix

COMPOSITION *Silicate.*
CRYSTAL SYSTEM *Orthorhombic.*
CLEAVAGE/FRACTURE *Perfect/Uneven, subconchoidal.*
LUSTRE/STREAK *Vitreous, adamantine, or pearly/White.*
HARDNESS/DENSITY *4.5–5 / 3.47.*
KEY PROPERTIES *Crystal shape and habit.*

Copper

Cu

THIS SAMPLE *of native copper is associated with red cuprite and green malachite. It is from Leicestershire, England.*

Copper is one of the few metals that occurs naturally in 'native' form, not bonded to other chemical elements. It is opaque and bright metallic salmon pink when fresh, but soon turns dull brown. Most copper is found as irregular, flattened, branching, or dendritic masses. Crystals, which are usually cubic or dodecahedral, are uncommon.

Native copper forms in the oxidized zone of copper deposits, and is found in basic and ultrabasic igneous rocks.

dendritic mass of crystals

bends very easily

pinkish brown colour

hackly surface when broken

COMPOSITION	*Element.*
CRYSTAL SYSTEM	*Cubic.*
CLEAVAGE/FRACTURE	*None/Hackly.*
LUSTRE/STREAK	*Metallic/Shiny pinkish brown.*
HARDNESS/DENSITY	*2.5–3 / 8.95.*
KEY PROPERTIES	*A pinkish brown metal that is easily bent.*

Chalcocite

Cu$_2$S

RICH *chalcocite 'blankets' form where water alters primary copper minerals.*

An important ore of copper, chalcocite is opaque, dark metallic grey, becoming dull on exposure to light. Crystals are striated, and prismatic or tabular, or form pseudo-hexagonal twins. Most chalcocite is massive or granular. It occurs in hydrothermal and porphyry copper deposits.

pseudo-hexagonal twins

massive habit

conchoidal fracture

metallic lustre

matrix contains other copper sulphides

COMPOSITION	*Sulphide.*
CRYSTAL SYSTEM	*Monoclinic.*
CLEAVAGE/FRACTURE	*Indistinct/ Conchoidal.*
LUSTRE/STREAK	*Metallic/Blackish grey.*
HARDNESS/DENSITY	*2.5–3 / 5.5–5.8.*
KEY PROPERTIES	*Crystal shape, but can resemble rarer enargite (p.111).*

Bornite

Cu_5FeS_4

This important ore of copper is opaque, metallic brownish red in colour, but develops an iridescent purple tarnish. Although it has orthorhombic symmetry, crystals are cubic, octahedral, or dodecahedral; granular or massive aggregates are common. Bornite is found in hydrothermal copper ore deposits, pegmatites, basic and ultrabasic igneous rocks, and skarns.

BORNITE *in Arizona is associated with Precambian volcanic activity and more recent granite intrusions.*

purple tarnish

massive bornite

metallic brownish red on fresh surfaces

crystals appear cubic

COMPOSITION *Sulphide.*
CRYSTAL SYSTEM *Orthorhombic.*
CLEAVAGE/FRACTURE *None/Uneven, nearly conchoidal.*
LUSTRE/STREAK *Metallic/Greyish black.*
HARDNESS/DENSITY *3–3.25 / 5.06.*
KEY PROPERTIES *Metallic brownish red, purple tarnish and pseudo-cubic symmetry.*

Covellite

CuS

Opaque, with a bright metallic blue colour and purple iridescence, covellite is easy to recognize. It is found as hexagonal platy crystals, foliated, or massive aggregates, and as a superficial coating on other copper sulphide minerals. It forms in the oxidized zone of copper sulphide deposits in association with bornite, chalcocite, and chalcopyrite.

DISTINCT *crystals and massive aggregates of covellite come from Butte, Montana, USA.*

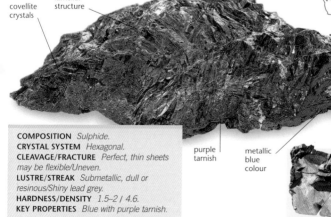

covellite crystals

lamellar structure

purple tarnish

metallic blue colour

COMPOSITION *Sulphide.*
CRYSTAL SYSTEM *Hexagonal.*
CLEAVAGE/FRACTURE *Perfect, thin sheets may be flexible/Uneven.*
LUSTRE/STREAK *Submetallic, dull or resinous/Shiny lead grey.*
HARDNESS/DENSITY *1.5–2 / 4.6.*
KEY PROPERTIES *Blue with purple tarnish.*

Chalcopyrite

$CuFeS_2$

THIS OPENCAST *copper mine at Phalaborwa, South Africa, extracts chalcopyrite, one of the principal ores of copper.*

Fresh chalcopyrite is opaque, brassy yellow, but on exposure it develops an iridescent tarnish. Its crystals appear tetrahedral, and massive aggregates are common, botryoidal masses less so. Chalcopyrite is a constituent of hydrothermal sulphide deposits. It is found as disseminated grains in igneous rocks and is an important ore mineral in porphyry copper deposits. More rarely it occurs in metamorphic rocks.

uneven fracture

brassy tetrahedral crystal

iridescent tarnish

massive chalcopyrite

COMPOSITION *Sulphide.*
CRYSTAL SYSTEM *Tetragonal.*
CLEAVAGE/FRACTURE *Poor/Uneven.*
LUSTRE/STREAK *Metallic/Greenish black.*
HARDNESS/DENSITY *3.5–4 / 4.1–4.3.*
KEY PROPERTIES *Brassy yellow colour, hardness, and tarnish distinguish this 'fool's gold' from real gold (p.87) and pyrite (p.124).*

Tetrahedrite

$Cu_{10}(Fe,Zn)_2(Sb,As)_4S_{13}$

TETRAHEDRITE *crystals from Cornwall, England, are often coated in yellow chalcopyrite.*

The name comes from this mineral's characteristic tetrahedral crystals, although it also occurs as massive or granular aggregates. This mineral is opaque, metallic grey, or nearly black, and it sometimes coats or is coated by brassy yellow chalcopyrite. It is found in hydro-thermal veins or contact metamorphic rocks.

mixed sulphide minerals

white quartz crystals

tetrahedral crystal

COMPOSITION *Sulphosalt.*
CRYSTAL SYSTEM *Cubic.*
CLEAVAGE/FRACTURE *None/Subconchoidal.*
LUSTRE/STREAK *Metallic/Black to brown.*
HARDNESS/DENSITY *3–4.5 / 4.97.*
KEY PROPERTIES *Tetrahedral crystals look like its arsenic-bearing counterpart tennantite, which associates with other arsenic minerals.*

Enargite

Cu_3AsS_4

Like many sulphide minerals, enargite has a bright metallic lustre and is opaque grey when fresh. On exposure to light and pollutants, it turns dull black. Crystals are tabular or prismatic, commonly striated along the prism faces. Twins are common, and may appear hexagonal. Enargite occurs in hydrothermal vein deposits, and exceptional crystals come from Quiruvilca, Peru and Butte, Montana, USA.

HYDROTHERMAL *veins that contain enargite in the Red Mountain mining district of Colorado, USA.*

striated grey crystal

perfect cleavage

bright metallic lustre

SECTION SHOWN

COMPOSITION *Sulphide.*
CRYSTAL SYSTEM *Orthorhombic.*
CLEAVAGE/FRACTURE *Perfect/Uneven.*
LUSTRE/STREAK *Metallic/Greyish black.*
HARDNESS/DENSITY *3 / 4.45.*
KEY PROPERTIES *Crystal shape, but can resemble more common chalcocite (p.108).*

Cuprite

$Cu_2^{1+}O$

Cuprite crystals are usually octahedral or cubic in shape, and massive or granular aggregates are common. Fresh cuprite is translucent bright red, but exposure to light and pollutants can turn surfaces dull metallic grey. An exception is chalcotrichite, a fibrous variety that retains its red coloration. Cuprite is an important ore of copper found in the oxidized zone of ore deposits.

RED *crystals of cuprite come from Brisbee and other locations in Arizona, USA.*

red, hair-like crystals

CHALCOTRICHITE

bright adamantine lustre

translucent red

COMPOSITION *Oxide.*
CRYSTAL SYSTEM *Cubic.*
CLEAVAGE/FRACTURE *Poor/Conchoidal or uneven.*
LUSTRE/STREAK *Adamantine or sub-metallic/Brownish red, shiny.*
HARDNESS/DENSITY *3.5–4 / 6.14.*
KEY PROPERTIES *Red; found with copper ores.*

Malachite

$Cu_2^{2+}(CO_3)(OH)_2$

Malachite is the most common of the copper secondary minerals and is always pale to dark green in colour. Crystals can be tabular but are usually prismatic or acicular, forming tufts and drusy coatings, which may be velvety in appearance. Botryoidal aggregates of malachite are also common, and when cut and polished, make a beautiful, banded, decorative stone. Malachite from the Ural Mountains of Russia was extensively used to decorate the palaces of the tsars, but today the malachite used in jewellery comes from the copper belt of the Democratic Republic of Congo.

GREEN *malachite and blue azurite occur together in the orange-brown goethite that forms 'gossan' caps on copper deposits.*

SECTION SHOWN

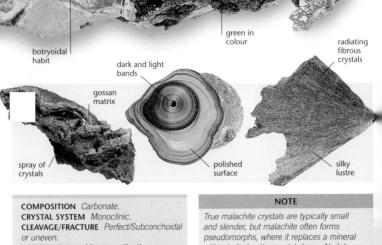

vitreous lustre

green in colour

botryoidal habit

radiating fibrous crystals

dark and light bands

gossan matrix

spray of crystals

polished surface

silky lustre

COMPOSITION *Carbonate.*
CRYSTAL SYSTEM *Monoclinic.*
CLEAVAGE/FRACTURE *Perfect/Subconchoidal or uneven.*
LUSTRE/STREAK *Vitreous; silky if fibrous/Pale green.*
HARDNESS/DENSITY *3.5–4 / 4.05.*
KEY PROPERTIES *Green; fizzes in diluted HCl.*

NOTE

True malachite crystals are typically small and slender, but malachite often forms pseudomorphs, where it replaces a mineral without altering the crystal shape. Nodules are found containing azurite that is partially altered to malachite, but the tabular shape of the azurite crystals (above right) is retained.

Azurite

$Cu_3^{2+}(CO_3)_2(OH)_2$

Azurite crystals are complex, often tabular with wedge-shaped terminations, and can form rosette-shaped aggregates. Well-developed crystals are dark azure blue, but massive or earthy aggregates may be paler. Azurite is common in the oxidized zones of copper deposits formed in carbonate rocks, such as limestone.

FINE *crystals of azurite come from the Touissit lead mine in the Atlas Mountains, Morocco.*

vitreous lustre

SECTION SHOWN

blocky azure blue crystals

thin, tabular crystals

COMPOSITION *Carbonate.*
CRYSTAL SYSTEM *Monoclinic.*
CLEAVAGE/FRACTURE *Perfect/Conchoidal.*
LUSTRE/STREAK *Vitreous/Pale blue.*
HARDNESS/DENSITY *3.5–4 / 3.77.*
KEY PROPERTIES *Bright to deep blue mineral that fizzes in diluted HCl.*

Atacamite

$Cu_2^{2+}Cl(OH)_3$

Bright or dark emerald green crystals of atacamite are typically prismatic or tabular, striated along the length, and have wedge-shaped terminations. Fibrous, granular, or massive aggregates also occur. Atacamite forms in the oxidation zone of copper deposits in salt-rich, arid environments. It also forms in volcanic fumaroles and in ocean-bottom black smoker deposits.

ATACAMITE *forms readily in arid environments, such as this opencast copper mine in Peru.*

radiating acicular crystal

prismatic crystal

associated quartz

dark green crystals

COMPOSITION *Halide.*
CRYSTAL SYSTEM *Orthorhombic.*
CLEAVAGE/FRACTURE *Perfect/Conchoidal.*
LUSTRE/STREAK *Adamantine or vitreous/Apple green.*
HARDNESS/DENSITY *3–3.5 / 3.74–3.78.*
KEY PROPERTIES *Green mineral forms in salty arid places. Does not fizz in diluted HCl.*

light green malachite

Brochantite

$Cu_4^{2+}(SO_4)(OH)_6$

Brochantite is emerald green or blue-green and forms acicular or fibrous crystals, usually in tufts, drusy coatings, and crusts. It is found in the oxidized zones of copper deposits, especially those in arid regions of the world. Excellent examples of brochantite come from copper mines in Chile, the Democratic Republic of Congo, and Arizona, USA.

THIS COMMON *secondary mineral was once found in the metal mines of Cornwall, England.*

brochantite with blue azurite

vitreous lustre

fibrous green crystal

iron-rich gossan

COMPOSITION *Sulphate.*
CRYSTAL SYSTEM *Monoclinic.*
CLEAVAGE/FRACTURE *Perfect/Uneven or conchoidal.*
LUSTRE/STREAK *Vitreous/Pale green.*
HARDNESS/DENSITY *3.5–4 / 3.97.*
KEY PROPERTIES *Bright green crystals that do not fizz in diluted HCl.*

Cyanotrichite

$Cu_4^{2+}Al_2(SO_4)(OH)_{12} \cdot 2H_2O$

Cyanotrichite is one of several copper minerals that are sky blue to azure blue in colour. Its name, from the Greek for 'blue' and 'hair', describes it very well. Crystals are acicular or fibrous, and form tufts, velvety coatings and delicate radiating groups. Cyanotrichite is found in the oxidized zone of copper sulphide deposits. The specimen below comes from Cap Garonne, Var, France.

BEAUTIFUL *examples of cyanotrichite come from Bisbee and elsewhere in the Arizona copper belt, USA.*

sky blue, hair-like crystals

green brochantite

SECTION SHOWN

rock matrix

COMPOSITION *Sulphate.*
CRYSTAL SYSTEM *Orthorhombic.*
CLEAVAGE/FRACTURE *Uneven/Uneven.*
LUSTRE/STREAK *Silky/Pale blue.*
HARDNESS/DENSITY *Not determined / 2.74–2.95.*
KEY PROPERTIES *Fine, fibrous sky blue crystals.*

Libethenite

$Cu_2^{2+}(PO_4)(OH)$

Crystals of libethenite are usually short, prismatic with wedge-shaped terminations, or appear octahedral and rather rounded. It is dark emerald or olive green, sometimes nearly black. Libethenite is found as clusters of crystals, drusy coatings, and crusts in the oxidized zones of copper deposits, often associated with other phosphate minerals. It was first discovered at Libethen (now L'ubietová), Slovakia, and small quantities occur in many places.

LIBETHENITE *occurs as small, lustrous crystals at Villa Vicosa, Portugal.*

blackish green colour

crystals appear octahedral

SECTION SHOWN

rock matrix

COMPOSITION *Phosphate.*
CRYSTAL SYSTEM *Monoclinic.*
CLEAVAGE/FRACTURE *Imperfect/Conchoidal or uneven.*
LUSTRE/STREAK *Vitreous or greasy/Green.*
HARDNESS/DENSITY *4 / 3.97.*
KEY PROPERTIES *Colour and crystal shape; less fibrous than olivenite (below).*

Olivenite

$Cu_2^{2+}(AsO_4)(OH)$

Olivenite gets its name from its typical olive green coloration, although it can also be grey, pale yellow, or white. Crystals are prismatic or fibrous, and earthy or matted aggregates are common. If dense masses of crystals are banded like wood grain, it is given the name wood copper. Olivenite is the most common copper arsenate mineral found in the oxidized zones of hydrothermal copper deposits.

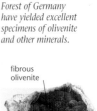

THE DUMPS *of Clara mine in the Black Forest of Germany have yielded excellent specimens of olivenite and other minerals.*

quartz matrix

short, prismatic, olive green crystals

SECTION SHOWN

fibrous olivenite

rock matrix

COMPOSITION *Arsenate.*
CRYSTAL SYSTEM *Monoclinic.*
CLEAVAGE/FRACTURE *Indistinct/Conchoidal or uneven.*
LUSTRE/STREAK *Adamantine, vitreous or silky/Yellowish green.*
HARDNESS/DENSITY *3 / 4.46.*
KEY PROPERTIES *Colour and fibrous habit.*

Chrysocolla

$(Cu,Al)_2H_2Si_2O_5(OH)_4 \cdot nH_2O$

Crystals of chrysocolla are acicular but uncommon, and it is usually found as fine-grained, sometimes botryoidal masses. The colour is rich blue-green. Chrysocolla is a common mineral in the oxidized zones of copper ore deposits, often intimately mixed with quartz or opal, which makes it hard enough to be polished as a semi-precious gemstone. Fine chrysocolla comes from the copper belt of Congo and from mines in Peru and Arizona, USA.

CHRYSOCOLLA *mixed with other copper minerals is an ornamental stone from Israel, known as Eilat stone.*

bluish green

associated azurite

orange iron-rich matrix

conchoidal fracture

COMPOSITION *Silicate.*
CRYSTAL SYSTEM *Probably orthorhombic.*
CLEAVAGE/FRACTURE *None/Conchoidal or brittle.*
LUSTRE/STREAK *Usually earthy/White or pale green.*
HARDNESS/DENSITY *2–4 / 1.93–2.4.*
KEY PROPERTIES *Absence of crystals.*

Dioptase

$Cu_6Si_6O_{18} \cdot 6H_2O$

Distinctive, vibrant, bluish green colour and its tendency to occur as well-formed crystals makes dioptase very popular with collectors. Crystals are blocky with rhombohedral terminations, or more rarely, elongate prisms. Dioptase can also be granular or massive. It forms in the oxidized zones of some copper deposits, and the most famous localities are Tsumeb in Namibia, Renéville in Congo Republic, and Altyn-Tyube in Kazakhstan.

THE MINE *at Tsumeb, Namibia has yielded a number of superb dioptase crystals.*

short prismatic crystals

intense bluish green

earthy chrysocolla

COMPOSITION *Silicate.*
CRYSTAL SYSTEM *Hexagonal.*
CLEAVAGE/FRACTURE *Perfect/Conchoidal.*
LUSTRE/STREAK *Vitreous/Green.*
HARDNESS/DENSITY *5 / 3.28–3.35.*
KEY PROPERTIES *Vibrant green colour and crystal shape are distinctive.*

Manganite

$Mn^{3+}O(OH)$

Opaque, metallic dark grey or black manganite crystals are prismatic and striated lengthways. They typically have flat or blunt terminations and are often grouped in bundles. Manganite can also be massive or granular and is then hard to distinguish from other manganese oxides, such as pyrolusite. Usually, manganite forms in low temperature hydrothermal veins, hot spring manganese deposits, and by alteration of other manganese minerals.

MANGANITE *occurs with other manganese oxides and minerals, such as rhodonite (shown here) and rhodochrosite.*

striations on faces

flat terminations

bundles of crystals

COMPOSITION *Oxide.*
CRYSTAL SYSTEM *Monoclinic.*
CLEAVAGE/FRACTURE *Perfect/Uneven.*
LUSTRE/STREAK *Metallic or submetallic/Dark reddish brown.*
HARDNESS/DENSITY *4 / 4.29–4.34.*
KEY PROPERTIES *Black mineral distinguished from pyrolusite (p.118) by streak.*

Hausmannite

$Mn^{2+}Mn_2^{3+}O_4$

Hausmannite is dark brown or black and is usually granular or massive. Well-formed crystals, although less common, are more distinctive. They appear octahedral in shape, but often have additional faces. An ore of manganese, hausmannite forms in hydrothermal veins. It also occurs where manganese-rich rocks have been metamorphosed.

AN ORE *mineral of the Kalahari manganese field in South Africa, hausmannite forms massive aggregates and fine crystals.*

massive habit

submetallic lustre

crystals appear octahedral

COMPOSITION *Oxide.*
CRYSTAL SYSTEM *Tetragonal.*
CLEAVAGE/FRACTURE *Perfect/Uneven.*
LUSTRE/STREAK *Submetallic/Reddish brown.*
HARDNESS/DENSITY *5.5 / 4.84.*
KEY PROPERTIES *Black octahedral-shaped crystals, perfect cleavage, reddish brown streak.*

Pyrolusite

$Mn^{4+}O_2$

This common opaque black or dark grey mineral is usually fibrous or fine-grained; prismatic crystals are rare. It is found as botryoidal masses, concretions, and as coatings that may be powdery or dendritic. Pyrolusite, a secondary mineral in manganese deposits, also forms in bogs, lakes, and shallow seas.

PYROLUSITE *occurs in the metamorphosed sedimentary rocks of the Green Mountains, Vermont, USA.*

marly limestone

black dendritic pyrolusite

earthy habit

black mass

COMPOSITION *Oxide.*
CRYSTAL SYSTEM *Tetragonal.*
CLEAVAGE/FRACTURE *Perfect/Uneven.*
LUSTRE/STREAK *Metallic to dull/Bluish black.*
HARDNESS/DENSITY 6–6.5 / 5.06.
KEY PROPERTIES *Black mineral, distinguished from other manganese oxides by streak, crystal shape, or chemical analysis.*

Psilomelane, Wad

Mixed manganese oxides

Black manganese oxides that lack distinct crystals are difficult to tell apart, and the problem is greater when they occur in mixtures. Soft, unidentified manganese oxides are known in general terms as wad, and when they are hard, as psilomelane. In the past, psilomelane has also been used as a name for the barium manganese oxide romanèchite and it often contains this mineral.

MANGANESE, *iron, and copper oxide minerals colour Castle Rocks, Michigan, USA.*

botryoidal habit

hard, black mass

COMPOSITION *Oxides and hydroxides.*
CRYSTAL SYSTEM *Various.*
CLEAVAGE/FRACTURE *None/Uneven.*
LUSTRE/STREAK *Earthy/Usually black.*
HARDNESS/DENSITY *Varies according to composition.*
KEY PROPERTIES *Soft or hard black masses; no distinct crystals visible.*

soft powdery mass

no obvious crystals

WAD

Rhodochrosite

$Mg^{2+}CO_3$

Rhodochrosite is usually pink, rarely brown, and forms rhombohedral or dog-tooth crystals like calcite. Banded rhodochrosite comes from Argentina and Peru, and makes an attractive decorative stone, but the finest crystals are from the Sweet Home mine and elsewhere in Colorado, USA, and are bright cherry red. Rhodochrosite is found mainly in hydrothermal deposits with black manganese oxides and minerals such as fluorite, galena, and sphalerite.

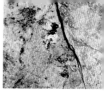

THESE HYDROTHERMAL *veins of rhodochrosite, galena, and fluorite are in the roof of the Sweet Home mine, Colorado, USA, and other localities.*

rhombohedral crystal

cherry red crystals

quartz crystal

vitreous lustre

pale silvery-yellow pyrite

pink rhodochrosite

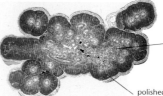

bands of pink and red

polished surface

COMPOSITION *Carbonate.*
CRYSTAL SYSTEM *Trigonal.*
CLEAVAGE/FRACTURE *Perfect, rhombohedral/Uneven or conchoidal.*
LUSTRE/STREAK *Vitreous/White.*
HARDNESS/DENSITY *3.5-4 / 3.7.*
KEY PROPERTIES *Pink mineral that fizzes in dilute HCl; does not fluoresce under UV light.*

NOTE

Manganese secondary minerals tend to be pink or black. Minerals containing other chemical elements can also be a particular colour. Copper secondaries are blue or green; those of cobalt, lilac pink, and of nickel, apple green. Chromium secondaries are green or purple-red, while iron minerals are often yellow, brown, or green.

Rhodonite

THIS RHODONITE *nodule contains black manganese oxides and brown bustamite.*

$CaMn_4Si_5O_{15}$

Rhodonite is a pink manganese mineral and an attractive semi-precious gemstone. It is usually found as coarse, cleavable or fine-grained compact masses veined with black manganese oxides. It can also be granular, but crystals are much less common. Rhodonite comes from manganese deposits formed by hydrothermal, metamorphic, and sedimentary processes.

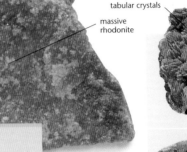

tabular crystals

massive rhodonite

polished pebble

black manganese oxides

COMPOSITION *Silicate.*
CRYSTAL SYSTEM *Triclinic.*
CLEAVAGE/FRACTURE *Perfect/Conchoidal to uneven.*
LUSTRE/STREAK *Vitreous/White.*
HARDNESS/DENSITY *5.5–6.5 / 3.57–3.76.*
KEY PROPERTIES *Harder than rhodochrosite (p.119) and does not fizz in dilute HCl.*

Braunite

BRAUNITE *is an important manganese ore in South Africa.*

$Mn^{2+}Mn_6^{3+}SiO_{12}$

Not the most striking of minerals, braunite is an important ore of manganese. It is opaque, brown-black, or dark grey, and is typically granular or massive. Crystals are less common and are pyramidal, nearly octahedral in shape. Braunite is found with manganese oxides and forms by metamorphism or the weathering of manganese deposits.

submetallic lustre

mass of small crystals

crystal appears octahedral

COMPOSITION *Oxide or silicate.*
CRYSTAL SYSTEM *Tetragonal.*
CLEAVAGE/FRACTURE *Perfect/Uneven to subconchoidal.*
LUSTRE/STREAK *Submetallic/Brownish black to steel grey.*
HARDNESS/DENSITY *6–6.5 / 4.72–4.83.*
KEY PROPERTIES *Shape, streak, and association.*

Anatase

TiO_2

Elongate octahedral crystals are the most common habit of anatase. It also occurs as tabular and, rarely, prismatic crystals. Anatase varies in colour from yellow- or red-brown to black, blue, grey, or lilac. It occurs, usually in small quantities, in various igneous and metamorphic rocks, and as a detrital mineral in sediments.

THE FINEST *crystals of anatase are found in the lens-shaped hydro-thermal veins typical of the European Alps.*

modified octahedral crystals

elongate octahedral crystals

rock matrix

metallic lustre

COMPOSITION *Oxide.*
CRYSTAL SYSTEM *Tetragonal.*
CLEAVAGE/FRACTURE *Perfect/Subconchoidal.*
LUSTRE/STREAK *Adamantine or metallic/White or pale yellow.*
HARDNESS/DENSITY *5.5–6.0 / 3.79–3.97.*
KEY PROPERTIES *Crystal form and absence of magnetism.*

Brookite

TiO_2

Brookite has the same chemical composition as anatase (above) but has orthorhombic symmetry. Crystals are thin or thick, tabular, or less commonly, pyramidal or pseudo-hexagonal. It is always red- or yellow-brown, dark brown or black. Brookite occurs in alpine-type hydrothermal veins, in some contact metamorphic rocks, and as a detrital mineral in sedimentary deposits.

THE AREA *around Snowdon, Wales, has yielded thin tabular crystals of brookite.*

dipyramidal crystal

SECTION SHOWN

transparent lustre

COMPOSITION *Oxide.*
CRYSTAL SYSTEM *Orthorhombic.*
CLEAVAGE/FRACTURE *Indistinct/Subconchoidal.*
LUSTRE/STREAK *Metallic, submetallic, or adamantine/White, greyish, or yellowish.*
HARDNESS/DENSITY *5.5–6 / 4.08–4.18.*
KEY PROPERTIES *Colour and lack of cleavage.*

Rutile

TiO$_2$

CHINA *has become a major supplier of rutile for industry, with important mines in the Hubei province.*

This mineral is familiar to many people as the pale golden, acicular crystals trapped inside crystals of quartz. When not enclosed in quartz, it is usually darker in colour, yellowish or reddish brown, dark brown or black. It forms striated, prismatic crystals and massive aggregates. Twins are very common and may be geniculate (knee-shaped), cyclic, or reticulated (net-like). Rutile is an accessory mineral in various igneous and metamorphic rocks, and occurs in alpine-type hydrothermal veins, and in some clastic sediments. Star-like sprays of rutile crystals, radiating from the faces of hematite crystals, come from Novo Horizonte, Bahia, Brazil and elsewhere.

NOTE

Like rutile crystals in quartz (p.143), inclusions in crystals are very common, although most are usually microscopic in size. Bubbles of gas or mineralising fluid can sometimes form inclusions.

cyclic twin

adamantine lustre

striations along length of crystal

rutile crystals in quartz

massive rutile

prismatic crystal

COMPOSITION *Oxide.*
CRYSTAL SYSTEM *Tetragonal.*
CLEAVAGE/FRACTURE *Good/Conchoidal to uneven.*
LUSTRE/STREAK *Adamantine or submetallic/Light brown or grey.*
HARDNESS/DENSITY *6–6.5 / 4.23.*
KEY PROPERTIES *Colour, striations, twinning.*

Ilmenite

$Fe^{2+}TiO_3$

Ilmenite is opaque and metallic grey-black but may weather dull brown. It occurs as tabular crystals and granular or massive aggregates. Intergrowths with hematite or magnetite are common. Found in many igneous and high-grade metamorphic rocks, economic deposits occur in anorthosites and other layered basic igneous rocks and as placer sand deposits.

PLACER *deposits of black ilmenite sands are dredged for this important ore of titanium.*

metallic lustre

well-formed crystal

thin, grey, tabular crystals

COMPOSITION *Oxide.*
CRYSTAL SYSTEM *Hexagonal.*
CLEAVAGE/FRACTURE *Parting/Conchoidal.*
LUSTRE/STREAK *Metallic or submetallic/Black or reddish brown.*
HARDNESS/DENSITY *5–6 / 4.72.*
KEY PROPERTIES *Colour, crystal shape, and weak magnetism.*

Titanite

$CaTiOSiO_4$

The crystals have a distinctive flattened wedge-shape, but they can also be prismatic or form massive aggregates. The colour is normally black, brown, grey, green, or yellow. Titanite is found in metamorphic rocks such as gneisses, schists, and marbles; in skarns, alpine-type hydrothermal veins, and as an accessory mineral in acid and intermediate plutonic igneous rocks.

MANY *famous localities for titanite, a mineral formerly known as sphene, are in the European Alps.*

wedge shape

small orange crystals

rock matrix

COMPOSITION *Silicate.*
CRYSTAL SYSTEM *Monoclinic.*
CLEAVAGE/FRACTURE *Good/Subconchoidal.*
LUSTRE/STREAK *Adamantine or resinous/White.*
HARDNESS *5–5.5.*
DENSITY *3.48–3.60.*
KEY PROPERTIES *Wedge-shaped crystals.*

large, translucent, brown crystal

Pyrite

FeS₂

PYRITE *crystals cover this mould of an ammonite shell in clay. The example shown here comes from Oxfordshire, England.*

A remarkably common mineral, pyrite is easy to distinguish from most other sulphides. It is opaque and pale silvery-yellow when fresh, turning darker and tarnishing with exposure. Crystals are cubic, octahedral, or twelve-sided 'pyritohedral', and are often striated. Pyrite can also be massive or granular, or form flattened discs or nodules of radiating elongate crystals. Discs and nodules are found in many kinds of sedimentary rocks, where pyrite can also fill or replace fossils. Crystals and crystalline masses of pyrite occur in many igneous, metamorphic, and sedimentary rocks, and extensively in hydrothermal deposits.

marl matrix

metallic, pale yellow cube

octahedral crystal

striations

five-sided face

radiating crystals

COMPOSITION	*Sulphide.*
CRYSTAL SYSTEM	*Cubic.*
CLEAVAGE/FRACTURE	*Indistinct partings/Conchoidal to uneven.*
LUSTRE/STREAK	*Metallic/Greenish black.*
HARDNESS/DENSITY	*6–6.5 / 5.02.*
KEY PROPERTIES	*Crystal shape and colour paler than chalcopyrite (p.110).*

NOTE

Both pyrite and marcasite (above right) react with water vapour in the air, decomposing to form powdery yellow and white iron sulphates and sulphuric acid, which can burn holes in containers and labels. To prevent 'pyrite decay', specimens must be stored in a dry atmosphere.

Marcasite

FeS₂

Marcasite is opaque and very pale silvery-yellow when fresh, darkening and tarnishing after exposure. Crystals are tabular, pyramidal, or prismatic, or form spear-shaped twins. It is found in granular, stalactitic, or massive aggregates and often infills or replaces fossils. Less widely distributed than pyrite, marcasite is found in sedimentary rocks.

NODULES *composed of marcasite crystals come from the chalk deposits of France and England.*

spear-shaped twin

pointed orthorhombic crystals

chalk matrix

SECTION SHOWN

COMPOSITION *Sulphide.*	
CRYSTAL SYSTEM *Orthorhombic.*	
CLEAVAGE/FRACTURE *Distinct/Uneven, brittle.*	
LUSTRE/STREAK *Metallic/Greyish black.*	
HARDNESS/DENSITY *6–6.5 / 4.89.*	
KEY PROPERTIES *Crystal shape and paler colour distinguishes marcasite from pyrite (left).*	

Pyrrhotite

Fe₁₋ₓS (x=0.1 to 0.2)

Often seen mixed with other sulphide minerals in massive or granular aggregates, pyrrhotite also occurs as tabular or platy hexagonal crystals, or rosette-shaped crystal clusters. It is opaque and bronze-yellow to pink-yellow in colour, readily tarnishing brown. Pyrrhotite forms in basic and ultrabasic igneous rocks, pegmatites, high-temperature hydrothermal veins, and less often in some metamorphic and sedimentary rocks.

GOLD *prospecting has revealed deposits of pyrrhotite and other sulphide minerals in the Alaska Range, USA.*

brown tarnish

group of hexagonal crystals

COMPOSITION *Sulphide.*	
CRYSTAL SYSTEM *Monoclinic and hexagonal.*	
CLEAVAGE/FRACTURE *Cleavage-like parting/Uneven to subconchoidal.*	
LUSTRE/STREAK *Metallic/Greyish black.*	
HARDNESS/DENSITY *3.5–4.5 / 4.58–4.65.*	
KEY PROPERTIES *Slight magnetism, crystal shape, and colour.*	

Arsenopyrite

FeAsS

LARGE *aggregates of arsenopyrite crystals come from mines at Panasqueira, Portugal.*

Light silvery grey arsenopyrite gives off the odour of garlic if crushed – a sign that it contains arsenic. Crystals are blocky or prismatic, often diamond-shaped in section. They are usually striated and often twinned. Massive or granular aggregates also occur. Arsenopyrite is a hydrothermal mineral often found in pegmatites and gold- or tin-bearing veins. It also occurs in contact metamorphic sulphide deposits and other metamorphic rocks.

striations on surface

bright metallic lustre

blocky crystals

siderite

diamond-shaped in section

SECTION SHOWN

COMPOSITION *Sulphide.*
CRYSTAL SYSTEM *Monoclinic, pseudo-orthorhombic.*
CLEAVAGE/FRACTURE *Distinct/Uneven.*
LUSTRE/STREAK *Metallic/Greyish black.*
HARDNESS/DENSITY *5.5–6 / 6.07.*
KEY PROPERTIES *Silvery grey; less dense than iron arsenide (löllingite).*

Magnetite

$Fe^{2+}Fe^{3+}{}_2O_4$

IGNEOUS *intrusions at South Africa's Bushveld Complex are a rich source of magnetite.*

Magnetite is a strong natural magnet. It is grey or black, weathering rusty brown. Crystals are octahedral, more rarely dodecahedral, and may be striated. Massive or granular aggregates are very common. Magnetite is an accessory mineral in many igneous and metamorphic rocks and a detrital mineral in some sediments. Economically important deposits occur in layered basic and ultrabasic igneous intrusions and banded ironstones.

octahedral crystal

metallic lustre

granular mass of magnetite

COMPOSITION *Oxide.*
CRYSTAL SYSTEM *Cubic.*
CLEAVAGE/FRACTURE *Cleavage-like parting/Uneven.*
LUSTRE/STREAK *Metallic to dull/Black.*
HARDNESS/DENSITY *5.5–6.5 / 5.18.*
KEY PROPERTIES *Strongly magnetic, grey octahedral mineral with a black streak.*

Hematite

α-Fe_2O_3

The names of the different varieties of hematite are very descriptive. Opaque grey crystals with a mirror-like lustre are known as specular hematite. Crystals are complex rhombohedral, pyramidal, or tabular, and sometimes thin and platy; triangular striations are often seen. Rosette-shaped groups of crystals are known as eisenrose. Where crystals have grown tightly together to form compact masses, hematite is always red. Red reniform masses are known as kidney ore. Hematite is found in volcanic fumeroles and hydrothermal veins, in contact metamorphic rocks, banded ironstones, oolitic ironstones, and as an alteration product of other iron minerals.

BANDED *ironstone formations are rich in hematite and important iron ores.*

NOTE

Whether in metallic grey crystals or brownish red masses, hematite has a brick red streak, which aids identification. Goethite (p.128) can also form botryoidal brown masses but its streak is always yellowish brown.

reniform red mass

KIDNEY ORE

colourful tarnish on surface

nearly cubic crystals

highly reflective

hexagonal platy crystal

SPECULAR HEMATITE

uneven broken surface

COMPOSITION *Oxide.*
CRYSTAL SYSTEM *Trigonal.*
CLEAVAGE/FRACTURE *Cleavage-like parting/Uneven or subconchoidal.*
LUSTRE/STREAK *Metallic, submetallic, or dull/Cherry red or reddish brown.*
HARDNESS/DENSITY *5–6 / 5.26.*
KEY PROPERTIES *Colour and streak.*

SECTION SHOWN

Goethite

$\alpha\text{-}Fe^{3+}O(OH)$

Goethite is an exceptionally common mineral. Crystals are brown to nearly black. They are small, prismatic, and usually occur in tufts and drusy coatings. But most goethite is found as coatings and botryoidal, reniform, stalactitic, or massive aggregates. These can be brownish yellow, reddish brown, or dark brown. Goethite is an alteration product in iron-bearing deposits; present in gossans, laterites, and many ironstones.

GOETHITE is one of the iron oxides extracted from the Kremikovtsi iron deposit at this mine in Bulgaria.

SECTION SHOWN

mass of close-packed dark brown crystals

small, adamantine prismatic crystals

COMPOSITION *Oxide.*
CRYSTAL SYSTEM *Orthorhombic.*
CLEAVAGE/FRACTURE *Perfect/Uneven.*
LUSTRE/STREAK *Adamantine, dull, earthy, or silky/Yellowish brown.*
HARDNESS/DENSITY *5–5.5 / 4.28.*
KEY PROPERTIES *Yellowish brown streak; is like naturally occurring rust.*

Limonite

Mixed hydrated iron hydroxides

To modern geologists, limonite is a general name for mixtures of the hydrated iron hydroxide minerals goethite, lepidocrocite, and akaganéite. Some hematite, clay, and other impurities may also be present. Limonite is yellow, brownish yellow or orange-brown with a yellowish brown streak. It is fine-grained, massive, stalactitic, or powdery. When analysed, many specimens of limonite turn out to be pure goethite.

COATINGS of limonite, where iron-rich rocks have been weathered, give this landscape its rusty colour.

brownish yellow mass

individual crystals cannot be seen

spherical masses

PEA IRON ORE

COMPOSITION *Oxides.*
CRYSTAL SYSTEM *Various.*
CLEAVAGE/FRACTURE *None/Uneven.*
LUSTRE/STREAK *Dull, earthy, or waxy/Yellowish brown.*
HARDNESS/DENSITY *Varies according to composition / 3.5–4.3.*
KEY PROPERTIES *Colour, streak, and habit.*

Siderite

$Fe^{2+}CO_3$

Siderite typically forms irregular crystalline masses or rhombohedral crystals with curved faces, so rarer elongate, prismatic crystals are highly prized. This common mineral is usually found in hydrothermal veins and in the oxidized zones of iron ore deposits. Remarkably lustrous, dark brown crystalline masses have come from the rare cryolite-bearing pegmatite at Ivigtut, Greenland.

A COMMON *mineral in hydrothermal veins, siderite is associated here with colourless quartz and dark brown sphalerite.*

unusual botryoidal siderite

typical rhombohedral crystals

colourless quartz

pearly lustre

COMPOSITION *Carbonate.*
CRYSTAL SYSTEM *Trigonal.*
CLEAVAGE/FRACTURE *Perfect, rhombohedral/Uneven or conchoidal.*
LUSTRE/STREAK *Vitreous or pearly/White.*
HARDNESS/DENSITY *3.75–4.25 / 3.96.*
KEY PROPERTIES *Fizzes slowly in dilute HCl; usually darker brown than ankerite (p.152).*

Dufrénite

$CaFe^{2+}_2Fe^{3+}_{10}(OH)_{12}(PO_4)_8 \cdot 4H_2O$

Dufrenite is found as crusts, spherical aggregates of radiating crystals, and botryoidal coatings. These are often colour-banded, with the fresh centre being dark green or greenish black and the weathered surface being olive green or brown. Crystals are tabular and rather rounded, and occur in sheaf-like aggregates. Dufrénite is found with other phosphate minerals mainly in the secondary zone of iron-rich deposits.

DARK GREEN *spherules of dufrénite with yellow cyrilovite are found in joints in the kaolinized granite of Cornwall, England.*

dark brown goethite

botryoidal. olive green dufrénite

SECTION SHOWN

COMPOSITION *Phosphate.*
CRYSTAL SYSTEM *Monoclinic.*
CLEAVAGE/FRACTURE *Perfect/Uneven.*
LUSTRE/STREAK *Vitreous or silky/Green or yellowish green.*
HARDNESS/DENSITY *3.5–4.5 / 3.1–3.34.*
KEY PROPERTIES *Habit, colour-banding, and association with other phosphates.*

Vivianite

Fe²⁺₃(PO₄)₂·8H₂O

$Fe^{2+}_3(PO_4)_2\cdot 8H_2O$

POWDERY *blue vivianite is found in sedimentary clays, for example, at this pit in Oxfordshire, England.*

Vivianite crystals are prismatic, blocky, or bladed, and occur singly or in radiating groups. While crystals are dark indigo blue or green and sometimes nearly black, this mineral often occurs as coatings, nodules, and powdery masses, which are a much lighter blue. Vivianite forms in the secondary zone of ore deposits, and as a result of the weathering of phosphate minerals in granite pegmatites. It also occurs in lake sediments and bog iron ores, and in other sedimentary rocks rich in bone and organic matter. Here, the crystals can line cavities in fossil shells or form a blue coating on bones. The delicate-bladed crystals, shown below, fill cavities and moulds left by fossil bivalves in an ironstone from Kerch, Ukraine.

radiating blue and green bladed crystals

SECTION SHOWN

transparent when crystals are thin

crystals in cavity left by fossil shell

vitreous lustre

earthy, pale blue vivianite

clay matrix

prismatic crystals

NOTE

When vivianite is first exposed to light it may be colourless, but it very quickly turns blue or green as ferrous iron changes to ferric iron. Continued exposure to light causes some crystals to fracture and should be avoided. Blocky crystals are most likely to crack than slender or thin-bladed ones.

COMPOSITION *Phosphate.*
CRYSTAL SYSTEM *Monoclinic.*
CLEAVAGE/FRACTURE *Perfect/Splintery.*
LUSTRE/STREAK *Vitreous; dull when earthy/Colourless, turns blue or brown.*
HARDNESS/DENSITY *1.5–2 / 2.68.*
KEY PROPERTIES *Indigo blue or green mineral, dissolves in diluted HCl without fizz.*

Scorodite

$Fe^{3+}AsO_4 \cdot 2H_2O$

Scorodite is violet, bluish green, leek green, grey, brown, or brownish yellow. Crystals may be tabular or short prismatic but usually they are di-pyramidal, appearing octahedral. Drusy coatings are common, but scorodite can also be porous and earthy, or massive. It is formed by the weathering of arsenopyrite and other arsenic-bearing minerals.

AN EXCAVATION *of the Ting Tang mine dumps in Cornwall yielded good scorodite crystals.*

poor cleavage

arsenic-rich matrix

violet, tabular crystals

COMPOSITION *Arsenate.*
CRYSTAL SYSTEM *Orthorhombic.*
CLEAVAGE/FRACTURE *Imperfect/ Subconchoidal.*
LUSTRE/STREAK *Vitreous or resinous/White.*
HARDNESS/DENSITY *3.5–4 / 3.27.*
KEY PROPERTIES *Unlike adamite (p.107), scorodite does not fluoresce under UV light.*

Pharmacosiderite

$KFe^{3+}_4(AsO_4)_3(OH)_4 \cdot 6–7H_2O$

Simple cubic crystals are unusual for phosphate and arsenate minerals, but they are typical of pharmacosiderite. It is olive green, grass green, yellow, brown, or red, and the crystals are rarely more than a few millimetres across. It can be deposited by hydrothermal solutions but usually forms by weathering of arsenopyrite and other arsenic minerals. Brown crystals are difficult to distinguish from the rarer but related barium pharmacosiderite.

THIS MINERAL *is never abundant, but it occurs at many localities worldwide, including the Lake District, England.*

quartz matrix

COMPOSITION *Arsenate.*
CRYSTAL SYSTEM *Cubic.*
CLEAVAGE/FRACTURE *Poor/Uneven.*
LUSTRE/STREAK *Adamantine to greasy/White.*
HARDNESS/DENSITY *2.5 / 2.8.*
KEY PROPERTIES *Cubic crystals that lack the perfect octahedral cleavage of fluorite (p.156).*

green cubic crystals

Bauxite

Mixed aluminium oxides and hydroxides

Gibbsite, diaspore, and böhmite are all aluminium oxides or hydroxides that occur in altered or metamorphosed aluminium-rich rocks but are most abundant, mixed together in a rock called bauxite. These are pale-coloured minerals, but bauxite also contains quartz, clays, hematite, and other iron oxides, so it is variably creamy yellow, orange, pink, and red in colour. It is by far the most important ore of aluminium. Bauxite forms as extensive but quite shallow deposits where aluminium-rich rocks have been heavily weathered in a humid tropical environment. It may be nodular, pisolitic, or earthy in structure. Bauxite is named after the deposits at Les Baux-de-Provence in France.

pisolitic structure

red, where it is iron-rich

dull to earthy lustre

earthy habit

lamellar crystals

minute yellow crystals

BÖHMITE

trace chromium gives lilac colour

GIBBSITE

DIASPORE

COMPOSITION *Oxides and hydroxides.*
CRYSTAL SYSTEM *Various.*
CLEAVAGE/FRACTURE *None/Irregular.*
LUSTRE/STREAK *Dull, waxy or earthy/White, yellow, or reddish brown.*
HARDNESS/DENSITY *Varies according to composition.*
KEY PROPERTIES *Colour; pisolitic habit.*

NOTE

Aluminium is a strong, lightweight metal and an excellent conductor of heat. It is abundant in the crust of the Earth and present in many minerals. The only important ore is bauxite; this is because too much costly energy is required to extract aluminium from other minerals that contain the metal.

Wavellite

$Al_3(PO_4)_2(OH,F)_3 \cdot 5H_2O$

Globules, hemispheres, or flat aggregates of radiating acicular crystals are typical of wavellite. This aluminium phosphate mineral is usually green but can also be white, yellow, brown, or black. Wavellite is nearly always a secondary mineral found lining joints and fractures in low-grade metamorphic rocks, in phosphate deposits, and where phosphate minerals have been weathered in granites and granite pegmatites.

WAVELLITE *has been found in a number of places in Ireland, including Kinsale.*

unbroken spherule

SECTION SHOWN

radiating crystals with vitreous lustre

joint in rock

COMPOSITION *Phosphate.*
CRYSTAL SYSTEM *Orthorhombic.*
CLEAVAGE/FRACTURE *Perfect/Uneven or subconchoidal.*
LUSTRE/STREAK *Vitreous, resinous, or pearly/White.*
HARDNESS/DENSITY *3.5–4 / 2.36.*
KEY PROPERTIES *Colour and habit.*

Turquoise

$Cu^{2+}Al_6(PO_4)_4(OH)_8 \cdot 4H_2O$

The colour of turquoise varies from sky blue to green, and crystals are rare. Nodules or fine-grained masses are more abundant, and are found where copper-bearing surface water reacts with aluminium-rich rocks. Turquoise is prized as a gemstone. Material used in native American jewellery comes from southwestern USA, while famous sources of Middle Eastern turquoise include Neyshabur, Iran.

TURQUOISE *crystals line small cavities in massive turquoise in this clay pit in Cornwall, England.*

massive habit

minute crystals line the cavity

nodular mass

COMPOSITION *Phosphate.*
CRYSTAL SYSTEM *Triclinic.*
CLEAVAGE/FRACTURE *Perfect/Conchoidal or smooth.*
LUSTRE/STREAK *Dull or waxy/White or pale greenish blue.*
HARDNESS/DENSITY *5–6 / 2.86.*
KEY PROPERTIES *Blue to green; massive.*

Cassiterite

SnO_2

Cassiterite is tin oxide and the only ore of tin. It is brown or black, rarely grey or white. Crystals are short prismatic and often twinned, or form botryoidal aggregates known as wood tin. Cassiterite is found in granitic rocks and high-temperature hydrothermal veins, and in placer deposits derived from them. The main sources are in China, Indonesia, and Peru.

THIS RUINED *engine house is in Cornwall, England, where cassiterite was mined from Roman times until the 20th century.*

yellow variety tin oxide

twinned crystals

VARLAMOFFITE

crystals of muscovite mica

adamantine black crystals

COMPOSITION *Oxide.*
CRYSTAL SYSTEM *Tetragonal.*
CLEAVAGE/FRACTURE *Poor/Uneven or subconchoidal.*
LUSTRE/STREAK *Adamantine; greasy on fractures/White to pale brown or grey.*
HARDNESS/DENSITY *6–7 / 6.98.*
KEY PROPERTIES *More dense than sphalerite.*

Wolframite

$Mn^{2+}WO_4$ *(hübnerite)* – $Fe^{2+}WO_4$ *(ferberite)*

The name wolframite is given to a mineral intermediate in composition between hübnerite (manganese tungstate) and ferberite (iron tungstate). It typically forms prismatic or bladed, opaque dark grey crystals and is found in granitic rocks and high-temperature hydrothermal veins. Wolframite is an important ore of tungsten.

EXTENSIVE *dumps of waste rock are brought out from the wolframite mine at Panasqueira, Portugal.*

tabular crystal

translucent red

HÜBNERITE

sub-metallic lustre

opaque grey

COMPOSITION *Tungstate.*
CRYSTAL SYSTEM *Monoclinic.*
CLEAVAGE/FRACTURE *Perfect/Uneven.*
LUSTRE/STREAK *Sub metallic/Brownish black.*
HARDNESS/DENSITY *4–4.5 / 7.12–7.58.*
KEY PROPERTIES *Ferberite is opaque and nearly black; pure hübnerite is translucent, and red or reddish brown.*

Scheelite

CaWO₄

Irregular masses of colourless, grey, orange, or pale brown scheelite can be difficult to spot, but they fluoresce vivid bluish white under a short-wave UV light. Well-formed crystals appear octahedral in shape and are found in high-temperature hydrothermal veins and greisens, and in certain contact metamorphic rocks. Fine examples come from Chungju, South Korea, near Pingwu in Sichuan Province, China, as well as in Bispberg, Sweden, and other European localities.

HIGH-TEMPERATURE *hydrothermal quartz veins contain scheelite and wolframite in Cumbria, England.*

translucent pale brown

pseudooctahedral shape

SECTION SHOWN

COMPOSITION *Tungstate.*
CRYSTAL SYSTEM *Tetragonal.*
CLEAVAGE/FRACTURE *Distinct/ Subconchoidal or uneven.*
LUSTRE/STREAK *Vitreous or adamantine/White.*
HARDNESS/DENSITY *4.5–5 / 6.1.*
KEY PROPERTIES *Shape and fluorescence.*

Molybdenite

MoS₂

Molybdenite is a very soft, bluish grey, opaque, metallic mineral that forms tabular hexagonal crystals, foliated masses, scales, and disseminated grains. It is found in high-temperature hydrothermal veins with wolframite and scheelite, in porphyry ores, granites, and pegmatites, and in contact metamorphic deposits.

MOLYBDENUM *ore often occurs with chalcopyrite. Both are extracted from this giant opencast mine at Bingham in Utah, USA.*

quartz grains

cleaves into thin sheets

granite matrix

massive molybdenite

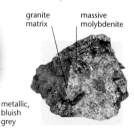

metallic, bluish grey

tabular hexagonal crystals

COMPOSITION *Sulphide.*
CRYSTAL SYSTEM *Hexagonal and trigonal.*
CLEAVAGE/FRACTURE *Perfect/Flaky.*
LUSTRE/STREAK *Metallic/Bluish grey.*
HARDNESS/DENSITY *1–1.5 / 4.62–4.73.*
KEY PROPERTIES *Flexible, sectile, and greasy; more dense than graphite (p.216), and has a blue tinge to colour and streak.*

Uraninite

UO_2

THIS IMPORTANT *ore of uranium is mined at the Rossing opencast mine in Namibia.*

Uraninite is black, sometimes tinted green or brown; fine modified cubic crystals are found in a few localities. Usually it is botryoidal or banded, or the massive variety known as pitchblende. Uraninite is found in granites, syenites, pegmatites, and in hydrothermal sulphide veins. Important deposits are also hosted in sandstones altered by uranium- and vanadium-rich fluids, and in ancient conglomerates. Uraninite is highly radioactive, so special precautions are needed to store and handle it safely.

yellow uranium secondary mineral

black botryoidal uraninite

SECTION SHOWN

COMPOSITION *Oxide.*
CRYSTAL SYSTEM *Cubic.*
CLEAVAGE/FRACTURE *Good, octahedral/Uneven to conchoidal.*
LUSTRE/STREAK *Submetallic, greasy, or dull/Green or grey shining.*
HARDNESS/DENSITY *5–6 / 10.63–10.95.*
KEY PROPERTIES *Highly radioactive mineral.*

Carnotite

$K_2(UO_2)_2(VO_4)_2 \cdot 3H_2O$

GEOLOGISTS *prospect for carnotite in the tuffs at Cook Inlet, Alaska, USA.*

Bright yellow carnotite normally occurs as coatings and massive or powdery aggregates. It is found in shallow surface deposits formed by the weathering of rocks rich in uraninite and other uranium minerals. It also occurs in sandstones that have been altered by vanadium- and uranium-bearing solutions. Special precautions are needed to store and handle this radioactive mineral.

powdery yellow radioactive coating

sandstone

COMPOSITION *Vanadate.*
CRYSTAL SYSTEM *Monoclinic.*
CLEAVAGE/FRACTURE *Perfect/None.*
LUSTRE/STREAK *Earthy, dull, or silky/Bright yellow.*
HARDNESS/DENSITY *Softer than 2 / 4.7.*
KEY PROPERTIES *Radioactive, powdery yellow mineral; crystals rarely seen.*

Autunite

$Ca(UO_2)_2(PO_4)_2 \cdot 10\text{-}12H_2O$

Greenish or lemon yellow tabular crystals of autunite have a rectangular or octagonal outline. Coarse groups are found, but scaly coatings are more common. Autunite forms in the oxidization zone of uranium deposits such as uraninite-bearing igneous rocks and hydrothermal veins. It dehydrates to form meta-autunite. Both minerals fluoresce yellow-green under UV light and are radioactive.

BRIGHT *yellow micro-crystals of autunite coat a joint in granite from Devon, England.*

tabular, octagonal in section

vitreous lustre (much duller in meta-autunite)

perfect cleavage into thin layers

SECTION SHOWN

COMPOSITION *Phosphate.*
CRYSTAL SYSTEM *Tetragonal.*
CLEAVAGE/FRACTURE *Perfect, rather micaceous/Uneven.*
LUSTRE/STREAK *Vitreous or pearly/Pale yellow.*
HARDNESS/DENSITY *2–2.5 / 3.05–3.2.*
KEY PROPERTIES *Radioactive tabular or platy yellow crystals.*

Torbernite

$Cu^{2+}(UO_2)_2(PO_4)_2 \cdot 8\text{-}12H_2O$

This radioactive mineral is bright mid-green, and occurs as isolated, square, tabular crystals, lamellar or sheaf-like crystal groups, or scaly coatings. It is found in the oxidation zone of deposits containing uranium and copper, and is associated with other phosphate minerals. Exceptional crystals come from the Democratic Republic of Congo.

SMALL *amounts of torbernite and other uranium minerals have been discovered in Cornwall, England.*

iron-stained rock matrix

square, tabular crystals

perfect mica-like cleavage

SECTION SHOWN

COMPOSITION *Phosphate.*
CRYSTAL SYSTEM *Tetragonal.*
CLEAVAGE/FRACTURE *Perfect micaceous/Uneven.*
LUSTRE/STREAK *Vitreous or waxy/Pale green.*
HARDNESS/DENSITY *2–2.5 / 3.22.*
KEY PROPERTIES *Radioactive square green tabular crystals look like metatorbernite.*

Columbite-tantalite

$(Fe,Mn)(Nb,Ta)_2O_6 - (Fe,Mn)(Ta,Nb)_2O_6$

Minerals at the columbite end of this coltan series are niobium-rich, and those at the tantalite end are tantalum-rich. Either iron or manganese is nearly always the other major element, in which case the name is prefixed 'ferro' or 'mangano'. Coltan minerals are brown or black, massive, or form tabular or short prismatic crystals. They occur in granite pegmatites and in detrital deposits.

THESE ORES *of niobium and tantalum are mined from granite pegmatites in South Dakota, USA.*

thin tabular crystal

typical submetallic lustre

SECTION SHOWN

COMPOSITION *Oxide.*
CRYSTAL SYSTEM *Orthorhombic.*
CLEAVAGE/FRACTURE *Distinct/ Subconchoidal or uneven.*
LUSTRE/STREAK *Submetallic to vitreous/Red, brown, or black.*
HARDNESS/DENSITY *6–6.5 / 5.17–8.0.*
KEY PROPERTIES *Dense, dark minerals.*

Pyrochlore

$(Ca,Na)_2Nb_2O_6F$

Pyrochlore is orange, brownish red, brown, or black. Crystals are octahedral with modified faces, or in granular or massive aggregates. Pyrochlore forms in carbonatites, pegmatites, and is an accessory mineral in alkaline rocks. It also accumulates in some detrital deposits. As it often contains traces of uranium and thorium, it may be radioactive.

THIS PYROCHLORE *comes from the Dande-Doma carbonatite in Zimbabwe.*

uneven surface where broken

modified octahedron

two intergrown octahedra

COMPOSITION *Oxide.*
CRYSTAL SYSTEM *Cubic.*
CLEAVAGE/FRACTURE *Indistinct/Uneven, splintery.*
LUSTRE/STREAK *Vitreous to resinous/Yellow or brown.*
HARDNESS/DENSITY *5–5.5 / 4.45–4.9.*
KEY PROPERTIES *Shape; slight radioactivity.*

Monazite-(Ce)

(Ce,La,Nd,Th)PO₄

Cerium-rich monazite-(Ce) is the most common of the four
minerals known as monazite. It is brown, pink, or grey.
Crystals are tabular, prismatic, or wedge-shaped, or
form granular or massive aggregates. Sources
include carbonatites, pegmatites, gneisses,
and fissure veins, and monazite also
accumulates in rich sand deposits. It
is radioactive if thorium is present.

CARBONATITE *from
Katete, northwestern
Zimbabwe, is a source
of monazite.*

translucent
brown crystal

waxy
lustre

uneven
fracture

COMPOSITION *Phosphate.*
CRYSTAL SYSTEM *Monoclinic.*
CLEAVAGE/FRACTURE *Distinct/Conchoidal
or uneven.*
LUSTRE/STREAK *Resinous, waxy, vitreous
or adamantine/White or pale brown.*
HARDNESS/DENSITY *5–5.5 / 4.98–5.43.*
KEY PROPERTIES *Crystal shape; radioactivity.*

Xenotime-(Y)

YPO₄

The yttrium phosphate xenotime-(Y) is brown, red, yellow,
or grey, and crystals are prismatic or equant, often with
pyramidal terminations. These may form radiating or
rosette-shaped aggregates. Xenotime-(Y), an important ore
of yttrium, is an accessory mineral in
granitic and alkaline intrusive
igneous rocks, gneisses, alpine-
type hydrothermal veins,
and clastic sediments. It
may contain traces
of radioactive
uranium or
thorium.

splintery
fracture

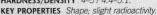

TRACE *uranium in
xenotime is used to
date unfossiliferous
sedimentary rocks such
as the Precambrian
rocks in Kimberley,
Western Australia.*

SECTION SHOWN

pyrimidal crystals

resinous lustre on
broken surface

COMPOSITION *Phosphate.*
CRYSTAL SYSTEM *Tetragonal.*
CLEAVAGE/FRACTURE *Good/Uneven or
splintery.*
LUSTRE/STREAK *Vitreous or resinous/Pale
brown or yellow.*
HARDNESS/DENSITY *4–5 / 4.4–5.1.*
KEY PROPERTIES *Shape; slight radioactivity.*

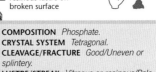

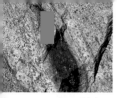

A DARK *layer rich in brown allanite-(Ce) from Namaqualand, South Africa.*

Allanite-(Ce)

$(Ca,Ce,La)_2(Al,Fe^{2+},Fe^{3+})_3(Si_3O_{12})(OH)$

Allanite used to be called orthite; it is now divided into allanite-(Ce), if cerium is dominant, and rarer allanite-(Y), if yttrium is dominant. Both can contain radioactive trace elements. Allanite-(Ce) forms tabular or prismatic brown or black crystals, but also occurs as bladed or massive aggregates or embedded grains. It is found in granites, syenites, pegmatites, and certain metamorphic rocks. Important localities are found in Norway, Sweden, Finland, and Greenland.

mass of elongate black crystals

rather resinous lustre

SECTION SHOWN

COMPOSITION *Disilicate.*
CRYSTAL SYSTEM *Monoclinic.*
CLEAVAGE/FRACTURE *Imperfect/Conchoidal to uneven.*
LUSTRE/STREAK *Vitreous, resinous, or submetallic/Greyish brown.*
HARDNESS/DENSITY *5.5–6 / 3.5–4.2.*
KEY PROPERTIES *Shape, colour, and lustre.*

THIS PEGMATITE *sample from Ytterby, Sweden, contains black gadolinite-(Y) with biotite and pale-coloured feldspar.*

Gadolinite-(Y)

$Y_2Fe^{2+}Be_2Si_2O_{10}$

Gadolinite-(Ce) contains more cerium than yttrium but the opposite applies to the more common gadolinite-(Y). It forms black, greenish black, or dark brown prismatic crystals and massive aggregates, and has thin splinters that are translucent green. Gadolinite-(Y) is mainly found in granites and granitic pegmatites. Traces of uranium and thorium can make it slightly radioactive.

conchoidal fracture

well-formed crystals

black massive gadolinite-(Y)

COMPOSITION *Ring silicate.*
CRYSTAL SYSTEM *Monoclinic.*
CLEAVAGE/FRACTURE *None/Conchoidal or splintery.*
LUSTRE/STREAK *Vitreous or greasy/Greenish grey.*
HARDNESS/DENSITY *6.5–7 / 4.36–4.77*
KEY PROPERTIES *Translucent green splinters.*

rock matrix

Chromite

$Fe^{2+}Cr_2O_4$

This most important ore of chromium, chromite is opaque black or dark brown and has octahedral crystals, often in granular or massive aggregates. It forms large deposits in layered basic and ultrabasic igneous intrusions, and is preserved when these rocks are metamorphosed to form serpentinites.

rounded weathered crystals

DARK *chromite-rich bands in anorthosite, a cumulate deposit at Dwars River, Eastern Bushveld, South Africa.*

granular chromite

serpentinite matrix

COMPOSITION *Oxide.*
CRYSTAL SYSTEM *Cubic.*
CLEAVAGE/FRACTURE *None/Uneven.*
LUSTRE/STREAK *Metallic or submetallic/Brown.*
HARDNESS/DENSITY *5.5 / 4.5–4.8.*
KEY PROPERTIES *Weakly magnetic; resembles magnetite (p.126).*

Platinum

Pt

This precious metal is opaque, silvery grey, and markedly dense. The cubic crystals are rarely seen, and platinum usually occurs as disseminated grains associated with chromium and copper ores in layered basic and ultrabasic igneous rocks. When these are weathered, platinum accumulates as grains and nuggets in the resulting placer deposits. It often forms an alloy with iron and so may be magnetic.

PLATINUM *is mined at the Merensky Reef deposit of South Africa, one of the world's most important sources of this metal.*

cube-shaped crystal

platinum nugget

COMPOSITION *Element.*
CRYSTAL SYSTEM *Cubic.*
CLEAVAGE/FRACTURE *None/Hackly.*
LUSTRE/STREAK *Metallic lustre/Silvery metallic.*
HARDNESS/DENSITY *4–4.5 / 14–19.*
KEY PROPERTIES *Very dense, silvery, malleable metal; lacks secondary alteration.*

Rock-forming Minerals

The bulk of minerals that constitute rocks are not ores, although some have important uses in industry. This chapter features minerals that are found in a wide range of rock types (pp.143–67), and those found mainly or exclusively in sedimentary rocks (pp.168–75), igneous rocks (pp.176–96), and metamorphic rocks (pp.197–216). Talc, for example, is found exclusively in metamorphic rocks, such as the cliffs of Kynance Cove, England (below). Hydrothermal minerals that are neither ores nor their secondary minerals are also included in this chapter.

MUSCOVITE   BERYL   GYPSUM   SERPENTI

Quartz

SiO₂

An exceptionally common mineral, quartz forms six-sided crystals with pyramidal terminations. The crystals are often prismatic, usually with striations at right angles to the length. They can also be massive, or granular as in common beach sand. Extremely fine-grained compact quartz is called chalcedony. The colour of quartz is highly variable, but mostly it is a colourless rock crystal or white. Purple amethyst and brown smoky quartz are relatively common, but the natural yellow variety, citrine, is rare – most so-called citrine is actually heat-treated amethyst. Rarer still are well-formed crystals of pink rose quartz, although rose quartz is more abundant in its massive form. Quartz is an essential constitutent of granites and granite pegmatites, quartzites, and many sandstones. It is frequently found in hydrothermal veins.

THE CAIRNGORM *mountains in Scotland are famous for the yellowish brown quartz variety called cairngorm.*

SMOKY QUARTZ GEMSTONE

ROSE QUARTZ GEMSTONE

vitreous lustre

pyramidal terminations

clear quartz grading into purple amethyst

AMETHYST

pink crystals

striations

ROSE QUARTZ

ROCK CRYSTAL

conchoidal fracture

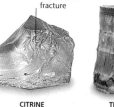

CITRINE

silky, fibrous appearance

TIGER EYE

COMPOSITION *Oxide or silicate.*
CRYSTAL SYSTEM *Trigonal.*
CLEAVAGE/FRACTURE *None/Conchoidal.*
LUSTRE/STREAK *Vitreous/White.*
HARDNESS/DENSITY *7 / 2.65.*
KEY PROPERTIES *A hard mineral with conchoidal fracture, usually with striations across prism faces.*

NOTE

Orangish brown tiger-eye and blue hawk's-eye (see Lustre, p.17) are both pseudomorphs where quartz (p.143) has replaced riebeckite(p.163) asbestos. These varieties are carved or cut into smooth-topped dome-shaped gems called cabochons; they have all the beauty of the blue asbestos without any of its dangers.

Chalcedony

SiO₂

Chalcedony is extremely fine-grained quartz and occurs in many geological environments. Commonly, it is white, brown, grey, or greyish blue, and is often botryoidal. Varieties include flint and chert, jasper, carnelian, chrysoprase, sard (translucent brown), prase (leek green), and plasma (dark green). Plasma with red hematite-rich spots is called heliotrope or bloodstone. Agate is banded chalcedony formed in gas bubbles in volcanic lava. The bands are colourless, white, grey, greyish blue, brown, yellow, pink, red, or black. When they are in flat parallel layers it is onyx, a name also given to creamy white agate or when the bands are black and white. Sardonyx has bands of sard, and in blue lace agate, they are light blue. Moss agate is not banded; it has moss-like green chlorite, brown goethite, or black manganese oxides in the chalcedony.

AGATES *weather out of the basaltic rocks at Agate Beach on the island of Haida Gwaii in British Columbia, Canada.*

surface often botryoidal

natural waxy lustre

patchy brown and white colours

SECTION SHOWN

typical apple green colour

CHRYSOPRASE

red, hematite-rich spots

always translucent orange or red

red, brown, yellow, or green, and opaque

HELIOTROPE/BLOODSTONE

CARNELIAN

JASPER

dendritic goethite looks like moss

colourless chalcedony

MOSS AGATE

swirled, lacy appearance

polished stone

flat, parallel layers

rough, uneven surface

translucent brown sard

SARDONYX

BLUE LACE AGATE

rounded shape of original gas bubble

colourless, white, and bluish grey bands

AGATE

banding best seen on a polished surface

natural fracture

COMPOSITION *Oxide or framework silicate.*
CRYSTAL SYSTEM *Trigonal.*
CLEAVAGE/FRACTURE *None/Uneven.*
LUSTRE/STREAK *Waxy to dull/White.*
HARDNESS/DENSITY *7 / 2.59–2.63.*
KEY PROPERTIES *Shows no crystal faces; any 'crystals' are pseudomorphs of other minerals.*

NOTE

Vivid pink, green, blue, purple, red, or brown agates that are often seen for sale in shops are artificially dyed. Originally they were bluish grey in colour and most have come from basalt quarries in Brazil. Chalcedony can absorb artificial dyes very well although not all the bands in an agate are equally porous.

Opal

SiO₂·nH₂O

THE OPAL-MINING *town of Coober Pedy, Australia, has grown around the place where a 14-year-old boy first discovered precious opal in 1915.*

Opal is unusual among minerals in being amorphous, and never forming crystals. Common opal is usually white, grey, pale brown, or yellow and has a waxy lustre. By comparison, precious opal is strikingly beautiful, showing flashes of vibrant colour as it is turned in the light. Most precious opal comes from Australia, but orange-red fire opal comes mainly from Mexico. Other varieties of opal include spherular pearly fiorite and the curious colourless, botryoidal hyalite. Fossil wood preserved in opal is called wood opal. Opal solidifies from a gel under low temperature conditions in a variety of rocks. It is also deposited around fumaroles and hot springs.

orange red

flashes of colour

conchoidal fracture

translucent with flashes of blue and green

SECTION SHOWN

waxy lustre

COMMON OPAL

translucent red mass

FIRE OPAL

pearly spherules

FIORITE

fossil wood

WOOD OPAL

NOTE

Opal is made up of spherules of silicon dioxide, which, in precious opal, are neatly stacked. The gaps between the spherules are the right size to break up white light into spectral colours, and, depending on the size of the spherules, they are able to flash certain colours back to the viewer.

COMPOSITION *Silicate.*
CRYSTAL SYSTEM *Amorphous.*
CLEAVAGE/FRACTURE *None/Conchoidal.*
LUSTRE/STREAK *Vitreous or waxy/ White.*
HARDNESS/DENSITY *5.5–6.5 / 1.99–2.25.*
KEY PROPERTIES *Crystals are never seen; the lustre is often waxy.*

Corundum

Al_2O_3

Surprisingly, ruby and sapphire are gem varieties of the same mineral, corundum. Commonly it is white, grey, or brown, but gem colours include red ruby, orange-pink padparadscha, and colourless, blue, green, yellow, orange, violet, and pink sapphire. Crystals are rough and generally hexagonal, either tabular, tapering barrel-shaped, or dipyramidal. It can also be massive or granular, and when mixed with magnetite, it is the abrasive known as emery. Corundum forms in syenites, certain pegmatites, and in high grade metamorphic rocks. It is concentrated in placer deposits.

MULTICOLOURED *gem sapphires can be collected from the gravels at Eldorado Bar in Montana, USA.*

tapering barrel-shaped crystals

rich red colour

rock matrix

RUBY

colour may be patchy

vitreous lustre

SAPPHIRE

pink feldspar

parting

drab greyish brown

COMMON CORUNDUM

| WHITE SAPPHIRE | YELLOW SAPPHIRE | GREEN SAPPHIRE | SAPPHIRE | PADPARADSCHA | RUBY |

COMPOSITION *Oxide.*
CRYSTAL SYSTEM *Trigonal.*
CLEAVAGE/FRACTURE *None, cleavage-like parting/Conchoidal to uneven.*
LUSTRE/STREAK *Vitreous to adamantine, sometimes pearly/White.*
HARDNESS/DENSITY *9 / 4.00–4.10.*
KEY PROPERTIES *Hardness, crystal shape.*

NOTE

Red ruby is coloured by trace chromium. The blue of sapphire is due to a little titanium and iron. All other gem colours are also called sapphire but named with the colour as well, for example pink sapphire, yellow sapphire, or colourless white sapphire. Colours result from traces of iron, chromium, and other metals.

Chrysoberyl

BeAl₂O₄

Chrysoberyl is typically yellow, green, or brown, and forms tabular or short prismatic crystals and heart-shaped or pseudohexagonal twins. It occurs in certain granite pegmatites, gneisses, mica schists, and marbles, and in detrital sands and gravels. Two varieties, alexandrite and cat's eye, are especially prized as unusual gemstones. Cat's eye contains parallel fibrous crystals of other minerals which reflect light across the surface of a polished gemstone, an effect known as chatoyancy.

THE MASVINGO *granite rocks in Zimbabwe are a modern source of alexandrite chrysoberyl.*

band of light

ALEXANDRITE

greenish yellow twinned crystal

transparent with vitreous lustre

pseudohexagonal crystal

green (in daylight)

brownish red (in tungsten light)

CAT'S EYE

ALEXANDRITE GEMSTONES

COMPOSITION *Oxide.*
CRYSTAL SYSTEM *Orthorhombic.*
CLEAVAGE/FRACTURE *Distinct/Uneven or conchoidal.*
LUSTRE/STREAK *Vitreous/White.*
HARDNESS/DENSITY 8.5 / 3.75.
KEY PROPERTIES *A hard green mineral that may appear red under incandescent light.*

NOTE

Chromium makes emeralds green in colour and rubies red, but it makes alexandrite look green in daylight or fluorescent light, and red under an ordinary tungsten light bulb. First discovered in the Ural Mountains of Russia, today alexandrite comes mainly from Lavra di Hematita in Minas Gerais, Brazil.

Spinel

$MgAl_2O_4$

Although most familiar as a blue, purple, red, or pink gemstone, spinel can be other colours. Crystals are usually octahedral and sometimes twinned, and granular or massive aggregates are found. A minor constituent of basalts, kimberlites, peridotites, and other igneous rocks, spinel also forms in aluminium-rich schists and metamorphosed limestones. Water-worn crystals come from detrital stream deposits in Sri Lanka and Myanmar.

TOURISTS *can try their hand prospecting for spinel and sapphire in gem gravels at Anakie, Queensland, Australia.*

gem-like red waterworn crystals

octahedral shape

rounded blue crystal

COMPOSITION *Oxide.*
CRYSTAL SYSTEM *Cubic.*
CLEAVAGE/FRACTURE *None, cleavage-like parting/Conchoidal, uneven or splintery.*
LUSTRE/STREAK *Vitreous/White.*
HARDNESS/DENSITY *7.5-8 / 3.6-4.1.*
KEY PROPERTIES *A red, blue, or violet gem mineral found as octahedral crystals.*

Lazulite

$MgAl_2(PO_4)_2(OH)_2$

Sky blue, greenish blue, and dark green are the typical colours of lazulite, and crystals are pyramidal, tabular, granular, or massive. It occurs in metamorphic rocks, such as schists and quartzites, and is found in the rocks bordering granite pegmatites and in alluvial deposits. Crystals from Georgia, USA, are nearly opaque, but those of the Yukon, Canada, and from northwest Pakistan are translucent.

BLUE *lazulite, seen here with brown siderite, is the official gemstone of Yukon, Canada.*

appears octahedral

dull, sky blue crystal

bi-pyramidal crystal

quartz matrix

COMPOSITION *Phosphate.*
CRYSTAL SYSTEM *Monoclinic.*
CLEAVAGE/FRACTURE *Poor to good/Uneven to splintery.*
LUSTRE/STREAK *Vitreous to dull/White.*
HARDNESS/DENSITY *5.5–6 / 3.12–3.24.*
KEY PROPERTIES *Name may be confused with lazurite (p.215), found in lapis lazuli.*

Calcite

$CaCO_3$

CALCITE *is the mineral that most often forms stalagmites and stalactites in caves, and banded travertine deposits in hot springs.*

A particularly common mineral, calcite is colourless, white, or tinted by impurities. Scalenohedral, rhombohedral, and prismatic forms occur in combination. Crystals with shallow pointed ends are called nailhead spar but when they are steeply pointed, they are dog-tooth spar. Clear rhombohedral cleavage fragments are Iceland spar. Calcite is often granular or massive. A constituent of limestones, marbles, and other sedimentary and metamorphic deposits, it is also found in hydro-thermal veins and igneous rocks.

criss-cross lines show where it would cleave

six-sided crystals

translucent with subvitreous lustre

group of dog-tooth crystals

six-sided, pointed crystal

NAIL HEAD SPAR

steep pointed end

DOG-TOOTH SPAR

line appears double through crystal

cleavage rhomb

transparent

ICELAND SPAR

COMPOSITION *Carbonate.*
CRYSTAL SYSTEM *Trigonal.*
CLEAVAGE/FRACTURE *Perfect, rhombohedral/Conchoidal but rarely seen.*
LUSTRE/STREAK *Subvitreous/White.*
HARDNESS/DENSITY *3 / 2.71.*
KEY PROPERTIES *Perfect rhombohedral cleavage and fizzes in dilute HCl.*

NOTE

Light passing through crystals may be split into polarized rays which, travelling at different speeds, are bent or refracted by different amounts. This means that a double image is seen of an object viewed through the crystal. Calcite crystals shows this double refraction particularly well.

Aragonite

CaCO₃

Although it has the same chemical composition as calcite, aragonite crystals are different. They are tabular, prismatic, or acicular, often with steep pyramidal or chisel-shaped ends, and can form columnar or radiating aggregates. Multiple twinned crystals are common, appearing hexagonal in shape. Aragonite is deposited in marine sediments and constitutes the shells of many molluscs. Pearls are composed mainly of this mineral. It is found in evaporites, hot spring deposits, and in caves where it may form coral-like aggregates, known as flos ferri. It is also found in some metamorphic and igneous rocks.

THESE SPHERULES *of acicular aragonite crystals on specular hematite and quartz were found in Cumbria, England.*

modern shell composed of aragonite

twisted, coral-like aggregate

FLOS FERRI

pseudohexagonal multiple twins

transparent and colourless crystal

subvitreous lustre

acicular crystals

subconchoidal fracture where tips have broken off

fragile and easily broken

brown siderite crystals

COMPOSITION	Carbonate.

COMPOSITION *Carbonate.*
CRYSTAL SYSTEM *Orthorhombic.*
CLEAVAGE/FRACTURE *Distinct/Nearly conchoidal.*
LUSTRE/STREAK *Subvitreous/White.*
HARDNESS/DENSITY *3.5–4 / 2.95.*
KEY PROPERTIES *Aragonite tends to alter to calcite (left). It fizzes in dilute HCl.*

NOTE

Aragonite is common in modern sediments but tends to be found only in younger rocks. This is because it is relatively unstable and over geological time, converts to calcite (left). The exterior form may still be that of aragonite, but a rhombohedral cleavage gives away its new identity.

FINE crystals of dolomite accompany rare sulphide and sulphosalt minerals at the Lengenbach quarry in Binntal, Switzerland.

Dolomite

$CaMg(CO_3)_2$

Dolomite is a white, pale brown, or pink mineral. It forms rhombohedral crystals that often have curved faces or cluster in saddle-shaped aggregates. It can also be massive or granular. The main constituent of dolomite rocks and dolomitic marbles, dolomite is also present in hydrothermal veins, serpentinites, altered basic igneous rocks, and in some carbonatites.

rhombohedral crystals

pearly lustre

curved crystal face

COMPOSITION *Carbonate.*
CRYSTAL SYSTEM *Trigonal.*
CLEAVAGE/FRACTURE *Perfect, rhombohedral/Subconchoidal.*
LUSTRE/STREAK *Vitreous or pearly/White.*
HARDNESS/DENSITY *3.5–4 / 2.86.*
KEY PROPERTIES *Harder than calcite (p.150), and fizzes only slightly in dilute HCl.*

amethyst matrix

Ankerite

$Ca(Fe^{2+},Mg,Mn)(CO_3)_2$

Ankerite is brown, yellow, or buff-coloured, and is found as rhombohedral crystals, often with curved faces. These may form saddle-shaped groups, and resemble the related minerals dolomite (above) and siderite. Prismatic crystals also occur, and massive or granular aggregates are common. Ankerite is a gangue mineral in hydrothermal ore deposits and occurs in carbonatites, low-grade metamorphosed ironstones and banded ironstone formations, and in some carbonate sedimentary rocks.

BROWN ankerite crystals accompany chalcopyrite in this copper ore deposit.

light brown crystals

rhombohedral cleavage

COMPOSITION *Carbonate.*
CRYSTAL SYSTEM *Trigonal.*
CLEAVAGE/FRACTURE *Perfect, rhombohedral/Subconchoidal.*
LUSTRE/STREAK *Vitreous to pearly/White.*
HARDNESS/DENSITY *3.5–4 / 2.93–3.10.*
KEY PROPERTIES *Fizzes only slightly in dilute HCl.*

Barytocalcite

$BaCa(CO_3)_2$

Barytocalcite occurs as striated prismatic or bladed crystals and cleavable masses. It can be colourless, white, grey, pale yellow, or green, and it fluoresces under UV light. Barytocalcite forms in limestones that have been altered by lead and zinc-bearing hydrothermal veins, but it also occurs in carbonatites.

FIRST *discovered near Alston, Cumbria, barytocalcite comes from a number of old lead mines in northern England.*

limestone matrix

prismatic crystals

radiating group of bladed crystals

COMPOSITION *Carbonate.*
CRYSTAL SYSTEM *Monoclinic.*
CLEAVAGE/FRACTURE *Perfect/Uneven to nearly conchoidal.*
LUSTRE/STREAK *Vitreous or resinous/White.*
HARDNESS/DENSITY *3.5–4 / 3.66–3.71.*
KEY PROPERTIES *Crystal shape differs from other gangue minerals; dissolves in dilute HCl.*

Strontianite

$SrCO_3$

The chemical element strontium was first discovered in the mineral strontianite from Scotland. This mineral is typically colourless, white, yellow, green, or grey. Crystals are prismatic, often in acicular or fibrous radiating groups; it also forms columnar, granular or massive aggregates, or powdery coatings. It occurs in hydrothermal veins and is found in carbonatite deposits.

TINY *spherules of strontianite crystals occur with celestine in limestone cavities on the south Wales coast.*

sprays of needle-like crystals

SECTION SHOWN

translucent pale yellow

COMPOSITION *Carbonate.*
CRYSTAL SYSTEM *Orthorhombic.*
CLEAVAGE/FRACTURE *Nearly perfect/Uneven to subconchoidal.*
LUSTRE/STREAK *Vitreous to resinous/White.*
HARDNESS/DENSITY *3.5 / 3.76.*
KEY PROPERTIES *Often in tufts of radiating white or green crystals, dissolves in dilute HCl.*

Witherite

BaCO₃

Witherite crystals may be prismatic and they may be pyramidal, but they are always twinned, appearing hexagonal in shape. Striations run across prism faces. This mineral can also be fibrous, botryoidal, spherular, columnar, granular, or massive. It is usually white or grey. Most witherite comes from low-temperature hydrothermal veins, usually resulting from the alteration of baryte.

LARGE *deposits of witherite used to be mined as an ore of barium in the northern Pennines of England.*

SECTION SHOWN

six-sided crystal

vitreous lustre

distinct cleavage

COMPOSITION *Carbonate.*
CRYSTAL SYSTEM *Orthorhombic.*
CLEAVAGE/FRACTURE *Distinct/Uneven.*
LUSTRE/STREAK *Vitreous or resinous/White.*
HARDNESS/DENSITY *3–3.5 / 4.22–4.31.*
KEY PROPERTIES *Dense; usually in hexagonal crystals; dissolves in dilute HCl; fluoresces blue-white under UV.*

Celestine

SrSO₄

Celestine is often light blue, taking its name from the colour of the sky. Well-formed crystals are common and are tabular, blocky, bladed, or elongate pyramidal in shape. Aggregates are fibrous, lamellar, granular, or massive. Celestine is usually found in cavities and fractures in limestones and other sedimentary rocks, but may be present in hydrothermal veins and basic igneous rocks.

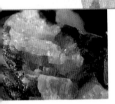

THIS CAVITY *in a septarian concretion from Oxfordshire, England, contains blue celestine with brown and white calcite.*

blocky, orthorhombic crystals

light blue colour

massive habit

sulphur

colourless crystals

COMPOSITION *Sulphate.*
CRYSTAL SYSTEM *Orthorhombic.*
CLEAVAGE/FRACTURE *Perfect/Uneven.*
LUSTRE/STREAK *Vitreous; pearly on cleavages/White.*
HARDNESS/DENSITY *3-3.5 / 3.97.*
KEY PROPERTIES *Colourless, orange, or white but usually blue; less dense than baryte (right).*

Baryte

BaSO₄

The most common barium mineral, baryte is generally colourless, white, grey, blue, pink, yellow, or brown. Crystals are usually thin or thick tabular; less commonly, they are prismatic. Cockscomb or crested aggregates of nearly parallel platy crystals are a distinctive habit of this mineral. It also occurs in rosette-shaped clusters of crystals, and banded, granular, or massive aggregates. Baryte is found as a gangue mineral in low-temperature hydrothermal veins or results from the weathering of barium-rich limestones. It is an accessory mineral in some igneous rocks.

LITTLE *remains of the baryte mine at Force Crag in Cumbria, England, where baryte and lead ore were mined until 1990.*

translucent, nearly opaque

sphalerite

cockscomb mass of platy crystals

tabular habit

colour-zoned tabular crystal

prismatic habit

COMPOSITION	Sulphate.
CRYSTAL SYSTEM	Orthorhombic.
CLEAVAGE/FRACTURE	Perfect/Uneven.
LUSTRE/STREAK	Vitreous to resinous/White.
HARDNESS/DENSITY	3–3.5 / 4.5.

KEY PROPERTIES A very dense mineral that may form distinctive cockscomb aggregates.

NOTE

The chemical element barium has a high density so baryte always feels distinctly heavy. It is used to make heavy drilling muds for oil and gas rigs, and it is a filler used to add weight to paper and rubber. It is also opaque to X-rays, and is used to make the 'barium meals' used in medicine.

Fluorite

CaF₂

In terms of colour, fluorite is a remarkable mineral. Most colours are found, often vibrant, and commonly as zones of different colours within a single crystal. Well-formed crystals are common. These may be octahedral but are usually cube-shaped. Additional faces can form bevelled edges, and the corners of cubic crystals are easily cleaved off. Colour-banded columnar or massive fluorite, such as the purple Blue John of Derbyshire, England, make beautiful but fragile ornamental stones. Fluorite occurs mainly as a gangue mineral in low temperature hydrothermal deposits, and, as an accessory mineral in acid and intermediate intrusive rocks.

LARGE *masses of purple fluorite can be seen in the roof of this mine at Foisches, Ardenne, France.*

banded white fluorite

purple fluorite

BLUE JOHN

zones of purple and green

cubic crystals

iron-stained coating

pink octahedral crystal

corner cleaved off

bevelled edges

NOTE

The phenomenon of fluorescence – where a substance glows under ultraviolet or other radiation – is named after fluorite, which often shows this property well. Fluorite comes from the Latin 'to flow' because it is an important flux, that is, it is used to lower other minerals' melting temperatures.

COMPOSITION *Halide.*
CRYSTAL SYSTEM *Cubic.*
CLEAVAGE/FRACTURE *Perfect, octahedral/Subconchoidal or uneven.*
LUSTRE/STREAK *Vitreous/White.*
HARDNESS/DENSITY *4 / 3.17–3.18.*
KEY PROPERTIES *Cubic mineral with octahedral cleavage; often fluorescent.*

Apatite

$Ca_5(PO_4)_3x$ or $Ca_5(PO_4,CO_3)_3x$ where $x = F, OH, Cl$

Apatite is the general name for a group of calcium phosphate minerals, the most common of which is fluorapatite. Others include hydroxylapatite, chlorapatite, carbonate-fluorapatite, and carbonate-hydroxylapatite. Apatite minerals occur as hexagonal or tabular crystals, and as nodular, globular, reniform, granular, or massive aggregates. They can be colourless, white, pink, yellow, green, blue, violet, brown, and black. Apatites are accessory minerals in nearly all igneous rocks, and large crystals come from pegmatites and hydrothermal veins. They occur in marbles, skarns, and other metamorphic deposits. In sedimentary rocks, rich deposits occur as phosphorites, derived from fossil bones and teeth, coprolites, and other organic debris.

VIOLET-BLUE *apatite, with yellow fluorite, topaz, and cassiterite, comes from Saxony, Germany.*

waxy lustre

HYDROXYLAPATITE

CHLORAPATITE

transparent with vitreous lustre

uneven where broken

colour-zoned crystal

siderite

well-formed hexagonal crystal

COMPOSITION	Phosphate.
CRYSTAL SYSTEM	*Hexagonal or monoclinic.*
CLEAVAGE/FRACTURE	*Poor/Conchoidal to uneven.*
LUSTRE/STREAK	*Vitreous or waxy; earthy when massive/White.*
HARDNESS/DENSITY	*5 / 3.1–3.25.*
KEY PROPERTIES	*Softer than beryl (p.179).*

NOTE

Bones and teeth are composed largely of apatite, and rocks rich in fossil bones and teeth are of huge interest to palaeontologists. Fossils can be composed of a number of different minerals, most commonly calcite, aragonite, quartz, or opal. Sometimes well-formed crystals can be found in cavities in fossils.

Zircon

ZrSiO₄

Zircon is reddish brown, green, yellow, blue, grey, or colourless. Controlled heating of brown zircon gives the sky blue and golden yellow stones preferred by jewellers. Zircon usually occurs as short, square prismatic crystals with pyramidal terminations, or as irregular grains. Traces of uranium and thorium can make it slightly radioactive. A common accessory mineral in many igneous and metamorphic rocks, zircon is also a particularly durable detrital mineral in sedimentary deposits. Much quality zircon comes from placer deposits. It is mined in Vietnam, Thailand, Myanmar, Sri Lanka, and elsewhere in southeast Asia.

ZIRCONS collected from Hanging Rock in Victoria, Australia, have been analysed for their trace element composition and age of formation.

heat treated

natural colour

GRAVEL

SECTION SHOWN

plagioclase feldspar

HEAT-TREATED BLUE GEMSTONE

typical tetragonal crystal

waterworn, rounded surface

reddish brown crystal has vitreous lustre

sawn and polished

black biotite

COMPOSITION *Silicate.*
CRYSTAL SYSTEM *Tetragonal or metamict.*
CLEAVAGE/FRACTURE *Indistinct/Conchoidal.*
LUSTRE/STREAK *Vitreous, adamantine, or resinous/White.*
HARDNESS/DENSITY *7.5 / 4.6–4.7.*
KEY PROPERTIES *Crystal shape; harder than vesuvianite (p.210).*

NOTE

In some minerals containing even traces of uranium or thorium, radioactive decay breaks down the crystal structure. These 'metamict' minerals become amorphous and some of their properties change. Metamict zircon is less dense than fresh zircon and often has a greasy lustre.

Olivine

Mg$_2$SiO$_4$ (forsterite) to Fe^{2+}$_2$SiO$_4$ (fayalite)

Olivine is the name of a group of silicate minerals, and most olivines have compositions ranging between magnesium-bearing forsterite and iron-bearing fayalite. Generally a distinctive yellowish green, they can also be yellow, white, grey, or brown. Rare well-formed crystals are tabular with wedge-shaped terminations, and may be striated lengthwise. Usually crystals are poorly formed; discrete grains and granular or massive aggregates are most common. Olivine occurs in mafic and ultramafic igneous rocks and is the main constituent of peridotites. It also forms by the metamorphism of iron-rich sediments and impure limestones. Tephroite, a manganese olivine occurs in skarns and metamorphosed manganese deposits.

NODULES *of green peridotite composed of coarse granular olivine are found in dark-coloured basalts on the volcanic island of Lanzarote.*

tabular crystals

dark brown (zinc- and manganese-rich)

pale tabular crystals

FAYALITE

distinctly resinous lustre

rounded, ill-formed crystal

FORSTERITE

typical yellowish green colour

granular mass

peridot gemstone

COMPOSITION *Silicate.*
CRYSTAL SYSTEM *Orthorhombic.*
CLEAVAGE/FRACTURE *Imperfect/Conchoidal.*
LUSTRE/STREAK *Vitreous to resinous/White.*
HARDNESS/DENSITY *6.5–7 / 3.28–4.39.*
KEY PROPERTIES *Rather rounded poorly formed yellow-green crystals with a conchoidal fracture.*

NOTE

Olivine was called topaz by ancient authors because it was found on Topazius, an island in the Red Sea now called Zebirget. This name was only restricted to the modern topaz (p.178) in 1747. Gem quality olivine is called peridot and today, superb crystals come from the North-West Frontier of Pakistan.

Muscovite

KAl₂AlSi₃O₁₀(OH)₂

$KAl_2AlSi_3O_{10}(OH)_2$

Muscovite is colourless, grey, pale pink, or green. When rich in chromium it is bright green and called fuchsite. As with all the micas, muscovite forms pseudohexagonal crystals which have a perfect, micaceous basal cleavage, splitting into thin, colourless, transparent sheets. In igneous rocks, muscovite is a constituent of granites and granite pegmatites. Some pegmatites contain huge crystalline masses. Muscovite is a key constituent of metamorphic rocks, such as phyllites, muscovite-schists, and some gneisses. It is also found in micaceous sandstones.

THIS GRANITE *pegmatite contains clusters of muscovite crystals with quartz and microcline.*

flaky crystals

bright green

FUCHSITE

six-sided pseudo-hexagonal crystal

cleaves into flexible sheets

greyish pink crystals

part of a large crystal

glass-like, vitreous lustre

SECTION SHOWN

COMPOSITION *Silicate, mica group.*
CRYSTAL SYSTEM *Monoclinic.*
CLEAVAGE/FRACTURE *Perfect, micaceous/None.*
LUSTRE/STREAK *Vitreous, pearly, or silky lustre/White.*
HARDNESS/DENSITY *2.5–4 / 2.77–2.88.*
KEY PROPERTIES *Pale; splits into thin sheets.*

NOTE

Muscovite has a much higher melting point than glass and can form large crystals, sometimes metres across, which cleave into thin, transparent sheets. This makes it suitable for blast furnace windows, and other situations in which glass would melt. India is the principal supplier of sheet muscovite for industry.

Biotite

Dark mica without lithium

This dark brown or black mica is found as pseudohexagonal crystals, lamellar or scaly aggregates, or disseminated grains. Biotite is a key constituent of many igneous and metamorphic rocks, including granites, nepheline syenites, schists, and gneisses. It is also found in potassium-rich hydrothermal deposits, and some clastic sedimentary rocks.

BIOTITE *and quartz crystals are seen in this pegmatite from Namaqualand, South Africa.*

PSEUDOHEXAGONAL CRYSTAL

flexible, thin sheets

COMPOSITION *Silicate, mica group.*
CRYSTAL SYSTEM *Monoclinic.*
CLEAVAGE/FRACTURE *Perfect, micaceous/None.*
LUSTRE/STREAK *Adamantine; pearly on cleavage/White.*
HARDNESS/DENSITY *2.5–3 / 2.7–3.3.*
KEY PROPERTIES *Dark; splits into thin sheets.*

Phlogopite

$KMg_3AlSi_3O_{10}(OH)_2$

Phlogopite crystals are tabular or prismatic, six-sided, and often tapered along the length. As with all micas, phlogopite cleaves easily into thin sheets. Lamellar or scaly masses are common. Phlogopite is red-brown, yellow-brown, green, or colourless. It is found in metamorphosed dolomites and dolomitic limestones, and in ultrabasic igneous rocks. Huge crystals of this important insulating material come from the Kovdor deposit on Russia's Kola peninsula.

RICH *deposits of apatite are associated with phlogopite at the Dorowa phosphate mine, Zimbabwe.*

COMPOSITION *Silicate, mica group.*
CRYSTAL SYSTEM *Monoclinic.*
CLEAVAGE/FRACTURE *Perfect, micaceous/None.*
LUSTRE/STREAK *Pearly; submetallic on cleavage/White.*
HARDNESS/DENSITY *2–3 / 2.78–2.85.*
KEY PROPERTIES *Paler than biotite (above).*

submetallic lustre

long, tapering crystal

Aegirine

$NaFe^{3+}Si_2O_6$

AEGIRINE *occurs with many rare minerals in the nepheline syenite of Mont St Hilaire in Quebec, Canada.*

Prismatic crystals of aegirine are often striated along the length, and have steep or blunt terminations. They can be acicular or fibrous, forming attractive radiating sprays. This pyroxene mineral is usually green or green-black, less commonly brown. Most aegirine is found as a characteristic constituent of syenites, carbonatites, and other alkaline rocks. To a lesser extent, it occurs in schists, granulites, and other metamorphic rocks. The fine large crystals shown here come from the Mount Malosa alkaline massif in southern Malawi.

dark green crystals

vitreous lustre

potassium feldspar

COMPOSITION *Silicate, pyroxene group.*
CRYSTAL SYSTEM *Monoclinic.*
CLEAVAGE/FRACTURE *Good, crossing at about 90°/Uneven.*
LUSTRE/STREAK *Vitreous or resinous/White or yellowish grey.*
HARDNESS/DENSITY *6 / 3.50–3.60.*
KEY PROPERTIES *Pyroxene cleavage; colour.*

Enstatite

$Mg_2Si_2O_6$

LARGE *brown enstatite crystals are seen here in a metamorphosed basic pegmatite.*

Enstatite, an orthopyroxene, forms white, grey, green, or brown prismatic crystals and columnar, fibrous, or massive aggregates. It is important in basic and ultrabasic igneous rocks, and occurs in granulites and other metamorphic rocks. Most so-called hypersthene is now considered to be enstatite.

large, green, prismatic crystal

metallic bronze lustre

BRONZITE

COMPOSITION *Silicate, pyroxene group.*
CRYSTAL SYSTEM *Orthorhombic.*
CLEAVAGE/FRACTURE *Good; crossing at about 90°/Uneven.*
LUSTRE/STREAK *Vitreous or sub-metallic; pearly on cleavages/White or pale grey.*
HARDNESS/DENSITY *6 / 3.50–3.60.*
KEY PROPERTIES *Pyroxene cleavage.*

Hornblende

$Ca_2[x4(AlFe_{3+})](Si7Al)O_{22}(OH)_2$ $(x= Fe^{2+}$ or $Mg)$

The hornblende series has compositions between ferro-hornblende and magnesiohornblende. Hornblendes are green, brown, or black. Crystals are prismatic, and usually dispersed through a rock, but can also form columnar, bladed, or massive aggregates. Hornblendes are important minerals in granodiorites, diorites, trachytes, amphibolites, hornblende schists, and many other rocks.

LARGE *hornblende crystals make up much of this pegmatite boulder at Glenbuchat in Aberdeenshire, Scotland.*

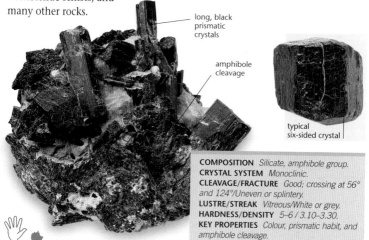

long, black prismatic crystals

amphibole cleavage

typical six-sided crystal

COMPOSITION *Silicate, amphibole group.*
CRYSTAL SYSTEM *Monoclinic.*
CLEAVAGE/FRACTURE *Good; crossing at 56° and 124°/Uneven or splintery.*
LUSTRE/STREAK *Vitreous/White or grey.*
HARDNESS/DENSITY *5–6 / 3.10–3.30.*
KEY PROPERTIES *Colour, prismatic habit, and amphibole cleavage.*

Riebeckite

$Na_2(Fe^{2+}_3Fe^{3+}_2)Si_8O_{22}(OH)_2$

Riebeckite is a greyish blue to dark blue amphibole. It is found as prismatic crystals and massive or fibrous aggregates in alkaline granites and syenites, their volcanic equivalents, and in some schists. It can also occur as blue asbestos, known to geologists as crocidolite. Riebeckite asbestos is formed where banded ironstones have been metamorphosed.

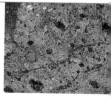

THE BLUE-GREY *flecks in this microgranite, from the island of Ailsa Craig in Scotland, are crystals of riebeckite.*

amphibole cleavage

blue, fibrous asbestos

SECTION SHOWN

deep greyish blue colour

CROCIDOLITE

COMPOSITION *Silicate, amphibole group.*
CRYSTAL SYSTEM *Monoclinic.*
CLEAVAGE/FRACTURE *Good; crossing at 56° and 124°/Uneven.*
LUSTRE/STREAK *Vitreous/Blue-grey.*
HARDNESS/DENSITY *6 / 3.28–3.34.*
KEY PROPERTIES *Blue asbestos causes fatal lung disease; inhalation must be avoided.*

Sanidine

(K,Na)AlSi₃O₈

$(K,Na)AlSi_3O_8$

SANIDINE, *as found in Vesuvius, Italy, is more likely to be transparent than other potassium feldspars.*

Sanidine is colourless, white, or cream, and has crystals that are usually tabular with a square cross-section. Twinned crystals are also common. Sanidine is a potassium feldspar that forms at high temperatures in volcanic rocks such as rhyolites, phonolites, and trachytes. It forms spherular masses of acicular crystals in obsidian, and also occurs in eclogites and contact metamorphic rocks.

large, translucent crystal

square cross-section

trachyte matrix

COMPOSITION *Silicate, feldspar group.*
CRYSTAL SYSTEM *Monoclinic.*
CLEAVAGE/FRACTURE *Perfect/Conchoidal to uneven.*
LUSTRE/STREAK *Vitreous; pearly on cleavages/White.*
HARDNESS/DENSITY 6 / 2.56–2.62.
KEY PROPERTIES *The nature of its twinning.*

Microcline

KAlSi₃O₈

$KAlSi_3O_8$

PIKES PEAK, *Colorado, USA, is the world's most famous locality for the amazonite variety of microcline.*

Microcline is often found as twinned crystals or massive aggregates. It is white, cream, pink, or pale brown, but amazonite is an attractive, bluish green variety. Microcline is a potassium feldspar that occurs in acid and intermediate intrusive rocks, some schists and gneisses, and as grains in sediment.

pegmatite

nearly opaque bluish green

white albite

smoky quartz

blocky, prismatic crystal

AMAZONITE

tartan twinning

COMPOSITION *Silicate, feldspar group.*
CRYSTAL SYSTEM *Triclinic.*
CLEAVAGE/FRACTURE *Perfect, at right angles/Uneven.*
LUSTRE/STREAK *Vitreous; pearly on cleavages/White.*
HARDNESS/DENSITY 6–6.5 / 2.54–2.57.
KEY PROPERTIES *Cross-hatched (tartan) twins.*

Orthoclase

KAlSi₃O₈

Orthoclase is usually white, cream, buff, or pink, and forms blocky prismatic crystals. Carlsbad twins are most common but other kinds occur. Orthoclase is a potassium feldspar that forms at medium to low temperatures. It is abundant in intrusive felsic rocks, such as granites, granite pegmatites, and syenites. It also occurs in high-grade metamorphic rocks and as coatings and grains in sedimentary deposits. Adularia is a very distinctive variety of orthoclase. It forms in low-temperature, alpine-type hydrothermal veins as simple, colourless crystals that are rhombohedral in section, and complex star-shaped twins. Adularia that shows a bluish white play of light is known as moonstone.

THIS SMALL *cavity in granite from Northern Ireland contains orthoclase, quartz, and beryl.*

milky colour

MOONSTONE CABOCHON

ADULARIA

diamond-shaped ends

rough crystal face

CARLSBAD TWIN

bluish white play of light

MOONSTONE

associated cleavelandite albite

translucent prismatic crystal

cavity in pegmatite

NOTE

Orthoclase, microcline, sanidine, anorthoclase, and the plagioclase albite are collectively known as alkali feldspars. The composition of anorthoclase is between albite and sanidine.

COMPOSITION *Silicate, feldspar group.*
CRYSTAL SYSTEM *Monoclinic.*
CLEAVAGE/FRACTURE *Perfect/Conchoidal to uneven.*
LUSTRE/STREAK *Vitreous; pearly on cleavages/White.*
HARDNESS/DENSITY *6–6.5 / 2.55–2.63.*
KEY PROPERTIES *The nature of its twinning.*

Plagioclase

NaAlSi$_3$O$_8$ (albite) – CaAl$_2$Si$_2$O$_8$ (anorthite)

WELL-FORMED *crystals of andesine, often twinned, are found in the blue porphyries of the Estérel Mountains in Var, France.*

Albite is the sodium end of this compositional series of feldspars and anorthite is the calcium end. In between, are varieties oligoclase, andesine, labradorite, and bytownite. Most plagioclases are colourless, white, grey, green, or brown. They form tabular or prismatic crystals or can be massive or granular. Simple twins are common, but lamellar plagioclase twinning is distinctive, seen as slender dark and light bands on some faces. A platy, transparent variety of albite found in pegmatites is called cleavelandite. Albite also occurs in granites, syenites, and alpine-type hydrothermal veins. Oligoclase and andesine are dominant in diorite and andesite. Labradorite and bytownite are found in gabbro, dolerite, basalt, and anorthosite. Anorthite is most often found in metamorphic rocks. Other plagioclases may also be metamorphic or form detrital grains in sedimentary rocks.

creamy white colour

uneven fracture

tabular, triclinic crystals

vitreous, pale brown crystals

natural fractures in mineral

ANORTHITE

COMPOSITION	*Silicate, feldspar group.*

COMPOSITION *Silicate, feldspar group.*
CRYSTAL SYSTEM *Triclinic.*
CLEAVAGE/FRACTURE *Perfect/Conchoidal to uneven.*
LUSTRE/STREAK *Vitreous, pearly on cleavages of albite/White.*
HARDNESS/DENSITY *6–6.5 / 2.60–2.76.*
KEY PROPERTIES *Shows lamellar twinning.*

NOTE

Perthites are feldspars that have separated into thin potassium- and sodium-rich layers as they cool. Light may be reflected off boundaries between layers to give beautiful colour effects. The schiller in moonstone (p.165) and blue iridescence shown by Norwegian larvikite (p.49) are due to perthitic structures.

coarse granular mass

BYTOWNITE

polished sunstone cabochon

sparkling flecks of hematite or copper

plagioclase twinning

OLIGOCLASE SUNSTONE

massive habit

conchoidal fracture

OLIGOCLASE

simple twinned crystal

ANDESINE

polished labradorite cabochon

coarse crystalline mass

grey where no flashes show

LABRADORITE

translucent with vitreous lustre

shows multicoloured flashes when turned in light

Illite

$$K_{0.65}Al_2Al_{0.65}Si_{3.35}O_{10}(OH)_2$$

Illite is one of the most common clay minerals, although it is now classed as a member of the mica group. It occurs as very fine-grained aggregates. Individual hexagonal crystals can only be seen using an electron microscope. It is white, but impurities may tint it grey and other pale colours. Illite is most commonly found in sedimentary rocks and is the most abundant clay mineral in shales and clays.

CLAY deposits rich in illite are used to make bricks. This brickpit is in Stewartby, Bedfordshire, England.

pale, earthy mass

SECTION SHOWN

COMPOSITION Silicate, mica group.
CRYSTAL SYSTEM Monoclinic.
CLEAVAGE/FRACTURE Perfect/None.
LUSTRE/STREAK Dull lustre/White.
HARDNESS 1–2.
DENSITY 2.6–2.9.
KEY PROPERTIES Fine-grained; important in sedimentary clay rocks.

Kaolinite

$$Al_2Si_2O_5(OH)_4$$

China clay is the more familiar name of kaolinite, which is used in porcelain manufacture. It is pure white and occurs as minute, hexagonal plates clustered into very fine-grained masses. Thick deposits of kaolinite result from hydrothermal alteration and weathering of aluminium silicates, for example, feldspars in granites. Kaolinite is also part of the clay in other sedimentary rocks.

HIGH-PRESSURE water jets wash kaolinite out of the granite in the china clay pits of Cornwall, England.

dull, pure white mass

SECTION SHOWN

very compact structure

quartz

LITHOMARGE

COMPOSITION Silicate.
CRYSTAL SYSTEM Triclinic.
CLEAVAGE/FRACTURE Perfect/None.
LUSTRE/STREAK Pearly to dull, earthy/white.
HARDNESS/DENSITY 2–2.5 / 2.61–2.68.
KEY PROPERTIES Fine-grained, white clay found in weathered granites (p.44) and granite pegmatites (p.46) replacing feldspars.

feldspar altered to kaolinite

Montmorillonite

$(Na,Ca)_{0.3}(Al,Mg)_2Si_4O_{10}(OH)_2 \cdot nH_2O$

This clay mineral occurs in fine-grained, massive aggregates, or in globular clusters of microscopic, scaly, tabular crystals. It is usually white, pink, or buff. Montmorillonite is the main constituent of fuller's earth or bentonite, a clay deposit formed by alteration of volcanic tuffs. Once used for cleaning (fulling) fleeces, it is now extracted as drilling mud for oil rigs.

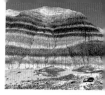

THESE BENTONITE *hills in the Petrified Forest National Park, Arizona, USA, have been stained by iron and manganese oxides.*

quartz crystal

tiny clusters of scaly crystals

dull, earthy surface

BENTONITE

COMPOSITION *Silicate.*
CRYSTAL SYSTEM *Monoclinic.*
CLEAVAGE/FRACTURE *Perfect/Uneven.*
LUSTRE/STREAK *Dull, earthy/White.*
HARDNESS/DENSITY *1–2 / 2–3.*
KEY PROPERTIES *A fine-grained clay mineral that swells as it absorbs water; found in altered volcanic rocks.*

Alunite

$KAl(SO_4)_2(OH)_6$

Alunite is usually granular or massive but can be fibrous or form tabular or cube-shaped crystals. It is colourless, white, or tinted grey, yellow or red-brown. Alunite forms where aluminium-rich rocks, such as volcanic ash deposits, have been altered by sulphur-rich fluids. The sulphur is derived from volcanic activity or the breakdown of pyrite in overlying rocks. Large deposits of alunite, called alumstone, are formed in some locations.

TAIWAN *is an important source of alum. Clusters of well-formed crystals come from Chinkuahshih mine in Taipeh Co.*

looks like marl or limestone

massive, creamy white alunite

SECTION SHOWN

COMPOSITION *Sulphate.*
CRYSTAL SYSTEM *Trigonal.*
CLEAVAGE/FRACTURE *Perfect/Conchoidal.*
LUSTRE/STREAK *Vitreous, pearly on some faces/White.*
HARDNESS/DENSITY *3.5–4 / 2.6–2.9.*
KEY PROPERTIES *Does not fizz in dilute HCl like calcite (p.150).*

Glauconite

$(K,Na)(Fe^{3+},Al,Mg_2)(Si,Al)_4O_{10}(OH)_2$

Bluish or yellowish green glauconite normally occurs as flakes, grains, pellets, or massive aggregates. Formed from iron-bearing micas and clays that are present in marine sediments rich in organic matter, glauconite is found disseminated in impure limestones, siltstones, and sandstones. Greensand rocks are particularly rich in this mineral.

FAMILIAR *to artists as the pigment 'green earth', glauconite was once quarried in these hills by Verona, Italy.*

rich bluish green mass

dull lustre

COMPOSITION *Silicate, mica group.*
CRYSTAL SYSTEM *Monoclinic.*
CLEAVAGE/FRACTURE *Perfect, micaceous/Not seen.*
LUSTRE/STREAK *Dull or glistening/Green.*
HARDNESS/DENSITY *2 / 2.4–2.95.*
KEY PROPERTIES *A flaky green mineral that is found in sedimentary rocks.*

Chamosite

$(Fe,Al,Mg)_6(Si,Al)_4O_{10}(OH)_8$

Often resembling glauconite in appearance, chamosite tends to be more yellowish or brownish green. It occurs as ooliths (grains composed of minute radiating crystals) and as scaly, foliated, or granular masses. Chamosite is a common constituent of ironstones formed from marine sediments rich in organic matter. It readily alters to orange-brown goethite.

LOCAL *chamosite oolite makes an attractive building stone in the area around Banbury, Oxfordshire, England.*

brownish green

fossilized shell fragment

tiny green chamosite ooliths

COMPOSITION *Silicate, chlorite group.*
CRYSTAL SYSTEM *Monoclinic.*
CLEAVAGE/FRACTURE *Perfect/Unknown.*
LUSTRE/STREAK *Pearly/Green to grey.*
HARDNESS/DENSITY *2–3 / 3.0–3.4.*
KEY PROPERTIES *Brownish green chlorite found in sedimentary ironstones.*

Epsomite

$MgSO_4 \cdot 7H_2O$

Epsom salts is the more familiar name for this hydrated magnesium sulphate mineral. Epsomite is colourless, white, pale pink, or green; its crystals are prismatic, but rarely seen. Usually, it occurs as crusts, powdery or woolly coatings, or as botryoidal or reniform masses. Epsomite is found in evaporite deposits and coats the walls of mine workings and caverns in dolomite and in dolomitic limestone.

EPSOMITE *is dissolved in salt lakes; it may be deposited along their shorelines during the dry summer season.*

SECTION SHOWN

powdery mass

woolly mass of fibrous crystals

powdery when dehydrated

COMPOSITION *Sulphate.*
CRYSTAL SYSTEM *Orthorhombic.*
CLEAVAGE/FRACTURE *Perfect/Conchoidal.*
LUSTRE/STREAK *Vitreous or silky/White.*
HARDNESS/DENSITY *2–2.5 / 1.68.*
KEY PROPERTIES *Dehydrates to form white powder in dry air; dissolves easily in water.*

Halite

NaCl

Culinary rock salt is actually a mineral called halite. Most halite is colourless, white, grey, orange, or brown, but it can be bright blue or purple. It usually occurs as cubic crystals and granular, compact, or coarse crystalline masses. Halite is found in evaporite deposits that form by the evaporation of salt pans and land-locked seas.

JAGGED *deposits of halite form the curious Devil's Golf Course in Death Valley, California, USA.*

orange crystalline mass

brown granular halite

colourless cubic crystals

COMPOSITION *Halide.*
CRYSTAL SYSTEM *Cubic.*
CLEAVAGE/FRACTURE *Perfect, cubic/Conchoidal.*
LUSTRE/STREAK *Vitreous/White.*
HARDNESS/DENSITY *2–2.5 / 2.17.*
KEY PROPERTIES *Brittle and water-soluble; feels greasy in a damp atmosphere.*

Sylvite

KCl

SYLVITE *is extracted from thick evaporite deposits in this potash mine in New Mexico, USA.*

Sylvite is usually colourless or white, but may be coloured by impurities. Crystals are cubic, octahedral, or combinations of these forms, but crusts and columnar, granular, or massive aggregates are more common. It is found in thick beds mixed or interbedded with halite and other evaporite minerals. It also forms in volcanic fumaroles and caves. Sylvite is very water-soluble and needs protection from moisture in the air.

octahedral face

pinkish tint

rare well-formed crystals

COMPOSITION *Halide.*
CRYSTAL SYSTEM *Cubic.*
CLEAVAGE/FRACTURE *Perfect, cubic/Uneven.*
LUSTRE/STREAK *Vitreous/White.*
HARDNESS/DENSITY *2 / 1.99.*
KEY PROPERTIES *Water-soluble but not brittle; fragments turn wax-like when crushed.*

Glauberite

$Na_2Ca(SO_4)_2$

ABUNDANT *glauberite and gypsum are formed in the mud flats of Death Valley, California, USA.*

Glauberite crystals are steep tabular or pyramidal, and may have rounded edges. Often they turn out to be pseudomorphs where glauberite has been replaced by another mineral, such as calcite or gypsum. Glauberite is colourless, pale yellow, or grey, and the surface may alter to white, powdery sodium sulphate. It forms mainly in evaporite deposits and in volcanic fumeroles.

crystals in the shape of glauberite

transparent and colourless

GLAUBERITE PSEUDOMORPH

pointed tabular crystals

COMPOSITION *Sulphate.*
CRYSTAL SYSTEM *Monoclinic.*
CLEAVAGE/FRACTURE *Perfect/Conchoidal.*
LUSTRE/STREAK *Vitreous to waxy; pearly on cleavages/White.*
HARDNESS/DENSITY *2.5–3 / 2.75–2.85.*
KEY PROPERTIES *Water-soluble, crystals are commonly replaced by other minerals.*

Gypsum

$CaSO_4 \cdot 2H_2O$

Many people call gypsum selenite, a name more correctly used for the transparent variety. This mineral is colourless or white, or tinted other colours by impurities. Crystals are tabular, lens-shaped, or prismatic. Fish-tail or swallow-tail contact twins are common. When gypsum occurs in closely packed, parallel fibrous crystal it is known as satin spar, but when it is compact and fine-grained, it is alabaster. Most gypsum forms in marine evaporite deposits, associated with anhydrite and halite. It is found as crystals and rosette-shaped aggregates in sands and clays, and occurs in volcanic fumeroles and in altered sulphide ore deposits.

THIS *extraordinary curled 'ram's horn' crystal of gypsum is in a cave in Mexico.*

tabular crystal

radiating crystals

inclusion of clay

packed full of sand grains

curved, lens-shaped crystals

DESERT ROSE

pearly lustre

swallow-tail twin

parallel fibrous crystals

SATIN SPAR

colourless, translucent

COMPOSITION	*Sulphate.*

COMPOSITION *Sulphate.*
CRYSTAL SYSTEM *Monoclinic.*
CLEAVAGE/FRACTURE *Perfect/Splintery.*
LUSTRE/STREAK *Subvitreous or pearly/White.*
HARDNESS/DENSITY *2 / 2.32.*
KEY PROPERTIES *Very common, easily scratched, does not fizz in dilute HCl.*

NOTE

Desert rose is the name given to rosette-shaped clusters of rounded gypsum crystals that form in desert sands, incorporating sand grains as they grow. They are common in Algeria and Tunisia. Baryte (p.155) also forms sand crystals which are more dense. Those of calcite (p.150) are rhombohedral and easy to distinguish.

Anhydrite

CaSO₄

Less common than gypsum, anhydrite is colourless, pale blue, violet, white, grey, pink, or brown. Crystals are tabular or equant, or in granular, fibrous, or massive aggregates. It is an important constituent of evaporite deposits and often forms by the dehydration of gypsum. Anhydrite is often a constituent of cap rocks above salt domes that act as reservoirs for natural oil. It also occurs in volcanic fumaroles and in sea-floor hydrothermal 'chimneys'.

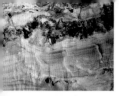

ANHYDRITE *is seen here mixed with gypsum in an evaporite deposit in Cyprus.*

pearly lustre

coarsely crystalline masses

perfect cleavage is nearly cubic

COMPOSITION *Sulphate.*
CRYSTAL SYSTEM *Orthorhombic.*
CLEAVAGE/FRACTURE *Perfect, nearly cubic/Uneven to splintery.*
LUSTRE/STREAK *Pearly or vitreous to greasy/White to pale grey.*
HARDNESS/DENSITY *3–3.5 / 2.98.*
KEY PROPERTIES *Harder than gypsum (p.173).*

Borax

Na₂B₄O₅(OH)₄·8H₂O

A hydrated sodium borate, borax is an important source of boron for industry. It occurs as flattened prismatic crystals or as massive aggregates, and is colourless, white, grey, pale green, or pale blue. Because borax is water-soluble, it is only found in arid regions of the world. It forms where water – enriched in boron from local volcanic activity – has evaporated from inland lakes. Borax readily dehydrates in air, turning to chalky white tincalconite.

BORAX *is mined from evaporite deposits at Death Valley, California, USA.*

flattened crystals

broken crystal shows transparent borax

coating of white tincalconite

dull on surface

COMPOSITION *Borate.*
CRYSTAL SYSTEM *Monoclinic.*
CLEAVAGE/FRACTURE *Perfect/Conchoidal.*
LUSTRE/STREAK *Vitreous to resinous or earthy/White.*
HARDNESS/DENSITY *2–2.5 / 1.71.*
KEY PROPERTIES *Water-soluble; dehydrates, turning powdery white.*

Colemanite

CaB$_3$O$_4$(OH)$_3$·H$_2$O

An important source of boron, colemanite is colourless, white, yellowish white, or grey and occurs as short prismatic or equant crystals, in nodules, or as granular or coarse massive aggregates. It forms by alteration of borax and ulexite in playa lake deposits in arid regions. Fine crystals come from California, USA, and large deposits occur in Turkey.

SPOIL *heaps mark the borate mines at Death Valley, California, USA; colemanite is mined here.*

vitreous lustre

transparent crystals

equant habit

COMPOSITION *Borate.*
CRYSTAL SYSTEM *Monoclinic.*
CLEAVAGE/FRACTURE *Perfect/Uneven to subconchoidal.*
LUSTRE/STREAK *Vitreous to adamantine/White.*
HARDNESS/DENSITY *4.5 / 2.42.*
KEY PROPERTIES *Harder than other borate minerals except boracite (Mg$_3$B$_7$O$_{13}$Cl).*

Ulexite

NaCaB$_5$O$_6$(OH)$_6$·5H$_2$O

A borate mineral with a number of curious habits, ulexite is colourless or white and is found in cotton wool-like masses, and in dense veins of parallel fibres. These behave like natural fibre-optics, transmitting light from one end of the crystals to the other. It also occurs in radiating or compact aggregates of crystals. Ulexite occurs with colemanite and borax in playa lake deposits.

THE UYUNI *salt flats near Potosí, Bolivia are an important commercial source of ulexite.*

natural fibreoptics

silky lustre

transmits light through crystal

mass of parallel fibres

COMPOSITION *Borate.*
CRYSTAL SYSTEM *Triclinic.*
CLEAVAGE/FRACTURE *Perfect/Uneven.*
LUSTRE/STREAK *Vitreous, silky or satiny/White.*
HARDNESS/DENSITY *2.5 / 1.95.*
KEY PROPERTIES *Slightly water-soluble; less dense than satin spar gypsum (p.173).*

usually colourless or white

Cryolite

Na_3AlF_6

Cryolite is usually colourless or white. It occurs rarely as nearly cubic crystals and most commonly as coarse granular or massive aggregates. The only major deposits were at Ivigtut, Greenland, where it occurred in layers and veins in pegmatites and granites. These were used as a flux for aluminium smelting but now synthetic cryolite is used instead.

CRYOLITE *forms crystalline masses with sphalerite and siderite (shown here), and other sulphides and halides.*

cleavage-like partings

nearly cubic crystals

brown siderite

rather greasy lustre

COMPOSITION *Halide.*
CRYSTAL SYSTEM *Monoclinic.*
CLEAVAGE/FRACTURE *Partings/Uneven.*
LUSTRE/STREAK *Vitreous to greasy; pearly on certain faces/White.*
HARDNESS/DENSITY *2.5 / 2.97.*
KEY PROPERTIES *Seems to disappear when in water as its refractive index is close to water.*

Amblygonite-montebrasite

$LiAl(PO_4)(F,OH)$ amblygonite - $LiAl(PO_4)(OH,F)$

In amblygonite, fluorine is more abundant than hydroxyl. The opposite is true in montebrasite at the other end of this compositional series. Both can be white or pale coloured. Blocky, poorly formed crystals are uncommon, coarse crystalline masses being more typical. These minerals occur in granite pegmatites.

AMBLYGONITE *and montebrasite are found in the Black Hills of South Dakota, USA.*

transparent yellow crystal fragment

massive, white

COMPOSITION *Phosphates.*
CRYSTAL SYSTEM *Triclinic.*
CLEAVAGE/FRACTURE *Perfect to distinct/Uneven to subconchoidal.*
LUSTRE/STREAK *Vitreous; pearly on cleavages/White.*
HARDNESS/DENSITY *5.5–6 / 2.98–3.11.*
KEY PROPERTIES *Four cleavage directions.*

Spessartine

$Mn_3^{2+}Al_2(SiO_4)_3$

This manganese-bearing garnet is orange, red, brown, or black. Crystals are dodecahedral or trapezohedral, or in granular or massive aggregates. Fine gem spessartine comes from granite pegmatites. It also occurs in granites, rhyolites, and metasomatic deposits.

THIS MINERAL *is associated with galena and other manganese minerals in metasomatic ore deposits.*

uneven fracture

vitreous lustre

dodecahedral crystal

cut facets

SPESSARTINE GEMSTONE

cabochon

SPESSARTINE GEMSTONE

COMPOSITION *Silicate, garnet group.*
CRYSTAL SYSTEM *Cubic.*
CLEAVAGE/FRACTURE *None/Uneven to conchoidal.*
LUSTRE/STREAK *Vitreous/White.*
HARDNESS/DENSITY *7–7.5 / 4.19.*
KEY PROPERTIES *Brownish red dodecahedral crystals without cleavage.*

Petalite

$LiAlSi_4O_{10}$

Petalite is colourless, white, grey, yellow, or pale pink and usually occurs as coarse cleavable masses or massive aggregates. Rare crystals are tabular or rather elongate. Petalite is found in granite pegmatites. It is a minor ore of lithium, and irregular crystals of colourless petalite from Minas Gerais, Brazil are cut as gemstones.

THE FIRST *petalite specimens came from Utö, Sweden.*

coarse cleavable mass

SECTION SHOWN

COMPOSITION *Silicate.*
CRYSTAL SYSTEM *Monoclinic.*
CLEAVAGE/FRACTURE *Perfect/Subconchoidal.*
LUSTRE/STREAK *Vitreous; pearly/White.*
HARDNESS/DENSITY *6.5 / 2.41–2.42.*
KEY PROPERTIES *Single perfect cleavage unlike quartz (pp.143–44) or feldspars.*

Topaz

$Al_2SiO_4(F,OH)_2$

SMALL *but beautifully formed topaz crystals come from the rounded granite hills of the Mourne Mountains in Northern Ireland.*

Most topaz is colourless or pale blue, but it is the yellow to orange-brown gemmy crystals from Minas Gerais in Brazil that are better known. Other colours include brown, pink, and red. Inferior-coloured gemstones may be irradiated and/or heat-treated to turn them pink or sky blue. Topaz crystals are short or long prismatic, with wedge-shaped terminations, or they form columnar, granular, or massive aggregates. Topaz is a hydrothermal mineral normally found in granites, granite pegmatites, and rhyolites, in detrital deposits and, occasionally, in high grade metamorphic rocks.

orange-brown colour

typical wedge-shaped termination

transparent crystal with vitreous lustre

platy, transparent albite feldspar

blue and colourless waterworn pebbles

cut faces

COLOURLESS GEMSTONE

natural colour

YELLOW GEMSTONE

COMPOSITION *Silicate.*
CRYSTAL SYSTEM *Orthorhombic.*
CLEAVAGE/FRACTURE *Single perfect/Subconchoidal or uneven.*
LUSTRE/STREAK *Vitreous/White.*
HARDNESS/DENSITY 8 / 3.49–3.57.
KEY PROPERTIES *Basal cleavage plane often visible inside crystals and waterworn pebbles.*

NOTE

For a mineral to be classed as a gemstone it has to be beautiful, durable, and rare. When gem-bearing rocks, such as pegmatites (p.46), are broken down over time in streams and rivers, topaz and other durable minerals may accumulate in gem gravels. Waterworn crystals can be cut to make fine gemstones.

Beryl

$Be_3Al_2Si_6O_{18}$

Two beautiful gem varieties of the mineral beryl are intense green emerald, coloured by trace chromium, and sea green to sky blue aquamarine, which contains trace iron. Others include pink morganite, yellow heliodor, colourless goshenite, and a raspberry red, manganese-bearing beryl from the Wah Wah Mountains of Utah, USA. Common beryl is usually pale green or white. This mineral occurs as hexagonal prismatic or tabular crystals with flat or pyramidal terminations, or as massive, columnar or granular aggregates. Most beryl is found in granites, granite pegmatites, and rhyolites, but can occur in metamorphic rocks such as schists.

PEGMATITES *from the North West Frontier province of Pakistan yield exceptional aquamarine and morganite crystals.*

aquamarine gemstone

emerald gemstone

typical oblong cut stone

mass of hexagonal crystals

transparent sky blue

iron-stained coating

AQUAMARINE

nearly opaque crystal

rich green colour

pink and tabular

pyramidal termination

COMMON BERYL

EMERALD

MORGANITE

HELIODOR

COMPOSITION *Silicate.* **CRYSTAL SYSTEM** *Hexagonal.* **CLEAVAGE/FRACTURE** *Imperfect/Conchoidal to uneven.* **LUSTRE/STREAK** *Vitreous or resinous/White.* **HARDNESS/DENSITY** *7.5–8 / 2.62–2.97.* **KEY PROPERTIES** *Forms hexagonal crystals like apatite (p.157) but is much harder.*	**NOTE** *The most important sources of emerald are in the Andes, in an area of Colombia, north of Bogotá. Unusually, Colombian emerald is hydrothermal and hosted in sedimentary limestones (p.32) and shales (p.31). Unflawed natural emerald is rare and very valuable. Inexpensive, gem-quality 'emerald' is usually synthetic.*

Euclase

BeAlSiO$_4$(OH)

Beryllium-bearing euclase is usually light or dark green or blue, but it can also be colourless or white. It is found as prismatic crystals with slanted terminations. This attractive gem mineral forms by the alteration of beryl in pegmatites, and is found in alpine veins. Exquisite colourless and blue colour-zoned crystals come from Karoi in Zimbabwe.

EUCLASE *was first discovered at Ouro Preto in Minas Gerais, Brazil, better known for its topaz crystals.*

colourless prismatic crystal

rich blue colour

altered pegmatite

perfect cleavage

COMPOSITION *Silicate.*
CRYSTAL SYSTEM *Monoclinic.*
CLEAVAGE/FRACTURE *Perfect/Conchoidal.*
LUSTRE/STREAK *Vitreous, pearly on cleavages/White.*
HARDNESS/DENSITY *7.5 / 2.99–3.10.*
KEY PROPERTIES *Crystal shape; cleavage differs from topaz (p.178).*

Schorl

NaFe$^{2+}_3$Al$_6$(BO$_3$)$_3$Si$_6$O$_{18}$(OH)$_4$

Schorl is black and like other tourmalines, forms six-sided prismatic crystals, with alternate narrow and wide faces, giving a roughly triangular cross-section. Acicular and fibrous crystals and massive aggregates are also found. Schorl occurs mainly in granites and granite pegmatites, and in high-temperature hydrothermal veins.

GRANITE *and pink orthoclase make up a tourmalinized granite named luxullianite, after a village in Cornwall, England.*

short prismatic crystal

striations are common

always black

massive habit

COMPOSITION *Silicate, tourmaline group.*
CRYSTAL SYSTEM *Trigonal.*
CLEAVAGE/FRACTURE *None/Uneven to conchoidal.*
LUSTRE/STREAK *Vitreous to resinous/White.*
HARDNESS/DENSITY *7 / 3.18–3.22.*
KEY PROPERTIES *Black and, unlike amphiboles and pyroxenes, has no cleavage.*

Elbaite

$Na(Al_{1.5}Li_{1.5})Al_6(BO_3)Si_6O_{18}(OH)_4$

Tourmalines are gem minerals renowned for their beautiful colours. Pink tourmaline is the variety rubellite; when blue, it is indicolite, and when colourless, it is achroite. Elbaite can be all these colours, and green, yellow, or orange too. It can even have zones of different colours within a single crystal. The forms and habits of elbaite are like those of schorl. Elbaite is found in granites and granite pegmatites, and also occurs in high-temperature hydrothermal veins and certain metamorphic rocks.

THE ISLAND of Elba, Italy, gave its name to the mineral elbaite, discovered in granite quarries on the island.

BICOLOURED ELBAITE GEMSTONE

green outside

pink in the middle

WATERMELON TOURMALINE

rich pink colour

BLUE INDICOLITE GEMSTONE

triangular cross-section

RUBELLITE

yellow colour

YELLOW ELBAITE GEMSTONE

pink crystal is green at base

SECTION SHOWN

pegmatite matrix

vitreous lustre

COMPOSITION Silicate, tourmaline group.
CRYSTAL SYSTEM Trigonal.
CLEAVAGE/FRACTURE None/Uneven to conchoidal.
LUSTRE/STREAK Vitreous to resinous/White.
HARDNESS/DENSITY 7 / 2.90–3.10.
KEY PROPERTIES Distinctive crystal shape, lack of cleavage, and possible colour zoning.

NOTE

Tourmaline crystals are pyroelectric, which means that when the crystals are heated, the ends of a crystal develop opposite electrical charges. This will attract dust and is the reason why elbaite gemstones that are left in a warm shop window or display case, develop a dirty halo over time.

Lepidolite

Light-coloured lithium-bearing mica

LOOK *for the geological hammer to gauge the size of these rosettes of lepidolite in a pegmatite outcrop in South Dakota, USA.*

Pale-coloured micas containing substantial lithium are called lepidolite. They are usually violet-pink and form hexagonal cleavable crystals and coarse to fine-grained masses. Lepidolite is found in granite pegmatites with elbaite tourmaline, spodumene, and amblygonite. Excellent crystals and unusual botryoidal aggregates come from Minas Gerais, Brazil.

violet-pink in colour

botryoidal habit

hexagonal crystals

COMPOSITION *Silicate, mica group.*
CRYSTAL SYSTEM *Monoclinic.*
CLEAVAGE/FRACTURE *Perfect, micaceous/None.*
LUSTRE/STREAK *Pearly or vitreous/Colourless.*
HARDNESS/DENSITY *2.5–4 / 2.80–2.90.*
KEY PROPERTIES *Pink mica that splits into paper-thin flexible sheets.*

Zinnwaldite

Dark-coloured lithium-bearing mica

ZINNWALDITE *is one of a large number of minerals to come from the tin-bearing granites at Greifenstein, Saxony, Germany.*

Any dark-coloured mica that contains lithium is known as zinnwaldite. The colour is typically brown or greyish brown, and crystals are six-sided with a perfect micaceous cleavage. These can form rosettes or fan-like groups, or lamellar or scaly masses. Zinnwaldite is found in greisens, granite pegmatites, and associated high-temperature hydrothermal veins.

split into thin sheets

pearly lustre

COMPOSITION *Silicate, mica group.*
CRYSTAL SYSTEM *Monoclinic.*
CLEAVAGE/FRACTURE *Perfect, micaceous/None.*
LUSTRE/STREAK *Vitreous or pearly/Colourless.*
HARDNESS/DENSITY *2.5–4 / 2.90–3.02.*
KEY PROPERTIES *Chemical analysis distinguishes it from other darker micas.*

Spodumene

$LiAlSi_2O_6$

Two varieties of spodumene are cut as gemstones. Rare hiddenite is light emerald green. More abundant is lilac or pink kunzite, which often occurs as superb transparent crystals. Most spodumene is not so gem-like but is still valued, as the main ore of lithium. Typically colourless, light green, pinkish brown, and other pale colours, it may fluoresce yellow, orange, or pink under UV light. Crystals are prismatic, usually flattened and striated along the length, or in massive aggregates. This pyroxene mineral comes mainly from granite pegmatites where it can form crystals several metres long. More rarely, it occurs in aplites and gneisses.

HUNDREDS *of tons of spodumene were extracted from a pegmatite at the Harding mine in New Mexico, USA.*

HIDDENITE

light green hiddenite gemstone

flattened prismatic crystals

deep striations

appears opaque

NOTE

Kunzite crystals may be deep violet, violet, or colourless, depending on the angle from which the crystal is viewed. This property is called pleochroism.

pink kunzite gemstone

crystal with subconchoidal fracture

KUNZITE

COMPOSITION *Silicate, pyroxene group.*
CRYSTAL SYSTEM *Monoclinic.*
CLEAVAGE/FRACTURE *Good, crossing at about 90°/Uneven or subconchoidal.*
LUSTRE/STREAK *Vitreous; pearly on cleavage/White.*
HARDNESS/DENSITY *6.5–7 / 3.03–3.23.*
KEY PROPERTIES *Often pleochroic.*

Astrophyllite

$$(K,Na)_3(Fe^{2+},Mn)_7Ti_2Si_8O_{24}(O,OH)_7$$

At first, the lustrous yellow, brown, or reddish brown crystals of astrophyllite may look like mica. They are tabular, bladed, or acicular with a perfect basal cleavage, often grouped in radiating star-like clusters. Astrophyllite forms mainly in nepheline syenites, alkaline granites, and their pegmatites. More rarely it occurs in gneisses and metasomatic deposits.

STAR-SHAPED *astrophyllite aggregates are found at various locations in the area around Pike's Peak, Colorado, USA.*

radiating reddish brown crystals

submetallic lustre

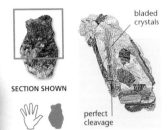

SECTION SHOWN

bladed crystals

perfect cleavage

COMPOSITION *Silicate.*
CRYSTAL SYSTEM *Triclinic.*
CLEAVAGE/FRACTURE *Perfect/Uneven.*
LUSTRE/STREAK *Submetallic, pearly, or greasy/Golden yellow.*
HARDNESS/DENSITY *3 / 3.2–3.4.*
KEY PROPERTIES *Brittle, mica-like mineral, often in star-shaped crystal groups.*

Eudialyte

$$Na_{15}(Ca,Ce)_2(Fe^{2+},Mn^{2+})ZrSi_8O_{22}(OH,Cl)_2$$

Eudialyte is best known as a deep pink mineral, but it can also be brown or yellow. It is usually found as irregular masses, more rarely as stubby or long prismatic crystals. Eudialyte is an important constituent of many nepheline syenites, alkaline granites, and their pegmatites.

IMPORTANT *localities for eudialyte include Mount St Hilaire, Canada, and the Ilimaussaq intrusion, Greenland.*

stubby crystals

dull pink, massive aggregates

black arfvedsonite

COMPOSITION *Silicate.*
CRYSTAL SYSTEM *Hexagonal.*
CLEAVAGE/FRACTURE *Perfect/Uneven.*
LUSTRE/STREAK *Vitreous to dull/White.*
HARDNESS/DENSITY *5–6 / 2.74–3.10.*
KEY PROPERTIES *Pink mineral found in nepheline syenites (p. 49) and alkaline granitic rocks with the sodium amphibole arfvedsonite.*

Augite

$(Ca,Na)(Mg,Fe,Al,Ti)(Si,Al)_2O_6$

Augite is a clinopyroxene and is dark green, black, or brown. Typical crystals are short prismatic with a square or octagonal cross-section, but augite can also be granular or massive. Augite is an essential component of basalts and gabbros, and is common in pyroxenites and other basic and ultrabasic igneous rocks. It also occurs in intermediate rocks, such as andesite.

DARK *augite crystals and pale labradorite in a gabbro pegmatite at Manacle Point on the Lizard Peninsula in Cornwall, England.*

good cleavages at right angles

dark coloured and nearly opaque

volcanic tuff

resinous brown crystal

COMPOSITION *Silicate, pyroxene group.*
CRYSTAL SYSTEM *Monoclinic.*
CLEAVAGE/FRACTURE *Good; crossing at about 90°/Uneven to conchoidal.*
LUSTRE/STREAK *Vitreous, resinous, or dull/Grey-green.*
HARDNESS/DENSITY *5.5–6 / 3.19–3.56.*
KEY PROPERTIES *Dark colour; cleavage.*

Pyrope

$Mg_3Al_2(SiO_4)_3$

Pyrope is magnesium aluminium garnet. The rich red colour may have a purple, pink, or orange tinge, or tend to black. Crystals are normally dodecahedral, trapezohedral, or form granular or massive aggregates. Unlike other garnets, pyrope is most common as a mineral of ultrabasic igneous rocks, such as eclogites and diamond-bearing kimberlites, and detrital deposits derived from them.

KIMBERLITE, *from diamond mines in South Africa, contains pyrope garnets, as well as diamonds.*

gem-like rounded grains

SECTION SHOWN

rich red colour

conchoidal fracture

COMPOSITION *Orthosilicate, garnet group.*
CRYSTAL SYSTEM *Cubic.*
CLEAVAGE/FRACTURE *None/Conchoidal.*
LUSTRE/STREAK *Vitreous lustre/White.*
HARDNESS/DENSITY *7–7.5 / 3.58.*
KEY PROPERTIES *Dodecahedral crystals that may be easily confused with almandine (p.207) and other garnets.*

Diamond

C

GRAVEL-FILLED *potholes at the Kleinsee diamond diggings, South Africa, are a source of alluvial diamonds.*

Not only is diamond remarkably hard and durable, it can also show great beauty in the form of 'fire', where light reflected inside a gemstone is split into its spectral colours. Crystals are octahedral or cubic, often with curved faces. Only the most flawless, colourless crystals and those rare and valuable stones with a clear colour are cut as gemstones. Fancy diamonds can be golden-yellow, blue, pink, red, green, orange, and violet. Most diamonds are yellow or brown and is used as an industrial abrasive, as are dark irregular masses called boart or bort, and fine-grained black carbonado. Diamond comes from kimberlites and lamproites, and because it is so durable, it is also obtained from placer deposits such as river and beach sands.

OCTAHEDRAL CRYSTAL

cubic crystal with adamantine lustre

CUBIC CRYSTAL

SECTION SHOWN

weathered kimberlite

curved face on an octahedral crystal

COLOURLESS GEMSTONE

GREY-GREEN GEMSTONE

YELLOW GEMSTONE

NOTE

Diamond and graphite (p.216) are both composed of carbon atoms. In diamond, they are evenly distributed and bonded closely together, making it the hardest of minerals. In graphite, they are arranged in layers, with strong bonds across layers but weak ones between layers. This makes graphite soft and slippery.

COMPOSITION *Element.*
CRYSTAL SYSTEM *Cubic.*
CLEAVAGE/FRACTURE *Perfect/Conchoidal.*
LUSTRE/STREAK *Adamantine to greasy/White.*
HARDNESS/DENSITY *10 / 3.51.*
KEY PROPERTIES *Brilliant adamantine lustre and extreme hardness are distinctive.*

Nepheline

(Na,K)AlSiO₄

Nepheline is an important rock-forming mineral but is not always easily identified. Crystals are prismatic but rarely well-formed and this mineral usually occurs as grains or massive aggregates. It is colourless, white, grey, yellow, or brown, often with a distinctly greasy lustre. Nepheline is a feldspathoid mineral that forms in silica-poor, alkaline rocks. It is also found in sodium-rich basalts and tuffs.

THE LARGE *pale-coloured crystals seen here are nepheline in a syenite at Spitskop, South Africa.*

massive habit

translucent with a vitreous lustre

CRYSTALS

COMPOSITION *Silicate.*
CRYSTAL SYSTEM *Hexagonal.*
CLEAVAGE/FRACTURE *Poor/Subconchoidal.*
LUSTRE/STREAK *Greasy or vitreous/White.*
HARDNESS *5.5–6.*
DENSITY *2.55–2.66.*
KEY PROPERTIES *Often has greasy lustre; never found with quartz (p.143).*

Sodalite

Na₈Al₆Si₆O₂₄Cl₂

Sodalite is nearly always massive or in disseminated grains so dodecahedral crystals are rarely seen. Blue sodalite is a popular decorative stone, but this mineral can also be colourless, grey, pink, and other pale shades. It fluoresces bright orange under UV light. Sodalite is a feldspathoid and occurs in alkaline igneous rocks, debris ejected from volcanoes, and in metasomatized calcareous rocks.

WHITE *dodecahedral crystals of sodalite occur in limestone blocks ejected from Mount Vesuvius, Italy.*

round polished surface

slightly greasy lustre

SODALITE CABOCHON

COMPOSITION *Silicate.*
CRYSTAL SYSTEM *Cubic.*
CLEAVAGE/FRACTURE *Poor/Uneven or conchoidal.*
LUSTRE/STREAK *Vitreous or greasy/White.*
HARDNESS/DENSITY *5.5–6 / 2.27–2.33.*
KEY PROPERTIES *Fluoresces orange; lacks lazurite's bright blue streak (p.215).*

typical massive sodalite

Haüyne

$Na_6Ca_2Al_6Si_6O_{24}(SO_4)_2$

Haüyne, pronounced 'how-een', is usually bright blue. It may fluoresce orange or pink under longwave UV light. Crystals are dodecahedral or octahedral but are relatively uncommon. Mostly haüyne occurs as irregular rounded grains and crystalline masses. It is a feldspathoid, and occurs in phonolites and other leucite- or nepheline-rich igneous rocks.

VIVID *blue grains of haüyne can be seen in this lava block taken from Laacher See, Eifel district, Germany.*

translucent blue grains

irregular shape

SECTION SHOWN

COMPOSITION *Silicate.*
CRYSTAL SYSTEM *Cubic.*
CLEAVAGE/FRACTURE *Distinct/Uneven to conchoidal.*
LUSTRE/STREAK *Vitreous or greasy/White or bluish white.*
HARDNESS/DENSITY *5.5–6 / 2.44–2.50.*
KEY PROPERTIES *Colour and fluorescence.*

Nosean

$Na_8Al_6Si_6O_{24}(SO_4).H_2O$

Nosean is also a feldspathoid and is colourless, white, grey, greyish brown, or blue. Crystals are rarely more than a few millimetres across and are dodecahedral or twinned with six-sided prisms. Disseminated crystals or grains are found in phonolites and related volcanic rocks that are low in silica, and in some volcanic bombs.

AMONG *the richest sources of nosean are the ancient volcanoes of the Eifel district, Germany.*

glassy sanidine feldspar

SECTION SHOWN

tiny crystals in cavity

COMPOSITION *Silicate.*
CRYSTAL SYSTEM *Cubic.*
CLEAVAGE/FRACTURE *Indistinct/Uneven to conchoidal.*
LUSTRE/STREAK *Vitreous/White.*
HARDNESS/DENSITY *5.5 / 2.30–2.40.*
KEY PROPERTIES *Crystal shape and lack of fluorescence under UV.*

Leucite

KALSi$_2$O$_6$

Leucite is colourless, white, or grey. At high temperatures, it is cubic and forms trapezohedral crystals. This form is preserved as the mineral cools and develops tetragonal symmetry. Good crystals are common; leucite is found more rarely as disseminated grains. A zeolite, leucite is a constituent of potassium-rich and silica-poor basic lavas, and sometimes makes up nearly the entire rock composition.

EXCELLENT *crystals come from Mount Vesuvius and Monte Somma, Italy.*

trapezohedral crystal

COMPOSITION *Silicate, zeolite group.*
CRYSTAL SYSTEM *Tetragonal (pseudocubic).*
CLEAVAGE/FRACTURE *Poor/Conchoidal.*
LUSTRE/STREAK *Vitreous/White.*
HARDNESS/DENSITY *5.5–6 / 2.45–2.50.*
KEY PROPERTIES *Trapezohedral crystals disseminated in rock.*

more crystals scattered through rock

basalt matrix

Analcime

NaAlSi$_2$O$_6$·H$_2$O

Like leucite, analcime is usually found as colourless, white, or grey trapezohedral crystals. It can also be pink, pale green, or yellow, and form granular or compact aggregates. Analcime is a zeolite that forms by hydrothermal alteration in joints and vesicles in silica-poor basic and intermediate igneous rocks.

DISTINCTIVE *crystals of analcime occur in altered igneous rocks of Cornwall, England.*

white translucent crystal

colourless analcime

COMPOSITION *Silicate, zeolite group.*
CRYSTAL SYSTEM *Cubic, tetragonal, orthorhombic, or monoclinic (pseudocubic).*
CLEAVAGE/FRACTURE *None/Conchoidal.*
LUSTRE/STREAK *Vitreous/White.*
HARDNESS/DENSITY *5–5.5 / 2.24–2.29.*
KEY PROPERTIES *Trapezohedral crystals found in cavities and joints in rocks.*

coating joint in rock

Natrolite

Na₂[Al₂Si₃O₁₀]·2H₂O

$Na_2[Al_2Si_3O_{10}] \cdot 2H_2O$

Natrolite is colourless, white, pale yellow, or pink, and crystals are prismatic, usually with a square cross-section. They can form fibrous, granular, or compact aggregates. Natrolite is typically found with other zeolites in cavities in marine-deposited basalts and trachytes. It also occurs in altered syenites, aplites, and dolerites.

SODIUM-RICH *zeolite often occurs in pillow lavas, which are basalts deposited in sea water.*

gas bubble

prismatic crystals with calcite

crystals are square in section

vitreous lustre

COMPOSITION *Silicate, zeolite group.*
CRYSTAL SYSTEM *Orthorhombic.*
CLEAVAGE/FRACTURE *Perfect/Uneven.*
LUSTRE/STREAK *Vitreous to pearly/White.*
HARDNESS/DENSITY *5–5.5 / 2.20–2.26.*
KEY PROPERTIES *Looks like mesolite (below) and scolecite (right), but found in pillow lavas (p.63) and some intrusive rocks.*

Mesolite

Na₂Ca₂[Al₆Si₉O₃₀]·8H₂O

$Na_2Ca_2[Al_6Si_9O_{30}] \cdot 8H_2O$

Intermediate in composition between natrolite and scolecite, this zeolite mesolite forms as colourless, white, or pale-coloured slender prismatic or fibrous crystals. These can form tuffs, radiating aggregates, or compact masses. Most mesolite is found in cavities in basalts, where delicate glassy prisms can occur with stilbite, heulandite, and green apophyllite.

A FINE-GRAINED *mixture of mesolite and thomsonite found on Northern Ireland's Antrim coast, is known as antrimolite.*

SECTION SHOWN

hair-like crystal basalt

COMPOSITION *Silicate, zeolite group.*
CRYSTAL SYSTEM *Orthorhombic.*
CLEAVAGE/FRACTURE *Perfect/Uneven.*
LUSTRE/STREAK *Vitreous; silky if fibrous/White.*
HARDNESS *5*
DENSITY *2.26.*
KEY PROPERTIES *Square-sectioned crystals.*

Scolecite

$Ca[Al_2Si_3O_{10}]\cdot3H_2O$

Like natrolite and mesolite, scolecite occurs as a white or colourless acicular prismatic crystals. These are generally striated and are often V-shaped, rather than square, in cross-section, which is a result of twinning. They typically form radiating sprays, fibrous masses, or massive aggregates. Scolecite – a zeolite – is found mainly in cavities in basalts.

FINE *sprays of scolecite come from Tertiary basalts at Berufjördur, in Iceland but it has also been detected in other igneous rocks in Iceland.*

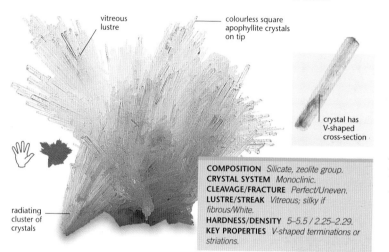

vitreous lustre

colourless square apophyllite crystals on tip

crystal has V-shaped cross-section

radiating cluster of crystals

COMPOSITION	*Silicate, zeolite group.*
CRYSTAL SYSTEM	*Monoclinic.*
CLEAVAGE/FRACTURE	*Perfect/Uneven.*
LUSTRE/STREAK	*Vitreous; silky if fibrous/White.*
HARDNESS/DENSITY	*5–5.5 / 2.25–2.29.*
KEY PROPERTIES	*V-shaped terminations or striations.*

Thomsonite

$Ca_2Na[Al_5Si_5O_{20}]\cdot6H_2O$

Thomsonite belongs to the zeolite group and is colourless, white, pink, yellow, or brown. Crystals are tabular, blocky, bladed, or radiating acicular. Globular, botryoidal, or massive aggregates are found and can have attractive concentric colour banding. Although most common in amygdaloidal basalts, thomsonite also occurs in some pegmatites and contact metamorphic rocks.

THOMSONITE *crystals from County Antrim, Northern Ireland, are typically tabular.*

acicular habit

tabular crystals

basalt

COMPOSITION	*Silicate, zeolite group.*
CRYSTAL SYSTEM	*Orthorhombic.*
CLEAVAGE/FRACTURE	*Perfect/Uneven or subconchoidal.*
LUSTRE/STREAK	*Vitreous lustre/White.*
HARDNESS/DENSITY	*5–5.5 / 2.23–2.39.*
KEY PROPERTIES	*Elongate crystals may be bladed.*

Heulandite

$(Ca_{0.5},Na,K)_9[Al_9Si_{27}O_{72}]\cdot\sim 24H_2O$ (heulandite-Ca)

Heulandite-Ca is the most common of four minerals called heulandite. All four look the same, forming coffin-shaped, tabular crystals and granular or massive aggregates. They are colourless, white, pink, red, yellow, or brown. Heulandite occurs with other zeolites and apophyllites in cavities in basalts and other volcanic rocks.

HEULANDITE *is found in cavities in basalt at Victoria Falls on the borders of Zimbabwe and Zambia.*

red crystals in basalt

crystal widest at centre

pearly lustre

COMPOSITION *Silicate, zeolite group.*
CRYSTAL SYSTEM *Monoclinic.*
CLEAVAGE/FRACTURE *Perfect/Subconchoidal to uneven.*
LUSTRE/STREAK *Vitreous, pearly/White.*
HARDNESS/DENSITY *3.5–4 / 2.10–2.20.*
KEY PROPERTIES *Elongate, coffin-shaped crystals, widest at centre.*

Stilbite

$(Ca_{0.5},Na,K)_9[Al_9Si_{27}O_{72}]\cdot 28H_2O$

Stilbite crystals are thin and tabular, but they often occur in distinctive wheatsheaf- or bow tie-shaped clusters, or in spherular aggregates. The crystals are colourless, white, pink, red, yellow, or brown. The two minerals of this name, stilbite-Na and stilbite-Ca, appear identical. Stilbite occurs with other zeolites in cavities in basalts, and andesites, and is found in some metamorphic and sedimentary rocks too.

FINE *crystals of stilbite come from the Bay of Fundy, Nova Scotia, Canada.*

bow tie clusters of crystals

pearly on cleavage

tabular crystal

COMPOSITION *Silicate, zeolite group.*
CRYSTAL SYSTEM *Monoclinic.*
CLEAVAGE/FRACTURE *Perfect/Uneven.*
LUSTRE/STREAK *Vitreous, pearly on cleavage/White.*
HARDNESS/DENSITY *3.5–4 / 2.19.*
KEY PROPERTIES *Wheatsheaf-, or bow tie shaped crystal clusters with a pearly lustre.*

Chabazite

$(Ca_{0.5},Na,K)_4[Al_4Si_8O_{24}]\cdot12H_2O$

Crystals of chabazite are normally rhombohedral, nearly cubic, or twins, which may be hexagonal and rounded. The crystals are colourless, white, yellow, pink, or red. Chabazite is now considered to be three minerals that look alike – chabazite-Ca, -K, and -Na. Like other zeolites, it occurs in cavities in basalts, andesites, and other volcanic rocks. It is also found in hydrothermal ore veins and bedded tuffs.

AMYGDULES in basalt lava flows of Quairang, Isle of Skye, Scotland, contain chabazite and other zeolites.

rhombohedron is nearly cubic

white translucent crystals

basalt

COMPOSITION Silicate, zeolite group.
CRYSTAL SYSTEM Trigonal.
CLEAVAGE/FRACTURE Distinct/Uneven.
LUSTRE/STREAK Vitreous/White.
HARDNESS/DENSITY 4–5 / 2.05–2.20.
KEY PROPERTIES Nearly cubic crystals that do not fizz in dilute HCl; found mainly in volcanic rocks.

Phillipsite

$(K,Na,Ca_{0.5},Ba_{0.5})_{4-7}[Al_{4-7}Si_{12-9}O_{32}]\cdot12H_2O$

Phillipsite, another zeolite, occurs as twinned prismatic crystals that often form spherular aggregates. It is usually colourless or white, but may be tinted yellow or red. The three minerals of this name, phillipsite-Ca, -K, -Na, are not distinguishable by eye. Most phillipsite is found with other zeolites in cavities in basalt, but it can also occur in some sedimentary deposits.

A FAMOUS locality for phillipsite is the Capo di Bove on the Appian Way near Rome, Italy.

vitreous lustre

tiny spherules

SECTION SHOWN

COMPOSITION Silicate, zeolite group.
CRYSTAL SYSTEM Monoclinic.
CLEAVAGE/FRACTURE Distinct/Uneven.
LUSTRE/STREAK Vitreous/White.
HARDNESS/DENSITY 4–4.5 / 2.20.
KEY PROPERTIES Spherular aggregates, but may resemble other zeolites in basalt (p.61).

Harmotome

$Ba_2(NaKCa_{0.5})(Al_5Si_{11}O_{32}) \cdot 12H_2O$

The barium zeolite harmotome is found as slightly elongate tabular crystals and simple or complex twins. It is normally colourless, white, or grey but may be tinted yellow or pink. Unlike other zeolites, it occurs more often in hydrothermal ore deposits than cavities in basalt and other volcanic rocks. Some of the finest crystals come from Strontian, Scotland, and the Harz Mountains, Germany.

WHITE *harmotome and purple amethyst line an amygdule from Idar Oberstein, Germany.*

vitreous lustre

thick tabular crystal

SECTION SHOWN

COMPOSITION *Silicate, zeolite group.*
CRYSTAL SYSTEM *Monoclinic.*
CLEAVAGE/FRACTURE *Distinct/Uneven to subconchoidal.*
LUSTRE/STREAK *Vitreous/White.*
HARDNESS/DENSITY *4.5 / 2.41–2.47.*
KEY PROPERTIES *Distinctive, blocky crystal shape.*

Laumontite

$Ca_4[Al_8Si_{16}O_{48}] \cdot 18H_2O$

Laumontite is a white, grey, pink, brown, or yellow zeolite. Crystals are square prisms with steep oblique terminations, but radiating fibrous or massive aggregates are more often seen. Laumontite is found in cavities in igneous rocks deposited by low-temperature hydrothermal solutions and can form thick sedimentary deposits.

FORMS *in the lavas of the Krafla volcano in Iceland, at relatively low temperatures of 100–230°C.*

crumbly dehydrated laumontite

steep oblique end

perfect cleavage

LEONHARDITE

COMPOSITION *Silicate, zeolite group.*
CRYSTAL SYSTEM *Monoclinic.*
CLEAVAGE/FRACTURE *Perfect/Uneven.*
LUSTRE/STREAK *Vitreous, pearly on cleavages, dull when dehydrated/White.*
HARDNESS/DENSITY *3–4 / 2.23–2.41.*
KEY PROPERTIES *Readily dehydrates to form the variety leonhardite.*

Apophyllite

$KCa_4Si_8O_{20}(F,OH)\cdot H_2O - KCa_4Si_8O_{20}(OH,F)\cdot H_2O$

An abundance of large transparent or translucent crystals, which are green, pink, colourless, or white, make apophyllite very popular with collectors. These are square-sided striated prisms with flat ends that may appear cubic, or can have steep pyramidal terminations. Apophyllite – a general name for minerals of the fluorapophyllite-hydroxyapophyllite series – is commonly found with zeolites in cavities in basalt.

APOPHYLLITE and a fine assemblage of zeolite minerals come from the volcanic cliffs of the Isle of Skye, Scotland.

pyramid

flat ends to crystals

square-sided crystal

pearly lustre

transparent with vitreous lustre

COMPOSITION Silicate.
CRYSTAL SYSTEM Tetragonal.
CLEAVAGE/FRACTURE Perfect/Uneven.
LUSTRE/STREAK Vitreous, pearly on some faces/White.
HARDNESS/DENSITY 4.5-5 / 2.33–2.37.
KEY PROPERTIES Large well-formed, square-sided crystals associated with zeolites.

Prehnite

$Ca_2Al_2Si_3O_{10}(OH)_2$

Crystals of prehnite are pale green, white, or yellow, and tabular or prismatic, but they are rarely seen. Usually they form fan-like, spherular, or botryoidal aggregates which tend to be more deeply coloured. Prehnite is generally found with calcite and zeolites in cavities in basic volcanic rocks. A common mineral, localities for exceptional specimens include Le Bourg d'Oisans, France.

PREHNITE was first discovered in the basalts of the Cape of Good Hope, South Africa.

yellowish green, spherular aggregate

COMPOSITION Silicate.
CRYSTAL SYSTEM Orthorhombic.
CLEAVAGE/FRACTURE Good/Uneven.
LUSTRE/STREAK Vitreous or slightly pearly/White.
HARDNESS/DENSITY 6–6.5 / 2.80–2.95.
KEY PROPERTIES Usually green and botryoidal, and found in volcanic rocks.

Cavansite

Ca(V⁴⁺O)Si₄O₁₀·4H₂O

$Ca(V^{4+}O)Si_4O_{10}\cdot 4H_2O$

Stunning peacock blue spheres and rosette-shaped clusters of prismatic cavansite crystals come from quarries near Poona (Pune), India. Here they are found associated with zeolites in cavities in altered andesite and basalt. Until the discovery of this deposit, cavansite was very rare. Its name is taken from the first letters of its principal chemical constituents, calcium, vanadium, and silicon.

THE DECCAN *basalt flows in India are host to the world's finest cavansite crystals.*

rossette-shaped mass of blue crystals

SECTION SHOWN

drusy coating of heulandite

COMPOSITION *Silicate.*
CRYSTAL SYSTEM *Orthorhombic.*
CLEAVAGE/FRACTURE *Good/Conchoidal.*
LUSTRE/STREAK *Vitreous/Blue.*
HARDNESS *3–4*
DENSITY *2.21–2.31.*
KEY PROPERTIES *Distinguished from copper minerals by association with zeolites.*

Okenite

Ca₅Si₉O₂₃·9H₂O

$Ca_5Si_9O_{23}\cdot 9H_2O$

Okenite from the Mumbai and Poona (Pune) regions of India look remarkably like white fur balls but the slender crystals are brittle and fragile. When found at other localities, its white or creamy white crystals are usually fibrous but can be bladed. It occurs in amygdules in basalt associated with zeolites, calcite, quartz, and pale green spherules of the silicate mineral gyrolite.

THIS AMYGDULE *contains hard white okenite and a single crystal of calcite on grey chalcedony.*

fragile, white hair-like crystals

SECTION SHOWN

COMPOSITION *Silicate.*
CRYSTAL SYSTEM *Triclinic.*
CLEAVAGE/FRACTURE *Perfect/Splintery.*
LUSTRE/STREAK *Vitreous to pearly/White.*
HARDNESS *4.5–5*
DENSITY *2.28–2.33.*
KEY PROPERTIES *White balls of fur-like crystals found in cavities in basalt (p.61).*

Actinolite

$Ca_2(Mg,Fe^{2+})_5Si_8O_{22}(OH)_2$

Green actinolite occurs as bladed, acicular, or fibrous crystals often in bent masses, or as asbestos. Massive fine-grained actinolite and tremolite are both called nephrite jade. Actinolite forms a compositional series with tremolite and is found in greenschists, blueschists, and other low- to medium-grade metamorphic rocks.

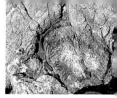

ELONGATE *bladed or fibrous green crystals give the metamorphic mineral actinolite a distinctive appearance in the field.*

green-bladed crystal

compact, fine-grained actinolite

polished surface

talc schist

NEPHRITE JADE

COMPOSITION *Silicate, amphibole group.*
CRYSTAL SYSTEM *Monoclinic.*
CLEAVAGE/FRACTURE *Good, crossing at 56° and 124°/Uneven or splintery.*
LUSTRE/STREAK *Vitreous or silky/White.*
HARDNESS/DENSITY *5–6 / 3.03–3.24.*
KEY PROPERTIES *Crystals show amphibole cleavages; less dense than jadeite jade (p.199).*

Tremolite

$Ca_2Mg_5Si_8O_{22}(OH)_2$

Tremolite, an amphibole mineral, is white becoming pale green as it grades towards the composition of actinolite. Traces of manganese may tint it pink or violet. It is found as bladed crystals, fibrous, or granular aggregates, and as asbestos. It can also be massive and fine grained when, like actinolite, it is known as nephrite jade. Tremolite is found in low-grade schists and in impure dolomitic limestones.

TREMOLITE *forms by metamorphism, like during the formation of the European Alps.*

thin white bladed crystals

fibrous crystals

vitreous lustre

COMPOSITION *Silicate, amphibole group.*
CRYSTAL SYSTEM *Monoclinic.*
CLEAVAGE/FRACTURE *Perfect, crossing at 56° and 124°/Uneven or splintery.*
LUSTRE/STREAK *Vitreous/White.*
HARDNESS/DENSITY *5–6 / 2.99–3.03.*
KEY PROPERTIES *Crystals show amphibole cleavages; less dense than jadeite jade (p.199).*

Clinochlore

$(Mg,Al_2)_6(Si,Al)_4O_{10}(OH)_8$

Clinochlore is a common chlorite; forms dark green foliated, granular, or scaly masses, disseminated grains, and tapering pseudohexagonal crystals. It is the main mineral in chlorite schists and occurs in serpentinites, marbles, amphibolites, and other metamorphic rocks, and in hydrothermal deposits. The chrome-bearing variety kämmererite is violet-pink, and found in chromium-bearing deposits.

THIS BOULDER of clinochlore with garnet is from Saas-Fee, Valais, in the Pennine Alps of Switzerland.

SECTION SHOWN

violet-pink coating

typical dark green colour

foliated mass

KAMMERERITE

COMPOSITION	Silicate, chlorite group.
CRYSTAL SYSTEM	Monoclinic.
CLEAVAGE/FRACTURE	Perfect, micaceous/None.
LUSTRE/STREAK	Pearly, greasy, or dull lustre/Pale green.
HARDNESS/DENSITY	2–2.5 / 2.6–3.02.
KEY PROPERTIES	Colour and cleavage.

Glaucophane

$Na_2(Mg_3Al_2)Si_8O_{22}(OH)_2$

A grey or greyish blue amphibole mineral, glaucophane is found in slender prismatic, acicular or fibrous crystals, and in granular masses. It is the mineral that is characteristic of blueschist metamorphic rocks. It also occurs in greenschist rocks and in some eclogites. Important localities are in the Italian Alps, Japan, and California, USA.

THE MOUNTAINS of Piedmont in Italy, seen here across Lake Orta, contain glaucophane-bearing blueschists.

SECTION SHOWN

monoclinic crystals

fuchsite (a variety of muscovite)

prismatic crystals

COMPOSITION	Silicate, amphibole group.
CRYSTAL SYSTEM	Monoclinic.
CLEAVAGE/FRACTURE	Perfect crossing at about 56° and 124°/Conchoidal to uneven.
LUSTRE/STREAK	Vitreous to pearly/Blue-grey.
HARDNESS/DENSITY	6 / 3.08–3.22.
KEY PROPERTIES	Blue-grey crystals in schists showing amphibole cleavages.

Jadeite

$Na(Al,Fe^{3+})Si_2O_6$

Massive jadeite, the most highly prized form of jade, is a tough, even-grained translucent stone, ideal for carving. When bright emerald green, it is called imperial jade, but jadeite can be many other colours, including white, yellow, violet, and other shades of green. Weathered surfaces are often brown. Jadeite can also be fibrous, and very rarely occurs as prismatic or platy crystals, usually in cavities in the massive stone. A pyroxene mineral, jadeite is found in high-pressure blueschist rocks, metamorphic rocks, and in eclogites. Important gem deposits are in the Uru River area of Myanmar and the Motagua Valley, Guatemala.

MOST *jadeite is a constituent of both eclogites and schists, such as these at As Sifah, Oman.*

rough lilac mass

pale greenish white

fine-grained, tough carving-stone

polished slab

translucent green cabochon

brown weathered surface

oriental carving

IMPERIAL JADE

COMPOSITION *Silicate, pyroxene group.*
CRYSTAL SYSTEM *Monoclinic.*
CLEAVAGE/FRACTURE *Good but rarely seen/Splintery when massive.*
LUSTRE/STREAK *Subvitreous, pearly on cleavages/White.*
HARDNESS/DENSITY *6–7 / 3.24–3.43.*
KEY PROPERTIES *Denser than nephrite jade.*

NOTE

Another member of the pyroxene group that often occurs with jadeite and glaucophane (left) is omphacite $(Ca,Na)(Mg,Fe,Al)Si_2O_6$. Omphacite is found in blueschists (p.71) and it is also the main green constituent of eclogites (p.71). Omphacite is nearly always granular or massive in habit.

Anthophyllite

$Mg_7Si_8O_{22}(OH)_2$

This amphibole mineral is generally found as aggregates of bladed or fibrous crystals but can also be massive or occur as asbestos. It is grey, purplish brown, or yellowish brown. Although only found in magnesium-rich metamorphic rocks, anthophyllite can form in rich deposits. It occurs in amphibolites, schists, gneisses, metaquartzites, metamorphic ironstone formations, and granulites.

THESE *rosette-shaped masses of anthophyllite in this boulder in South Africa are very typical of this mineral.*

purplish brown

perfect amphibole cleavage

radiating crystals

COMPOSITION	*Silicate, amphibole group.*
CRYSTAL SYSTEM	*Orthorhombic.*
CLEAVAGE/FRACTURE	*Perfect, crossing at about 56° and 124°/Splintery.*
LUSTRE/STREAK	*Vitreous, pearly on cleavage/White or grey.*
HARDNESS/DENSITY	*5.5–6 / 2.9–3.5.*
KEY PROPERTIES	*Colour and cleavages.*

Epidote

$Ca_2Al_3(Fe^{3+},Al)Si_3O_{12}(OH)$

Typically, epidote is yellowish to brownish pistachio green, but it can also be rather grey or yellow. Epidote crystals are prismatic and often striated. Aggregates are fibrous, granular, or massive. Epidote is found in metamorphic rocks, such as greenschists and amphibolites. It also forms by alteration of plagioclases in other rocks.

EPIDOTE *can be seen coating joints in these altered andesite from Somerset, England.*

striated prismatic crystals

vitreous lustre

yellowish green, slender crystals

perfect cleavage

COMPOSITION	*Silicate.*
CRYSTAL SYSTEM	*Monoclinic.*
CLEAVAGE/FRACTURE	*Perfect/Uneven.*
LUSTRE/STREAK	*Vitreous, pearly or resinous/Colourless or grey.*
HARDNESS/DENSITY	*6–7 / 3.38–3.49.*
KEY PROPERTIES	*Pistachio-green colour, prismatic crystals, and basal cleavage.*

Piemontite

$Ca_2(Al,Mn^{3+},Fe^{3+})_3Si_3O_{12}(OH)$

Piemontite is a manganese silicate closely related to epidote (left), that has a distinctive purplish red colour. Crystals are prismatic or bladed, and fine examples come from St Marcel, Val d'Aosta, in the Piedmont region of Italy where it was first discovered. It commonly occurs as grains and granular aggregates, and forms in low- to medium-grade metamorphic rocks, metasomatic deposits, low-temperature hydrothermal veins, and some altered igneous rocks.

AT ANDROS in Greece, piemontite is found with the closely related mineral androsite-(La).

rather contorted prismatic crystals

SECTION SHOWN

purplish red

COMPOSITION *Silicate.*
CRYSTAL SYSTEM *Monoclinic.*
CLEAVAGE/FRACTURE *Perfect/Uneven.*
LUSTRE/STREAK *Vitreous/Red.*
HARDNESS/DENSITY *6–6.5 / 3.46–3.54.*
KEY PROPERTIES *Distinctive purplish red, translucent to nearly opaque, rock-forming mineral.*

Talc

$Mg_3Si_4O_{10}(OH)_2$

Talc is white, brown, or green, and forms foliated, fibrous, or compact masses. It is exceptionally soft, and often has a pearly lustre. It is found in talc schists, forms hydrothermal veins in serpentinites, and results from metamorphism of siliceous dolomites. Talc is the main ingredient of talcum powder.

TALC is commonly found in the serpentinite on the Lizard Peninsula, Cornwall, England.

pearly lustre

perfect micaceous cleavage

SOAPSTONE LION

compact massive talc carving

pale green, foliated

COMPOSITION *Sheet silicate.*
CRYSTAL SYSTEM *Triclinic or monoclinic.*
CLEAVAGE/FRACTURE *Perfect/Uneven, sectile, and flexible.*
LUSTRE/STREAK *Pearly, greasy, or dull/White.*
HARDNESS/DENSITY *1 / 2.58–2.83.*
KEY PROPERTIES *Soft, greasy; like the igneous silicate pyrophyllite.*

Serpentine

Typically, $Mg_3Si_2O_5(OH)_4$

THIS SMALL, *polished slab from Italy shows the snake's skin appearance that gives serpentine its name.*

Resembling snake's skin in appearance, serpentine is a group of white, yellowish, or grey-green magnesium silicate minerals. Usually they are mixed but sometimes individual members can be distinguished. Antigorite is found as platy, bladed, or fibrous aggregates. Chrysotile consists of three minerals with different crystal symmetry – ortho-, para-, and clinochrysotile. Its crystals are fibrous and occur as veins of asbestos. Lizardite occurs as fine-grained massive aggregates. Serpentine minerals are the main constituents of serpentinites; rocks formed by the alteration and metamorphism of ultrabasic igneous rocks.

very fine grain

LIZARDITE

silky asbestos

CHRYSOTILE

vein of chrysotile

platy mass

green mixture of serpentine minerals

SECTION SHOWN

ANTIGORITE

COMPOSITION *Silicates.*
CRYSTAL SYSTEM *Varies with mineral.*
CLEAVAGE/FRACTURE *Perfect/Splintery; chrysotile crystals mat together.*
LUSTRE/STREAK *Dull, waxy or silky/White.*
HARDNESS/DENSITY *2.5–3.5 / 2.53–2.65.*
KEY PROPERTIES *Chrysotile fibres mat when rubbed together; hazardous if inhaled.*

NOTE

Rocks rich in serpentine minerals make attractive ornamental stones, and are often used in the cladding of public buildings. Ornaments and jewellery are made from a translucent serpentine called 'bowenite' or 'new jade' but this is inferior to true jade (p.197 and p.199) in hardness and value.

Brucite

Mg(OH)₂

Brucite is white, pale green, pale blue, grey, or brown. Crystals are tabular, often in platy or foliated aggregates, but fine large crystals have been collected. In the variety nemalite, they can also be fibrous. Brucite is found in serpentinite, but it also occurs in low-temperature hydrothermal veins in marbles and chlorite schists.

BEDS *of serpentinite, that host veins of brucite, are found in the Shetland Islands, Scotland.*

pearly green surface

flaky mass

perfect cleavage

long fibrous crystals

NEMALITE

> **COMPOSITION** *Hydroxide.*
> **CRYSTAL SYSTEM** *Trigonal.*
> **CLEAVAGE/FRACTURE** *Perfect/Flaky, splintery.*
> **LUSTRE/STREAK** *Waxy, pearly on cleavage surfaces/White.*
> **HARDNESS/DENSITY** *2.5 / 2.39.*
> **KEY PROPERTIES** *Soft, sectile, but less greasy to the touch than talc (p.201).*

Magnesite

MgCO₃

Magnesite rarely occurs as distinct rhombohedral or six-sided prismatic crystals. More typical are coarsely crystalline, granular, fibrous, and earthy masses. Magnesite forms as an alteration product of peridotites, serpentinites, talc schists, and other metamorphic rocks. Rich deposits make it an ore of magnesium. Occasionally, it is a primary mineral in carbonatites and sedimentary evaporite deposits.

MAGNESITE *from Snarum in Norway forms veins in green lizardite serpentine.*

typical coarsely crystalline mass

perfect rhombohedral cleavage

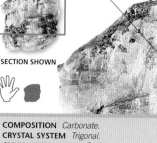

SECTION SHOWN

> **COMPOSITION** *Carbonate.*
> **CRYSTAL SYSTEM** *Trigonal.*
> **CLEAVAGE/FRACTURE** *Perfect, rhombohedral/Conchoidal.*
> **LUSTRE/STREAK** *Vitreous/White.*
> **HARDNESS/DENSITY** *3.5–4.5 / 3.*
> **KEY PROPERTIES** *Does not fizz in cold dilute HCl; rare in igneous and sedimentary rocks.*

Uvarovite

$Ca_3Cr_2(SiO_4)_3$

Uvarovite is calcium chromium garnet and is bright emerald green. Its crystals are dodecahedral or trapezohedral, or are in massive or granular aggregates. It forms by hydrothermal alteration of chromite-rich serpentinite and is also found in certain skarns and metamorphosed limestones in the Ural Mountains, Russia, and Outokumpu, Finland. It rarely forms crystals large enough for jewellery.

GREEN *coatings of uvarovite garnet come from chromium mines in the Ural Mountains, Russia.*

coating of emerald green crystals

vitreous lustre

dodecahedral crystal

COMPOSITION *Silicate, garnet group.*
CRYSTAL SYSTEM *Cubic.*
CLEAVAGE/FRACTURE *None/Uneven to conchoidal.*
LUSTRE/STREAK *Vitreous/White.*
HARDNESS/DENSITY *6.5–7 / 3.77–3.81.*
KEY PROPERTIES *Small, vivid green crystals in chromium-rich host rock.*

Benitoite

$BaTiSi_3O_9$

The rare gem mineral benitoite is normally sapphire blue, but can be colourless, white, or pink. Crystals are triangular and tabular or pyramidal, or form star-shaped twins. Nearly all benitoite comes from California, USA. Here, crystals are concealed in natrolite veins cutting a glaucophane schist within a large serpentinite deposit.

GEM-QUALITY *benitoite comes from the Dallas gem mine in the southern Diablo Range, San Benito county, California, USA.*

vitreous lustre

sapphire blue

natrolite

BENITOITE GEMSTONE

COMPOSITION *Silicate.*
CRYSTAL SYSTEM *Hexagonal.*
CLEAVAGE/FRACTURE *Poor/Conchoidal.*
LUSTRE/STREAK *Vitreous/White.*
HARDNESS/DENSITY *6–6.5 / 3.65.*
KEY PROPERTIES *Softer than sapphire (p.147) with unusual triangular crystals and blue, fluorescence under shortwave UV light.*

curious triangular shaped crystals

Andalusite

Al_2SiO_5

Crystals are prismatic, square in section, and creamy-white, pink, buff, or grey. It can be columnar or massive, but is most familiar as the variety chiastolite, which contains cross-shaped inclusions of dark carbonaceous matter. It is a polymorph of aluminium silicate, forming at low temperatures, and occurs in slates, schists, and other low-grade metamorphic rocks, and rarely in granites and pegmatites.

CHIASTOLITE *crystals are clearly visible in this outcrop of spotted slate near Threlkeld in Cumbria, England.*

square prismatic crystal

associated quartz

carbonaceous matter

andalusite

CHIASTOLITE

COMPOSITION *Silicate.*
CRYSTAL SYSTEM *Orthorhombic.*
CLEAVAGE/FRACTURE *Good/Uneven, subconchoidal.*
LUSTRE/STREAK *Vitreous/White.*
HARDNESS/DENSITY *6.5–7.5 / 3.13–3.16.*
KEY PROPERTIES *Square prismatic crystals; may have cross-shaped dark inclusions.*

Clinozoisite

$Ca_2Al_3Si_3O_{12}(OH)$

Crystals of clinozoisite are striated and prismatic, or in granular, fibrous, or massive aggregates. Clinozoisite is often pale yellow, pink, or red but may be colourless, grey, or green. It is found in low- to medium-grade regionally metamorphosed rocks, and in contact metamorphosed and metasomatized calcium-rich sediments.

CLINOZOISITE *forms where crustal plates collide to create mountain chains.*

radiating fibrous crystals

pink prismatic crystals

COMPOSITION *Silicate.*
CRYSTAL SYSTEM *Monoclinic.*
CLEAVAGE/FRACTURE *Perfect/Uneven.*
LUSTRE/STREAK *Vitreous/Greyish white.*
HARDNESS/DENSITY *6.5 / 3.21–3.38.*
KEY PROPERTIES *Different crystal forms to those of the polymorph zoisite (p.206), but are rarely visible.*

Zoisite

Ca₂Al₃Si₃O₁₂(OH)

Most zoisite is grey, white, light brown, or pale greenish grey. It is found as deeply striated prismatic crystals, disseminated grains, and columnar or massive aggregates. Zoisite typically occurs in medium-grade schists, gneisses, and amphibolites resulting from metamorphism of calcium-rich rocks. It also forms in eclogites. A lilac-blue precious gem variety of zoisite, discovered in the Merelani Hills of Tanzania in 1967, is called tanzanite. Tanzania is also the source of a zoisite amphibolite containing ruby crystals in vivid green chrome-zoisite and black hornblende.

TANZANIA *is the source of precious blue tanzanite and bright green chrome-zoisite.*

SECTION SHOWN

chromium-rich zoisite

ruby

CHROME-ZOISITE

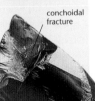

THULITE CABOCHON

conchoidal fracture

TANZANITE

cut face

GEMSTONE

striated crystals

perfect cleavage

COMPOSITION *Silicate.*
CRYSTAL SYSTEM *Orthorhombic.*
CLEAVAGE/FRACTURE *Perfect/Uneven or conchoidal.*
LUSTRE/STREAK *Vitreous/White.*
HARDNESS/DENSITY *6–7 / 3.15–3.36.*
KEY PROPERTIES *Like clinozoisite (p.205), the different crystal forms are rarely visible.*

NOTE

Manganese-rich thulite is a mottled pink, semi-precious variety of zoisite. It was named in 1823 after Thule, which was an ancient name for the far north of Europe. It was first discovered in Telemark, Norway, and it is the national stone of that country. As a gemstone, it is usually cut into cabochons.

Chloritoid

$(Fe^{2+},Mg,Mn)_2Al_4Si_2O_{10}(OH)_4$

Chloritoid looks very similar to chlorite. Crystals appear hexagonal and form rosette-like clusters, or more often occur as disseminated scales and foliated or massive aggregates. In colour, it is dark grey, greenish grey, or greenish black. Chloritoid forms in low- to medium-grade regionally metamorphosed rocks such as mica schists and phyllites. It also forms in hydrothermal veins and by hydrothermal alteration of lavas and other rocks.

CHLORITOID *is commonly present in the slates around Tintagel, England.*

perfect, mica-like cleavage

foliated mass of dark green crystals

COMPOSITION *Silicate.*
CRYSTAL SYSTEM *Monoclinic and triclinic.*
CLEAVAGE/FRACTURE *Perfect/Brittle.*
LUSTRE/STREAK *Pearly on cleavage surfaces/White, greenish, or greyish.*
HARDNESS/DENSITY *6.5 / 3.46–3.8.*
KEY PROPERTIES *Brittle, non-flexible; harder than clinochlore chlorite (p.198).*

Almandine

$Fe_3^{2+}Al_2(SiO_4)_3$

Iron aluminium garnet is called almandine. It is always red, often with a pink or violet tinge, and sometimes nearly black. Crystals often have well-developed faces and are dodecahedral, trapezohedral, or more complex forms; massive aggregates and rounded grains are also found. Almandine, the most common of the garnets, is found in mica schists and gneisses, hornfelses, granites, eclogites, and in detrital sediments.

THIS ALMANDINE *is with kyanite in a coarse-grained gneiss from Namaqualand, South Africa.*

mica schist

SECTION SHOWN

COMPOSITION *Silicate, garnet group.*
CRYSTAL SYSTEM *Cubic.*
CLEAVAGE/FRACTURE *None/Subconchoidal.*
LUSTRE/STREAK *Vitreous to resinous/White.*
HARDNESS/DENSITY *7–7.5 / 4.31.*
KEY PROPERTIES *Pink to red dodecahedral or trapezohedral crystals.*

well-formed crystal with cubic symmetry

translucent pinkish red

ALMANDINE GEMSTONE

Staurolite

$(Fe,Mg,Zn)_{3-4}(Al,Fe)_{18}(Si,Al)_8O_{48}H_{2-4}$

Staurolite is reddish brown, yellowish brown, or nearly black. It normally occurs as prismatic crystals, which are hexagonal or diamond-shaped in section, often with rough surfaces. Cross-shaped penetration twins are common. It forms by regional metamorphism of argillaceous (or clay) rocks, and is found in medium-grade schists and gneisses.

STAUROLITE *is often associated with kyanite, as in this muscovite schist from St Gotthard, Switzerland.*

pseudo-orthorhombic crystals

muscovite schist

cross-shaped twin

COMPOSITION *Silicate.*
CRYSTAL SYSTEM *Monoclinic, pseudo-orthorhombic.*
CLEAVAGE/FRACTURE *Distinct/Nearly conchoidal.*
LUSTRE/STREAK *Vitreous to dull/Pale grey.*
HARDNESS/DENSITY *7–7.5 / 3.74–3.83.*
KEY PROPERTIES *Brown; cross-shaped twins.*

Kyanite

Al_2SiO_5

Blue, white, and green are the usual colours of kyanite, and these are generally mixed or zoned within a single crystal. The elongate, flat, bladed crystals are often bent; hardness is markedly greater across a crystal than along its length. Kyanite forms at temperatures between those of its polymorphs andalusite and sillimanite. It occurs in mica schists, gneisses, and associated hydrothermal quartz veins and pegmatites.

THE FIRST *descriptions of kyanite were of crystals from the schists of Zillertal in the Austrian Alps.*

triclinic prismatic crystals

shades of blue

vitreous lustre

bladed crystals

COMPOSITION *Silicate*
CRYSTAL SYSTEM *Triclinic.*
CLEAVAGE/FRACTURE *Perfect and distinct cleavages at 90°/Splintery.*
LUSTRE/STREAK *Vitreous to pearly/Colourles*
HARDNESS/DENSITY *5.5 along crystal, 7 across crystal / 3.53–3.65.*
KEY PROPERTIES *Bladed, blue crystals.*

Cordierite

$Mg_2Al_4Si_5O_{18}$

Cordierite is blue, violet, grey, or brown, and it is pleochroic (different colours at different angles under light). Crystals are short and prismatic, but it is usually granular or massive. Mainly found in metamorphic rocks, it also occurs in contaminated igneous rocks and as detrital grains in sediments.

PURPLISH BLUE *cordierite, as in this South African gneiss, shows strong violet-blue/pale blue/yellow pleochroism.*

vitreous lustre

violet colour

distinct cleavage

GEMSTONE FORM

COMPOSITION *Silicates.*
CRYSTAL SYSTEM *Orthorhombic.*
CLEAVAGE/FRACTURE *Distinct/Conchoidal.*
LUSTRE/STREAK *Vitreous/Colourless.*
HARDNESS/DENSITY *7–7.5 / 2.60–2.66.*
KEY PROPERTIES *Pleochroic; it can resemble blue quartz, but has distinct cleavage.*

Sillimanite

Al_2SiO_5

Usually colourless, white, or grey, sillimanite can also be other pale tints. It occurs as prismatic or acicular striated crystals with square cross-section, or in fibrous mats. Sillimanite is the high-temperature polymorph of aluminium silicate and forms by high-grade metamorphism of aluminium-rich rocks. It is found in hornfelses, sillimanite schists, and gneisses, and in detrital sediments derived from these rocks.

FOUND IN *the region of Brandywine Springs Park, sillimanite is the official mineral of the State of Delaware, USA.*

mass of white acicular crystals

COMPOSITION *Silicate.*
CRYSTAL SYSTEM *Orthorhombic.*
CLEAVAGE/FRACTURE *Perfect/Uneven.*
LUSTRE/STREAK *Vitreous to silky/Colourless.*
HARDNESS/DENSITY *6.5–7.5 / 3.23–3.24.*
KEY PROPERTIES *Prismatic white crystals in high-grade metamorphic rocks that do not form rounded radiating aggregates.*

Axinite

$Ca_2Fe^{2+}Al_2BO(OH)(Si_2O_7)_2$ *(ferro-axinite)*

WELL-CRYSTALLIZED *axinite is found in skarn deposits around St Just near Lands End, Cornwall, England.*

The name axinite refers to ferro-axinite, rarer manganoaxinite, tinzenite, and very rare magnesioaxinite. All have flattened axe-shaped crystals but may be granular or massive. Axinites are typically clove brown, but can be grey, pink, blue, or when manganese-bearing, yellow. They are most commonly found in contact or regional metamorphic rocks, skarns, and alpine-type hydrothermal veins.

vitreous lustre

characteristic clove-brown colour

distinctive axe shape

alpine-type vein

> **COMPOSITION** *Silicate.*
> **CRYSTAL SYSTEM** *Triclinic.*
> **CLEAVAGE/FRACTURE** *Good/Uneven to conchoidal.*
> **LUSTRE/STREAK** *Vitreous/White.*
> **HARDNESS/DENSITY** *6.5–7 / 3.18–3.31.*
> **KEY PROPERTIES** *Axe-shaped crystals, commonly clove brown.*

Vesuvianite

$Ca_{19}(Al,Mg,Fe)_{13}Si_{18}O_{68}(OH,O,F)_{10}$

CRYSTALS *are found in limestone blocks ejected from the dormant volcano near Vesuvius in Italy.*

Vesuvianite, formerly known as idocrase, occurs as pyramidal or prismatic crystals, and columnar, granular, or massive aggregates. Yellow, green, and brown are the most common colours, but copper-bearing cyprine is greenish blue. Usually found in metamorphosed impure limestones and skarn deposits, vesuvianite also occurs in serpentinites and some igneous rocks.

CYPRINE

fine tetragonal crystals

square cross-section

> **COMPOSITION** *Silicate.*
> **CRYSTAL SYSTEM** *Tetragonal.*
> **CLEAVAGE/FRACTURE** *Poor/Subconchoidal or uneven.*
> **LUSTRE/STREAK** *Vitreous to resinous/White.*
> **HARDNESS/DENSITY** *6–7 / 3.32–3.43.*
> **KEY PROPERTIES** *Crystal shape; hardness.*

Andradite

$Ca_3Fe^{3+}_2(SiO_4)_3$

Andradite is calcium-iron garnet, and like other garnets it typically forms dodecahedral or trapezohedral crystals, and granular or massive aggregates. The colour of andradite can be very variable. Melanite is black and titanium rich, and forms in alkaline igneous rocks. Topazolite is brownish yellow and is found in chlorite schists and serpentinites. Bright green demantoid is coloured by trace chromium and comes mainly from serpentinite deposits in the Ural Mountains of Russia. Other shades of yellow, green, brown, or reddish brown are more common, and most andradite forms as a result of contact or regional metamorphism of impure limestones.

THE SERPENTINITES *at the foot of the Matterhorn in Switzerland are one of the best known sources of andradite garnet.*

cluster of black opaque crystals

cut faces

TOPAZOLITE GEMSTONE

bright green

DEMANTOID GEMSTONE

MELANITE

dodecahedral crystal

yellowish topaz-like colour

massive habit

TOPAZOLITE

crystals are dodecahedral

COMPOSITION *Silicate, garnet group.*
CRYSTAL SYSTEM *Cubic.*
CLEAVAGE/FRACTURE *None/Uneven to conchoidal.*
LUSTRE/STREAK *Adamantine, resinous or dull/White.*
HARDNESS/DENSITY *6.5–7 / 3.8.*
KEY PROPERTIES *Crystal shape and colour.*

NOTE

Garnets are rarely of pure composition. Pyrope, almandine, and spessartine belong to the pyralspite series; uvarovite, grossular, and andradite belong to the ugrandite series. Inter-mediate chemical compositions are common but only within a series, so most andradites contain some chromium or aluminium.

THE CHLORITE *clinochlore often accompanies the hessonite variety of grossular, as shown here.*

Grossular

$Ca_3Al_2(SiO_4)_3$

Grossular is calcium-aluminium garnet. Its name, from the Greek for gooseberry, alludes to its rounded dodecahedral or trapezohedral crystals and typical yellow, green, or honey colour. When orange-brown, it is called hessonite or cinnamon stone and these fine crystals come from Sri Lanka, Canada, and Italy. East Africa yields the precious emerald green variety tsavolite. Grossular may also be granular or massive. It forms in impure calcareous rocks that have undergone regional or contact metamorphism and in some schists and serpentinites.

impure marble

rounded pink crystals

grains of grossular

bright green irregular mass

conchoidal fracture

TSAVOLITE

orange-brown dodecahedral crystals

TSAVOLITE GEMSTONE   **HESSONITE GEMSTONE**

HESSONITE

NOTE

Tsavolite (also called tsavorite) was discovered in Tanzania in 1967. The same gem deposit was tracked over the border and mined in the Tsavo National Park in Kenya. Now, Madagascar and Pakistan are also sources of tsavolite. The intense green colour is due to traces of chromium and vanadium.

COMPOSITION *Silicate, garnet group.*
CRYSTAL SYSTEM *Cubic.*
CLEAVAGE/FRACTURE *None/Uneven or conchoidal.*
LUSTRE/STREAK *Vitreous or resinous/White.*
HARDNESS/DENSITY *6.5–7 / 3.59.*
KEY PROPERTIES *Dodecahedral or trapezohedral crystals.*

Diopside

$CaMgSi_2O_6$

Diopside, a clinopyroxene, is usually colourless, green, brown, or grey. It is violet-blue in manganese-bearing violan, and vibrant green in chromium-rich chrome diopside. Crystals are prismatic, usually nearly square in section. They can form columnar, lamellar, granular, or massive aggregates. Most diopside is metamorphic, found in marbles, hornfelses, schists, gneisses, and skarns. More rarely it occurs in peridotites, kimberlites, and other igneous rocks.

THIS TYPICAL *skarn assemblage, which shows green diopside with calcite and biotite, comes from Ontario, Canada.*

often light coloured

pyroxene cleavages cross nearly at right angles

SECTION SHOWN

vitreous lustre

hessonite grossular garnet

bright green crystals

VIOLAN

violet-blue lamellar mass

CHROME DIOPSIDE

COMPOSITION Silicate, pyroxene group.
CRYSTAL SYSTEM Monoclinic.
CLEAVAGE/FRACTURE Distinct, crossing at about 90%/Uneven to conchoidal.
LUSTRE/STREAK Vitreous or dull/White, grey, or greyish green.
HARDNESS/DENSITY 5.5–6.5 / 3.22–3.38.
KEY PROPERTIES Light colour; cleavage.

STAR DIOPSIDE

NOTE

Gemstones of star diopside show a four-rayed star effect when a beam of light crosses the stone. This property is called asterism.

Dravite

$NaMg_3Al_6(BO_3)Si_6O_{18}(OH)_4$

DRAVITE *is found on Manhattan Island, an important locality for this mineral in the State of New York, USA.*

Dravite is the sodium magnesium member of the tourmaline group of minerals, and is usually brown but can be black, dark red, or green. Crystals are prismatic, usually with a rather rounded triangular cross-section and different-shaped ends. Dravite can also be granular or massive. Generally, dravite forms in metamorphosed limestones and is only very rarely found in pegmatites.

vitreous lustre

large prismatic crystal

granular dravite

COMPOSITION *Silicate, tourmaline group.*
CRYSTAL SYSTEM *Trigonal.*
CLEAVAGE/FRACTURE *None/Uneven to conchoidal.*
LUSTRE/STREAK *Vitreous to resinous/White to light brown.*
HARDNESS/DENSITY *7 / 3.03–3.18.*
KEY PROPERTIES *Often brown; no cleavage.*

Wollastonite

$CaSiO_3$

WELL-FORMED *wollastonite crystals are found in metamorphosed limestone blocks ejected from Monte Somma, Italy.*

Wollastonite is usually white or grey but impurities can tint it other colours. Crystals are tabular, bladed, or fibrous, and normally occur in coarse masses, or in radiating, plumose, or massive aggregates. Most wollastonite comes from thermally metamorphosed siliceous limestones and from skarn deposits. Less often, it forms in carbonatites and alkaline igneous rocks.

white bladed crystals

vitreous lustre

cleavages cross at almost right angles

COMPOSITION *Silicate.*
CRYSTAL SYSTEM *Monoclinic or triclinic.*
CLEAVAGE/FRACTURE *Good to perfect, crossing at about 90°/Uneven.*
LUSTRE/STREAK *Vitreous; pearly on cleavages/White.*
HARDNESS/DENSITY *4.5–5 / 2.86–3.09.*
KEY PROPERTIES *Pyroxene-like cleavage.*

Lazurite

$(Na,Ca)_8Al_6Si_6O_{24}[(SO_4),S,Cl,(OH)]_2$

Since ancient times, lazurite has been highly prized for its exquisite blue coloration as the principal mineral in the rock known as lapis lazuli. Lazurite is a member of the feldspathoid group. It is always deep or vibrant blue, and it was once the source of the artist's pigment ultramarine. Most lazurite is massive or in disseminated grains, and distinct crystals – which are usually dodecahedral – are much sought after. Lapis lazuli forms by contact metamorphism of limestones. At its finest, this rock consists of lazurite speckled with golden pyrite, but white calcite and other feldspathoids are normally present too.

THE HIGH *mountains of Badakhshan in Afghanistan have been a rich source of lapis lazuli for thousands of years.*

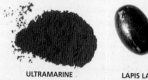

polished surface

ULTRAMARINE

LAPIS LAZULI CABOCHONS

dodecahedral crystals with dull lustre

white calcite

SECTION SHOWN

rich blue colour

POLISHED LAPIS LAZULI

golden pyrite grains

ROUGH LAPIS LAZULI

NOTE

The best lazurite crystals come from Badakhshan Province in Afghanistan, which is also the source of the many lapis lazuli specimens in old collections said to be from Persia (now Iran). The stone was traded, but not mined, in Persia. Other deposits of lapis lazuli are in the USA, Chile, and Russia.

COMPOSITION *Silicate.*
CRYSTAL SYSTEM *Cubic.*
CLEAVAGE/FRACTURE *Imperfect/Uneven.*
LUSTRE/STREAK *Vitreous to dull/Bright blue.*
HARDNESS/DENSITY *5–5.5 / 2.38–2.45.*
KEY PROPERTIES *Bright blue streak; does not fizz in dilute HCl like azurite (p.113). Should not be confused with lazulite (p.149).*

Scapolite

$$3NaAlSi_3O_8.NaCl - 3CaAl_2Si_2O_8.CaCO_3$$

The scapolite group of minerals has compositions ranging from sodium chloride-bearing marialite to calcium carbonate-bearing meionite. Crystals are prismatic with flattened pyramidal terminations or form massive or granular aggregates. They are colourless, white, grey, yellow, green, pink, or other colours. Scapolite, once known as wernerite or dipyre, is found in regionally metamorphosed rocks, skarns, altered basic and ultrabasic igneous rocks, and debris from volcanoes.

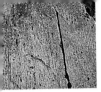

SCAPOLITE *is present in this outcrop at Mavuradonha, Zimbabwe.*

prismatic crystals

vitreous lustre

splintery fracture

pyramidal end to crystal

rather resinous lustre

COMPOSITION *Silicate, scapolite group.*
CRYSTAL SYSTEM *Tetragonal.*
CLEAVAGE/FRACTURE *Distinct, splintery or fibrous/Uneven to conchoidal.*
LUSTRE/STREAK *Vitreous, pearly or resinous/White.*
HARDNESS/DENSITY *5–6 / 2.50–2.78.*
KEY PROPERTIES *Splintery cleavage.*

Graphite

C

Graphite, like diamond, is composed of pure carbon, but has very different properties. It is very soft, opaque, dark grey or black, and is normally found as grains and scaly, foliated, or massive aggregates. Crystals are hexagonal and platy with triangular striations. Graphite forms by the metamorphism of organic material in sediments and occurs in schists and marbles. It is a rare constituutent of meteorites and igneous rocks.

MINED *at Borrowdale, in the Lake District, England, graphite is used to make the 'lead' in lead pencils.*

bright, metallic lustre

foliated mass with perfect cleavage

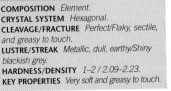

COMPOSITION *Element.*
CRYSTAL SYSTEM *Hexagonal.*
CLEAVAGE/FRACTURE *Perfect/Flaky, sectile, and greasy to touch.*
LUSTRE/STREAK *Metallic, dull, earthy/Shiny blackish grey.*
HARDNESS/DENSITY *1–2 / 2.09–2.23.*
KEY PROPERTIES *Very soft and greasy to touch.*

Glossary

For illustrations of many of the terms defined here, and additional definitions, see the general introduction (pp.8–19). Words in *italic* are defined elsewhere in the glossary.

ACICULAR Needle-shaped.

ACID A class of igneous rocks with the highest proportion of silica (SiO_2), including granite and rhyolite.

ADAMANTINE A particularly brilliant lustre as shown by diamond.

ALKALINE A class of igneous rocks rich in sodium- and potassium-bearing minerals; it includes syenite and phonolite.

ALPINE-TYPE VEINS Low-temperature *hydrothermal* veins typical of the European Alps, that contain a characteristic assemblage of minerals.

ALTERATION The change of rocks at or near the Earth's surface, which may result in the formation of new, *secondary minerals*.

ALUMINOSILICATE A mineral containing proportions of both aluminium and silicon.

AMPHIBOLES A complex group of at least 65 rock-forming silicate or *aluminosilicate* minerals, which typically form elongate crystals.

ASTERISM The star-shaped play of light caused by orientated microscopic crystal inclusions; best seen in minerals cut as *cabochons*.

BASIC A class of igneous rocks with a low proportion of silica (SiO_2), including basalt and gabbro.

BEDDING A flat structure in sedimentary rocks, that is the product of a period of sedimentation.

BLACK SMOKER DEPOSITS *Hydrothermal* minerals deposited from volcanic vents along geologically active mid-ocean ridges at the bottom of the sea.

BOTRYOIDAL Like a bunch of grapes.

CABOCHON Gemstone cut with a smooth, curved, polished surface.

CARBONIFEROUS A geological period, 299 to 359.2 million years ago. Named after its abundant coal deposits.

CHLORITES A group of nine hydrated *aluminosilicate* minerals with a sheet-like structure and perfect *cleavage*; most contain magnesium and/or iron.

CLAST (adj. **CLASTIC**) A grain in a sedimentary rock; usually a larger one than those in the surrounding *matrix*.

CLEAVAGE In rocks, a flat layer produced by *deformation* or metamorphism, along which the rock splits; in minerals, the flat plane where the crystal structure is weakest, along which a crystal tends to split.

CRETACEOUS A geological period, 65.5 to 145.5 million years ago. Named after the Latin for chalk, one of its characteristic rocks.

DEFORMATION ROCKS Rocks produced by stretching, squashing, or fracturing of a rock during Earth movements.

DENDRITIC Tree-like branching.

DETRITAL A type of sediment that has settled in water or been deposited by wind.

DEVITRIFICATION The process of turning from glass into a crystalline mineral.

DRUSY COATING Coating of many small, often parallel, well-formed crystals.

DYKE A vertical sheet of igneous rock; a minor intrusion (see also *intrusive*).

EQUANT Describes a crystal that is roughly equal sizes in all directions.

EXTRUSIVE Igneous rocks formed at the Earth's surface from lava.

FELDSPARS A group of 16 silicate or *aluminosilicate* minerals; the most important contain calcium or sodium (plagioclase) or potassium (potassium feldspar) and are major constituents of rocks.

FELDSPATHOIDS *Aluminosilicate* minerals that occur instead of *feldspars* in rocks low in silica (SiO_2). They are never found in the same rocks as quartz.

FLOW BANDING A structure within an igneous rock produced by drag during the final stages of crystallization of a lava.

FLUORESCENCE Glowing of a mineral when exposed to ultraviolet or other radiation, caused by the mineral's chemical composition or by traces of certain chemical impurities.

FLUX A substance used to promote the melting of an *ore* or metal and remove impurities.

FOLDING The bending of *bedding* or banding during *deformation* of a rock.

FRACTURE For rocks, the destruction of rock material during *deformation*; for minerals, the appearance of a broken surface which is not a *cleavage* or *parting*.

GANGUE A mineral in an *ore* deposit such as a *hydrothermal* vein, that is not itself an *ore*.

GARNETS A group of 15 silicate minerals with cubic symmetry that form dodecahedral or trapezohedral crystals.

GOSSAN An iron-rich residue at the top of an *ore* deposit left after ores have been leached away by downward-percolating water.

GRADED BEDDING A type of *bedding* where the grains are sorted by larger grains settling before smaller ones.

GROUNDMASS The fine-grained portion of an igneous rock, in which larger crystals are set.

HIGH GRADE Rocks formed at the highest temperatures and pressures during metamorphism.

HYDROTHERMAL A process by which minerals crystallize out of circulating, very hot water rich in dissolved chemicals; a mineral formed by this mechanism.

INTERMEDIATE A class of igneous rocks between *acid* and *basic* types.

INTRUSIVE Igneous rocks formed beneath the Earth's surface. Large bodies are major intrusions; smaller bodies, minor intrusions.

LAMELLAR In thin, flat sheets.

LOWER PALAEOZOIC A geological period, 416 to 542 million years ago.

MAGMA Molten rock – the source of igneous rocks.

MASSIVE In rocks, a texture showing little variation; in minerals, a sample not showing any crystal shape.

MATRIX In rocks, the finer portion of a *detrital* sedimentary rock in which larger grains are embedded; in minerals, the underlying mineral or rock on which a crystal has grown.

METASOMATISM A kind of metamorphism involving the introduction of new materials from outside, for example liquids or gases from a magma body.

MICAS A group of 41 rock-forming aluminium silicate minerals with a sheet-like structure and single perfect basal *cleavage*.

MODIFIED CRYSTAL A crystal with a particular form, but in which additional faces are also present.

ORE A mineral extracted from the ground as an economic source of a metal.

OXIDISED ZONE The area of an *ore* deposit above the water table, where circulating water has altered sulphide ores to form oxygen-bearing *secondary minerals*.

PARTING A flat plane along which a mineral tends to split, that is not a *cleavage*. May be caused by fracturing or *twinning*.

PHENOCRYST A large crystal in a *porphyritic* rock.

PLACER DEPOSITS Economic deposits where dense, durable minerals have been concentrated in sands and gravels by rivers or seas.

PLEOCHROISM When the colour of a crystal differs depending on its orientation.

PORPHYRITIC An igneous texture consisting of larger crystals (*phenocrysts*), in a mass of finer crystals (the *groundmass*).

PORPHYRY ORE DEPOSITS *Porphyritic* rocks containing finely dispersed ore minerals.

PRECAMBRIAN The oldest geological period on Earth, earlier than 542 million years ago; rocks of this period are usually metamorphic.

PRIMARY ORES Metal-bearing minerals that have not been altered by the action of rain or ground-water, or any other agency.

PSEUDOMORPH A mineral that replaces another but retains the original's outer crystal shape.

PYRITOHEDRON A form composed of twelve pentagonal faces; typically shown by the mineral pyrite.

PYROCLASTIC ROCK A rock formed from solid material, such as ash, ejected from a volcano.

PYROXENES A group of 21 rock-forming silicate minerals which typically form elongate crystals. Clinopyroxenes have monoclinic symmetry; orthopyroxenes have orthorhombic symmetry.

RENIFORM With a kidney-like appearance.

SCALENOHEDRON For trigonal minerals, a form composed of twelve unequal-sided triangles.

SCHILLER A milky or bluish play of light seen when a mineral is turned in the light; shown best by stones cut as *cabochons*.

SCREE Loose piles of fragmented rocks, for example on mine tips, mountain sides, and at the base of cliffs.

SECONDARY MINERALS Minerals formed by the action of rain or ground-water, or other *alteration* processes, on primary *ores*.

SECONDARY ZONE Part of an *ore* deposit in which *secondary minerals* form; often enriched where metals leached from above have been redeposited by percolating water.

SECTILE Can be cut with a knife.

SERIES A complete range of chemical compositions possible between two fixed end-members. For example, the plagioclase series albite ($NaAlSi_3O_8$) to anorthite ($CaAl_2Si_2O_8$). Sometimes known as a 'solid solution' series.

SHEAR ZONE Part of a rock body that has been stretched along a narrow, flat zone.

STRIATIONS Fine, parallel grooves and ridges on the surface of a crystal.

TERMINATIONS Faces making up the ends of a crystal.

THRUST A fault, a crack in the Earth's crust along which there has been movement, oriented at a low angle to the horizontal.

TOURMALINE A group of 11 boron-bearing silicate minerals having a ring-like structure and trigonal symmetry.

TWIN A crystal with one or more parts that have grown as mirror images of each other, joined along a crystal face edge or an internal plane.

ULTRABASIC A class of igneous rocks with the least amount of silica (SiO_2); it includes dunite and pyroxenite.

VESICULAR A term to describe lavas that are full of gas bubble holes, or vesicles.

ZEOLITES A group of 83 hydrated *aluminosilicate* minerals in which the other elements present are predominantly sodium, potassium, and calcium. They are commonly found in *altered basic* rocks.

Index

Acknowledgments

DORLING KINDERSLEY would like to thank David Summers, Jude Garlick, and Miezan van Zyl for editorial support; Louise Thomas, Neil Fletcher, Georgina Garner, Kevin Walsh, and Monica Price for picture research; Bob Gordon for design work; John Dinsdale for jacket design; Adam Powley for jacket copyediting; Mariza O'Keeffe for jacket editing; and Erin Richards for additional administrative help.

PICTURE CREDITS

Picture librarians: Richard Dabb, Claire Bowers
Abbreviations key: a = above, b = bottom, c = centre, f = far, l = left, t = top, r = right.

Key:
t=top; b=bottom; l=left; r=right; c=centre

alamy: 204 cl. **Ben Hoare:** 194 cl. **Chris Gibson:** 20 ca; 22 cl; 30 tl; 32 tl; 33 cr; 34 cl; 37 cr. **Colin MacFadyen:** 28 tl. **Dave Waters:** 13 cb, bc; 21 tr; 25 tr, cr; 26 cla; 27 cla, tr; 29 tr; 31 tr; 34 cla; 35 ca; 37 cra; 46 tl; 48 cl, crb; 49 cr; 50 tl, cl; 52 cl; 53 tr; 54 cl; 55 tr; 56 tl, cra; 58 crb; 60 tl; 65 tr; 70 tl; 73 cr; 74 tl; 75 tr; 76 tl; 77 tr; 78 tl; 81 cr; 82 tl; 110 tl; 140 tl; 141 tr, cr; 161 tr; 162 cl; 185 tr; 186 tl; 197 tr; 199 tr; 200 tl; 209 tr. **Dreamstime:** Daryl Faust 23tr. **Earl and Maureen Verbeek:** 104 tl, cl; 126 cl. **Frank de Wit:** 89 cr; 92 cl; 106 cl; 107 tr; 115 tr, cr; 126 tl; 152 tl, cl; 157 tr; 188 tl, cl; 197 cr; 198 tl. **Jim Stuby:** 55 cr; 69 cr; 135 cr; 182 tl. **Kevin Walsh:** 29 cr; 33 tr; 36 tl; 45 tr; 47 tr, cr; 48 tl; 49 cr; 51 tr; 53 cr; 54 tl; 57 tr; 62 cl; 72 tl; cl; 80 tl; 82 cl; 83 cr; 128 tl; 135 tr; 138 cl; 148 tl; 155 tr; 161 cr; 187 tr; 192 tl; 205 tr; 216 tl. **Kim Cofman:** 117 cr; 120 cl. **Monica Price:** 101 cr; 105 cr; 116 cl; 119 cr. **National Museum of Natural History, © 2004 Smithsonian Institution, Photographs by Chip Clark:** 92 bl; 100 cr; 102 tr; 119 c; 119 br; 120 tr, 148 bc; 148 br. **National Trust:** 43 c. **Neil Fletcher:** 13 ca; 21 cbr; 24 cl, cra; 25 cb; 26 cra, bl, crb; 27 br; 28 ca; 31 cl, cl; 35 cb; 36 bl, cb; 38 cl, bl; 45 tcr, ca, cb; 47 br, bl; 48 ca; 49 br; 51 bl; 52 cb; 54 ca, crb; 55 ca, cb; 59 br; 62 br; 63 ca, car, br; 64 ca, cal, bl; 67 cal, car; 69 car, clb, crb; 71 ca, cb; 72 bl; 73 cal, car; 74 cr; 75 cb, bl; 76 cal, car; 82 cal, cbl, br; 83 ca, cbl, cbr; 84 cbl; 89 car, cbl; 95 br; 98 cbr; 101 cal; 103 cl; 104 cr, br; 110 cb; 113 cbl; 117 car; 120 cbr; 121 crb; 122 cl; 128 cbr; 130 bc; 132 crb; 135 cbr; 141 cal; 143 cbr; 147 cbr; 153 cal; 160 br; 170 br; 171 cal; 172 bl; 182 cal; 184 car, cbr; 189 br; 190 cal, car; 191 clb; 197 cb; 200 bl; 202 br; 206 cr; 211 cb; 213 bc. **Oxford University Museum of Natural History:** Joseph Barrett: 124 tl; 154 cl. Helen Cowdy: 110 cl. Monica Price: 87 tr; 88 tl; 90 tl, cl; 91 tr; 93 br; 96 tl; 98 tl; 100 tl; 102 cl;

108 tl; 112 tl; 114 tl; 117 tr; 120 tl; 130 tl; 131 cr; 133 cr; 137 tr; 140 cl; 149 cr; 151 tr; 153 cr; 160 tl; 162 tl; 163 cr; 165 tr; 168 tl, cl; 176 tl; 177 tr; 180 cl; 184 cl; 194 tl; 196 cl; 200 cl; 202 tl; 203 cr; 212 tl; 213 tr; 214 cl. **Peter Rigg:** 73 tr. **R Prout:** 93 cr. **Ron Bonewitz:** 94 cl; 102 tl; 111 cr; 134 cl; 136 cl; 147 tr; 169 cl; 183 tr. **Roy Starkey:** 44 tl; 57 cr; 58 tl, cl; 61 tr; 76 cl; 86 ca; 100 cl; 163 tr. **Sandesh Bhandare:** 196 tl. **Stephen Kline:** 13 bl; 24 tl; 37 tr; 42 tl; 63 tr; 67 cr; 68 ca; 81 tr; 123 tr; 172 tl. **Stock.XCHNG:** 178 tl; Joerg Burkhardt 40cl; Oscar Dahl 105tr; Steve Dorrington 203tr; Hans-Günther Dreyer 121tr; Dynamite 118cl; Torsten Eismann 159tr; Alejandro González G. 211tr; Tom Haynes 22tl; Craig Johnson 38cl; Cerys Jones 27cr; Stephan Joos 45cr; Aneta Kowalski 13 crb; 41cl; Gregor Künzli 64cl; Stephan Langdon 175cr; LL 146tl; M Nota 208cl; Ville Pehkonen 177cr; Jim Robinson 35cr; Marcelo da Mota Silva 180tl; Moritz Speckamp 169cr; Deon Staffelbach 30cl; Stephanie Syjuco 36cl; Claire Talbot 207tr; Dennis Taufenbach 205cr; Jay Thompson 13 cra; 26tl; Tim & Annette 24cl; Tuomo Tormulainen 204tl; Rob Waterhouse 134tl; Emmanuel Wuyts 21cr; Binphon Yang 122tl. **© United States Geological Survey:** 63cr; Connie Hoong 59tr; R.G. McGimsey 190tl; C. Nye, Alaska Division of Geological and Geophysical Surveys 66tl; U.S. Department of the Interior, U.S. Geological Survey 84tl; U.S. Department of the Interior, U.S. Geological Survey, Coastal and Marine Geology Program 26cl.

© United States Geological Survey; Image courtesy Earth Science World ImageBank http://www.earthscienceworld.org/image bank: © ASARCO 92tl, 99cr, 103tr, 109tr; © Anne Dorr, American Geological Institute 113cr; © Larry Fellows, Arizona Geological Institute 169tr; © Chris Keane, American Geological Institute 88cl; © Louis Maher 59cr, 138tl; © Cindy Martinez, American Geological Institute 52tl, 174tl; © Thomas McGuire 127tr; © Martin Miller, University of Oregon 175tr; © Marcus Milling, American Geological Institute 109cr; © Bruce Molnia, Terra Photographics 108cl, 176cl; © National Park Service 125cr, 209cl; © Oklahoma University 150tl, 173tl, 192cl; © United States Geological Survey 13 tr; 28cl; © USGS Hawaiian Volcano Observatory 67tr.